Internet Trust and Security

The way ahead

James Essinger

Addison-Wesley

An imprint of Pearson Education

Harlow, England • London • New York Reading, Massachusetts • San Francisco • Toronto
Don Mills, Ontario • Sydney • Tokyo • Singapore • Hong Kong • Seoul • Taipei • Cape Town
Madrid • Mexico City • Amsterdam Munich • Paris • Milan

PEARSON EDUCATION LIMITED

Head Office:
Edinburgh Gate
Harlow CM20 2JE
Tel: +44 (0)1279 623623
Fax: +44 (0)1279 431059

London Office:
128 Long Acre
London WC2E 9AN
Tel: +44 (0)20 7447 2000
Fax: +44 (0)20 7240 5771

Website: *www.it-minds.com*
         www/aw.com/cseng

First published in Great Britain in 2001

© Pearson Education Limited 2001

The right of James Essinger to be identified as Author of this
Work has been asserted by him in accordance with the Copyright,
Designs and Patents Act 1988.

ISBN: 0 201 72589 4

British Library Cataloguing in Publication Data
A CIP catalogue record for this book can be obtained from the British Library.

Library of Congress Cataloging in Publication Data
Applied for.

This publication is designed to provide accurate and authoritative information in regard to the subject matter covered. It is sold with the understanding that neither the authors nor the publisher is engaged in rendering legal, investing, or any other professional service. If legal advice or other expert assistance is required, the service of a competent professional person should be sought.

The publisher and contributors make no representation, express or implied, with regard to the accuracy of the information contained in this book and cannot accept any responsibility or liability for any errors or omissions that it may contain.

10 9 8 7 6 5 4 3 2 1

Typeset by MCS Ltd, Devizes Road, Salisbury, Wiltshire.
Printed and bound in the UK by Biddles Ltd of Guildford and King's Lynn.

The Publishers' policy is to use paper manufactured from sustainable forests.

PARK LEARNING CENTRE

The Park Cheltenham
Gloucestershire GL50 2RH
Telephone: 01242 714333

UNIVERSITY OF
GLOUCESTERSHIRE
at Cheltenham and Gloucester

WEEK LOAN

WEEK LOAN

1 8 FEB 2002	2 4 FEB 2003	0 7 JUN 2004
1 7 APR 2002	- 7 APR 2003	2 6 OCT 2004
- 9 MAY 2002	- 4 JUN 2003	- 4 MAR 2005
2 3 MAY 2002	- 3 NOV 2003	2 1 APR 2005
2 7 MAY 2002	24 NOV 03 9 DEC 03	2 7 APR 2005
- 5 JUN 2002	16th Dec 03	- 8 JUN 2005
- 4 OCT 2002	16th Jan 03	- 1 OCT 2007
1 6 DEC 2002	1 5 MAR 2004	2 7 JAN 2012
1 5 JAN 2003	2 3 APR 2004 3 0 APR 2004	
2 7 JAN 2003	1 7 MAY 2004	

*If the purpose of a business is to acquire and retain customers,
how can the internet help you to do this
if you don't know who your customers are?*

FRÉDÉRIC ENGEL, ACTIVCARD INC.

*The security issue – knowing who is
communicating with you – will be crucial to realising
the commercial promise of the internet.*

BILL GATES, CHAIRMAN, MICROSOFT CORPORATION

Contents

Permission

We are grateful to the following for permission to reproduce copyright material:

Figures 1.1, 3.1, 3.2, 3.3, 3.4, 3.5 and 8.1 and Box 3.2 reprinted by permission of Deloitte & Touche.

Frédéric Engel for quotations on p. ii and p. 185; Her Majesty's Stationery Office for extracts from *Information Security and the Internet*, published DTI, Crown copyright is reproduced with permission of the Controller of Her Majesty's Stationery Office; Microsoft Corporation for the quotation by Bill Gates on p. ii; Ovum Ltd for extracts from *E-Business Security: New Directions and Successful Strategies*, published June 2000.

While every effort has been made to trace the owners of copyright material, in a few cases this has proved impossible and we take this opportunity to offer our apologies to any copyright holders whose rights we have unwittingly infringed.

Acknowledgements

My particular gratitude is due to Robert Coles of KPMG for allowing me to republish his article 'Secure Electronic Commerce in the Retail Financial Sector?' and to Paul Graham of Masons for providing the chapter on high-tech security and trust.

In addition, I extend my sincere gratitude to the following people who all gave up time from their busy schedules to assist me with the research for this book: Alan Brill (Kroll Associates), Scott Charney (PriceWaterhouseCoopers), Mike Conroy (HSBC), Donald R. Cressey, Paul Dhesi (SSE), Det. Supt. Ken Farrow (City of London Police Fraud Squad), Marina Geri (IBM), Andy Hunter (Royal Bank of Scotland), Yag Kanani (Deloitte & Touche), Caelen King (Baltimore Technologies), Cornelia Parchment-Horn (Ovum), Chris Potter (PriceWaterhouseCoopers), Matthew Rees (Charteris), Duncan Reid (Entrust Technologies), Andy Ross (Royal Bank of Scotland), Srivats Sampath (McAfee), Martin Samociuk (Network International), Alan Stevens (Consumers Association), DI Phil Swinburne (Metropolitan Police Computer Crime Unit), Graham Titterington (Ovum), John Todd (SafeStone Technologies), Alan Woodward (Charteris).

My thanks also go to Lloyds for allowing me permission to reproduce the material in Appendix I.

My warm thanks also to Steve Temblett, my editor at Pearson Education, to Mark Moore of the Inteligis Group, and to my colleagues Helen Wylie and Rebecca Taylor.

James Essinger

Introduction

E-business is arguably the most significant commercial revolution since the early nineteenth century. Yet issues of e-business trust and security potentially inhibit the growth and development of this revolution. By providing comprehensive discussion and analysis, this book sets out to address what is therefore a crucially important problem.

The rise of the internet has since the mid-1990s effected such a great change in how so much of business and leisure life is conducted that calling it a revolution in itself is in no way an exaggeration. Indeed, it could be argued that the impact of the internet revolution has actually been greater than that of the Industrial Revolution.

> It could be argued that the impact of the internet revolution has actually been greater than that of the Industrial Revolution.

Why? Because at heart the Industrial Revolution simply brought new resources to bear on producing goods that had already been produced for a long time. It created, to a certain extent, new opportunities for mass-production, and above all deployed steam power as the main source of energy for industry. But the products of the Revolution very much resembled what had been produced in the past, even if they were frequently of a higher quality than those produced by the old manual way of doing things. Furthermore, the Industrial Revolution made little or no impact on the way in which products were actually *delivered* to customers, and it is doubtful whether it really improved the quality of life for the majority of people it affected. Indeed, a strong case could be made for arguing that it had a *negative* effect on the lives of most people it touched as far as their quality of life was concerned. It made a few people very rich. Yet most of the workers who thronged its dark Satanic mills – to use William Blake's immortal phrase – were paid the very minimum their ironmaster could get away with paying and were worked for so many hours in a day that their health frequently suffered.

The internet revolution, on the other hand, has taken place within an economic framework that was already highly sophisticated and had already generated very great prosperity in the world's developed countries and also in many sectors of the developing world. The internet revolution benefits *everybody*. Commercial and industrial organizations enjoy a completely new dimension of delivery channel for distributing their products and services to customers and also for publicizing these to customers. It also benefits customers themselves, who have access to a prodigious range of products and services and total control over accessing information from these suppliers. If it is true that a customer can access information about one supplier rather than another by the simple expedient of clicking a mouse to change screens, it is also true that this creates a marketplace where customers have an unprecedentedly high knowledge about what is available and can select what they need from one vendor or another entirely at their own discretion. Of course, this scenario is challenging for vendors because they can no longer expect the same level of loyalty from customers that they were used to expecting in the past. However, this level of loyalty was often undeserved and stemmed more from the fact that customers did not know who else to turn to than because the quality of customer service provided by their vendor was so good that it left the customer wanting for nothing. A good case could be made for the argument that it is only with the advent of the internet that true democratic capitalism has been achieved, or is being achieved, depending on one's own perspective.

> A good case could be made that it is only with the advent of the internet that true democratic capitalism has been achieved.

Customers benefit enormously from the convenience and choice of the internet. They also benefit from the fact that the very nature of the internet means that there are entirely new products and services available which were not available before because the delivery channel made it impossible for them to be furnished. For example, customers who are accessing computer-based services are able to download software directly from vendors over the internet. They are also able to relay details of their own particular case or problems over the internet to whoever is going to be sorting this out. Online customer service is possible on a widespread basis for the first time since the development of computers, and has created an entirely new industry: the e-based Customer Relationship Management (CRM) industry. This industry is truly a phenomenon: providing the tools which allow an increasing number of organizations to give their customers a level of attentiveness and overall quality of customer service unprecedented in commercial history.

Which of us cannot remember the bad old days of customer service – even only a couple of decades ago – when any complaint or query meant having to write to the organization, which might deign to reply within a month so if it was inclined to do so?

The development and implementation of telephone helplines during the 1980s certainly made inroads into the formerly desperate way of doing things. But even telephone helplines were – and are – clumsy and ineffective resources in many cases, with customers frequently being held in long and irritating queues while they are subjected to the taste in music of whoever is running the helpline service and, when they finally do talk to an operator, all too often being subjected to a trite and demeaning script which reveals only too plainly the operator's comparative indifference to them and their particular query or problem. It is often quite clear that the whole telephone helpline scenario is structured by the organization not to help the customer, but to maximize the organization's advantage, whether this is in terms of its opportunity to use the customer's information for marketing purposes, to protect the organization's position, status and reputation, or generally to try to show to the customer that the organization is right and he or she is wrong.

Customer service delivered over the internet, on the other hand, has to be handled by an organization in a completely different way. The intimacy of the relationship between the internet user and the organization means that the organization has no choice but to treat the customer as an individual. When George Orwell – who, despite his own unnecessarily (and inaccurately) gloomy view of the future expressed in *Nineteen Eighty Four* was an extremely accurate commentator on the rise of the mass media and on many of the dynamics that would shape the modern world – first got to grips with radio broadcasting in the 1930s, he observed very shrewdly that radio broadcasting was always ultimately 'broadcasting to an audience of one'. This is also true of internet-based customer service. Furthermore, the very fact that customers can reasonably expect their query to be handled either in real time or very rapidly by the organization places another burden on organizations which is entirely to the customer's advantage. As for organizations, delivering customer service over the internet is far less expensive than doing so in any other way – including telephone helplines. Again, everyone benefits, or should do if organizations are shrewd enough to see that being able to deliver customer service this way is the best opportunity that has ever happened to them.

As for all the other opportunities which organizations of all kinds enjoy to use the internet to conduct a plethora of types of business with counterparties and customers around the world, any statement of the quantity of such business that can be conducted is inevitably going to date almost before it has been stated. Suffice it to say that the internet revolution is transforming the world into a vast network that connects customers, organizations, political parties, interest groups, public bodies and all other types of organization. Statistics about the number of people in a particular country who happen to be connected to the internet at present are of minimal interest. This is partly because they *will* date very quickly (and because this is a book which aims for a shelf-life of at least five years, I avoid quoting such figures in it), and also because nobody can realistically doubt that what is simply happening is the creation of a global scenario where most people in a developed economy or within a privileged section of a developing economy will – by around 2005 – have access to internet facilities in *all* of the following three locations:

- their homes
- their workplaces
- on the move.

I am aware that there is considerable discussion at present among sociologists of the dangers of a two-tier scenario being created in the world where there are

> The future of the internet is also in many respects the future of humankind.

> The very ubiquity and ease of access of the internet, and the widespread availability of the technology on which it runs, create unprecedented security dilemmas.

those who have access to the internet from a variety of locations, and those who are for ever cut off from the web due to their poverty. The extent to which this fear of the creation of such a two-tier society is justified remains to be seen. Certainly, those in unprivileged sections of developing countries are likely to find it more difficult to gain access to the internet than those in developed countries or in privileged sections of the developing world, but the very cheapness and ease of internet access makes it more than likely that in fact these people will be gaining internet access sooner than many expect. The very fact that geographical remoteness is in no way a difficulty when arranging internet access, as long as hardware can be supplied to the person in question, means that it is far from unrealistic to foresee a scenario where, for example, even a remote village in a poor country is likely to have at least one internet terminal somewhere in it.

For all these reasons, the future of the internet is also in many respects the future of humankind, and not just wealthy and technologically privileged humankind either. But there is a problem: the very ubiquity and ease of access of the internet, and the widespread availability of the technology on which it runs, also create unprecedented security dilemmas.

In his great novel of South America, *Nostromo*, the Anglo-Polish writer Joseph Conrad wryly comments at one point that human beings have never been at a loss to devise ways of inflicting torture and pain on their fellow men. By the same token, human beings have never been at a loss to use new types of technology for criminal purposes. In *The Victorian Internet*, an illuminating study of the origins of the first electricity-based remote communications system, the telegraph, Tom Standage makes the observation: 'Ever since people have invented things, other people have found ways to put those things to criminal use'. Standage quotes an Inspector John Bonfield, a Chicago policeman, who declared to the *Chicago Herald* in 1888:

> It is a well-known fact that no other section of the population avail themselves more readily and speedily of the latest triumphs of science than the criminal class. The educated criminal skims the cream from every new invention, if he can make use of it.

As Standage emphasizes, the telegraph – which in many respects was indeed a primitive form of internet first implemented in the nineteenth century – was no exception. He observes: 'It provided unscrupulous individuals with novel opportunities for fraud, theft and deception'.

Fraudsters and other criminals seeking to exploit the telegraph for financial gain would pay particular attention to the fact that the telegraph destroyed distance in a way entirely novel to nineteenth-century perceptions. A classic example was horse racing. Obviously, the result of a horse race was known as soon as the result was declared and made official. However, the information about the result could take hours or even days to reach bookmakers in other parts of the country using conventional messaging systems based around the mail or some other physical messenger. Consequently, anyone in possession of the results of a horse race before the news reached the bookmakers could then place a sure-fire bet on the winning horse.

This might seem implausible; after all, no bookmaker today would take a bet on a race after the race had been run. However, in a scenario where bookmakers were used to getting results of races only many hours or days after the race had been run, and where no bookmaker would expect any of his customers to get the results of the race any sooner, it is perfectly plausible that bookmakers would take bets after a race had been won. In the nineteenth century, rules were introduced almost immediately to prohibit the transmission of such information by telegraph. But, as is indeed always the case with any attempt to regulate new technologies, the criminals were no less ingenious than those who made the rules.

For example, in the 1940s a man went into the telegraph office at Shoreditch in East London on the day of the famous race, the Derby. He explained that he had left his luggage and a shawl in the care of a friend at another station, a station that just happened to be nearest the racetrack. He sent an apparently innocent-sounding message asking his friend to dispatch the luggage and the shawl down to London on the next train. Almost immediately, his friend sent a reply: 'YOUR LUGGAGE AND TARTAN WILL BE SAFE BY THE NEXT TRAIN'. The apparently harmless reference to 'TARTAN' revealed the colours of the winning horse and enabled the man to place the bet and make a huge profit. The method of making the profit was discovered but the man had escaped by the time this happened.

Today, the twenty-first-century internet is almost infinitely more extensive than the Victorian internet. It is also very considerably more sophisticated and subtle from a technological perspective, for it relies not on the passage of electrical current, but on the distribution of electrical signals that make use of much smaller current levels and can also be transmitted by radio and by satellite. Yet no matter how sophisticated the technology has become, Inspector Bonfield's adage that criminals are astonishingly ingenious at how they exploit the potential of new technology for illicit gain is found to be as true now as it was then. The difference is that the potential for illicit gain presented by the internet makes even the most successful fraudulent bet on a horse seem very small-time indeed. This book is about how and why security problems are part of the very framework of internet revolution, why people seek to cause security problems, and how organizations can prevent these problems and thereby maximize the potential for quality of customer service, excellence in marketing, efficiency in delivery and distribution and overall profitability and success which the internet can offer.

This book is deliberately written so as to be accessible by the non-technologist as much as by the technologist. Technical terms are therefore explained in detail when they arise. Two key terms should, however, be defined right away. I follow the increasing trend to see the concept of **e-business** as **the totality of all an organization's internet activities, including its internet-based relationships with its customers, suppliers, business partners and other associates**. The concept of **e-commerce**, on the other hand, is strictly a subset of e-business and can be defined more straightforwardly as **buying and selling over the internet**. The two concepts do need to be defined in this way to avoid confusion. Readers should note, however, that some sources do still define them in the increasingly outdated fashion, with e-commerce being used to mean what I regard here as e-business, and vice versa.

Readers should also note that this is a *general* book intended to cover the needs of e-business trust and security throughout all industrial and commercial sectors. Inevitably, there are some sectors where the trust and security problems identified and discussed in the book are particularly pressing. Examples of these sectors are the defence sector, where issues of national security are clearly at stake, and the banking sector, where information not only is likely to be particularly valuable in monetary terms but in many instances actually *is* money. But the fact that many of the illustrations are drawn from these two sectors, and especially from the banking sector, should not be taken to imply that the material in the book is *only* directed at these two sectors. In fact, internet-delivered information has a value in *all* sectors, and for this reason the book is also correspondingly relevant to all the industrial and commercial sectors where the internet is found to be a useful resource.

In practice, because the internet probably has implications for every industrial and commercial sector in the world, there are few areas of business where e-business security is not a critically important issue. Moreover, even if there are a small number of sectors where it is not a critically important issue now, it is likely to become so even in these sectors sooner rather than later.

Note

1. Tom Standage (1998) *The Victorian Internet*, Walker Publishing Company, New York, p. 105.

The internet explosion

Introduction

The internet is the most important new communications system developed during the second half of the twentieth century.

Figure 1.1 shows unequivocally the scale of the internet's importance and influence as of March 2000. This figure, supplied by one of the world's leading professional services organizations, illustrates not only the current scale of take-up of the internet but also the likely future growth. This is estimated to be greater than 50 per cent annually: a level of growth that is fabulous, in the old meaning of the word as something that seems unreal. Which is precisely the point. The growth of the internet *does* seem unreal, but it is really happening. The figure also shows the level of take-up that is still available to the expansion of the internet: 95 per cent of the global population still does not have any access to it.

> The internet is entirely a child of the high-tech 1990s.

The internet is entirely a child of the high-tech 1990s. Unlike other communication systems familiar today, which can trace their origins to early in the twentieth century or even before, the internet is an entirely modern invention.

What exactly *is* the internet? There is perhaps no better departure point for arriving at an answer to this question than the comments of the man who is, by universal consent, regarded as the inventor of the world wide web: Tim Berners-Lee. In *Weaving the Web*, Berners-Lee recalls:

> When I first began tinkering with a software program that eventually gave rise to the idea of the World Wide Web, I named it Enquire, short for *Enquire Within upon Everything*, a musty old book of Victorian advice I noticed as a child in my parents' house outside London. With its title suggestive of magic, the book served as a portal to a world of information, everything from how to remove clothing stains to tips on investing money. Not a perfect analogy for the Web, but a primitive starting-point.

Figure 1.1 The expansion in the use of the internet

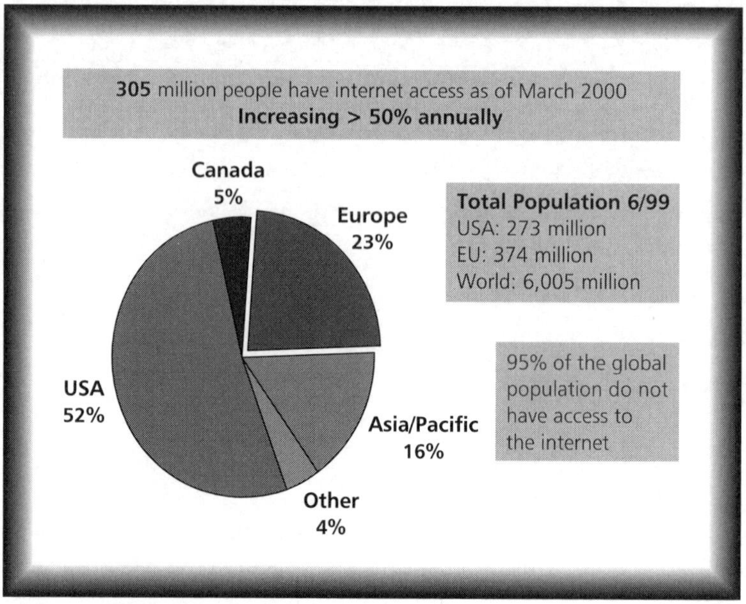

305 million people have internet access as of March 2000
Increasing > 50% annually

Canada
5%

Europe
23%

Total Population 6/99
USA: 273 million
EU: 374 million
World: 6,005 million

USA
52%

95% of the global
population do not
have access to
the internet

Asia/Pacific
16%

Other
4%

Source: Deloitte & Touche

And he continues:

> What that first bit of Enquire code led me to was something much larger, a vision encompassing the decentralised, organic growth of ideas, technology and society. The vision I have for the Web is about anything being potentially connected with anything. It is a vision that provides us with new freedom, and allows us to grow faster than we ever could when we were fettered by the hierarchical classification systems into which we bound ourselves. It leaves the entirety of our previous ways of working as just one tool among many. It leaves our previous fears for the future as one set among many. And it brings the workings of society closer to the workings of our minds.

These remarks provide a pretty accurate summary of what the internet is and what it offers its users.

To start with, it is indeed a sort of 'enquire within about everything' resource, as everyone familiar with using internet search engines will testify. Used in this way, the internet is simply like a gigantic online library that offers users access to all internet-published material anywhere in the world that happens to be connected to the web. This is not to say that *all* information is available on the web; it isn't, and in particular there is much historical material held in paper form in libraries which is not available for viewing over the web. But even here, the web will usually provide details of library catalogues, so the information is at least likely to be *listed*.

And if users can enquire via the internet about any topic they want to research from an academic standpoint, it is hardly surprising that the continual pressure on commercial organizations to find new markets has led to a prodigious amount of commercial information being available on the web, with the vast majority of commercial websites also offering users a direct purchasing facility whereby they can buy goods and services directly over the internet.

And in this, of course, the internet has become so much more than any mere paper-based book could ever be – even one with such an ambitious title as *Enquire Within upon Everything*. For the internet does not just offer a one-way transaction providing *information*; it is a 'living' book in which the information flow is two-way, and in which the whole concept of the website is that of a building which the user can explore at will by selecting different rooms (i.e. website pages) to enter and look around in. This concept makes one realize that the notion of the internet as a virtual world is very far from being contrived. It is, in fact, what really happens, and there is no greater beneficiary of the internet's remarkable ability to provide a wealth of information in a form that can be readily explored and navigated by users than commercial organizations.

Furthermore, the online, eternally updatable nature of the internet means that material available through it can be as topical as the provider of the material wants it to be. In practice, websites are updated regularly, and no more regularly than by commercial organizations, which have every motivation to place details on their website of new products and services, changes to the nature of existing products and services, and details of new deals on offer as soon as this information is released.

The capacity of the internet to respond to enquiries, then, is effectively limitless. Permitting what is indisputably the freest and easiest communications and information flow in all of human history, the state of the internet today already represents a total fulfilment of Tim Berners-Lee's stated vision to create a web of information that is 'about anything being potentially connected with anything'.

> The capacity of the internet to respond to enquiries is effectively limitless.

The limitless freedom and ease of information flow that this vision has already created – and which is only likely to become freer and easier in the future – has completely changed the commercial face of society. Already, many commercial organizations that have been established and trading for hundreds of years earn considerably more revenue (although not yet necessarily *profits*) from their internet trading subsidiary than from their traditional activities. The designation **e-** (an abbreviation of 'electronic') before the name of any trading department or indeed any entity at all has already come to be universally understood as indicating the internet version of that department or entity. For example, terms such as **e-banking**, **e-insurance**, **e-business**, **e-commerce** and so on, are all increasingly common usage and clearly heading to become familiar household terms. The best known 'e-term' of all, **e-mail**, already is.

One extremely important factor in the successful proliferation of the internet as a global medium for information flow is the point that the internet is not governed by any regulatory authority. This makes it highly attractive to people living in countries where the telecommunications system is poor due to problems with the national infrastructure and also in countries where the government has a strict control of other communications and broadcast systems. Indeed, the internet has many political implications in such countries. It might even be argued that it represents an electronic form of democratic capitalism whose tendrils reach around the world and into any country which has a telecommunications system at all, carrying unbiased and objective information around the world, and with it the e-catalogues and e-sales departments of millions of commercial organizations motivated by that most innocent of motivations: to make money.

Above all, the internet is, almost by definition, a strictly *virtual* medium. *The New Shorter Oxford English Dictionary* defines **virtual** in the computing sense as **not physically existing but made by software to appear to do so from the point of view of the program or the user**: an admirably concise and accurate definition which exemplifies how well work on the *Oxford English Dictionary* has accommodated the latest technological terms.

Strictly speaking, of course, the internet *does* have a physical existence in the wires, wireless systems, connections, switching devices and computer interfaces of which it is comprised. However, the network created by these cannot be said to exist in a physical sense: it is truly virtual.

The enormous, and rapidly increasing, popularity of the internet is undeniable. By 1 January 2001, about 400 million people worldwide had regular access to the internet. The volume of internet traffic continues to double about every 100 days. Extrapolating current figures, and taking into account the ongoing extremely significant development that internet access is becoming more and more something that people enjoy at home as well as at work, it is likely that by 2005 close to one billion people worldwide will have regular access to the internet. This would be equivalent to about 12 per cent of the world's *entire* population. When one considers the proportion of the world's population that will not be living in technologically developed countries in 2005, it is clear that by that year the proportion of the population in developed countries that will be regular users of the internet is likely to be up to around 25 per cent or even higher.

> By 2005 close to one billion people worldwide will have regular access to the internet.

In the same way that the number of internet users is surging, the number of internet websites is also increasing dramatically. Industry evidence proves that the number of websites on the internet worldwide (which reached 100 million at the start of 2001) is continuing to increase very rapidly. By 2005 there may well be close to 200 million websites for the billion-plus internet users to access.

Why should the internet be so popular? This is not difficult to explain. It is normally readily accessible, and it is certainly extremely easy to use. In principle, anyone who can use a computer can use the internet. Buying over the internet should be particularly easy. Some commercial websites are less easy to use, and less attractive, than their designers like to believe. But in principle, and for very good commercial reasons, website providers almost fall over themselves to make their sites user-friendly.

The problems which most users experience at some stage – such as slow access times, occasional impossibility of access and sudden interruptions to internet service – are due to the burgeoning demand for the service and the fact that the technology is sometimes overloaded as a result. These problems are gradually being solved by the increasing technological sophistication of internet communications technology and by the increasing extent of these connections. It is likely that by around 2005 these problems will have been comprehensibly solved, and will be relegated to technological history, just as problems with telephone connections such as crossed lines are no longer seen in telephone systems in developed countries.

For many businesspeople, an increasingly important benefit of the internet is its sheer portability. There are two aspects to this.

At one level, which might be termed the 'transportable hardware level', a palmtop, notebook or laptop PC can be plugged into any telephone socket around the world which has international access and have internet access provided within a matter of seconds. An American businessman visiting Europe, for example, can obtain access to his e-mail messages via the internet as easily as if he were in his office at home. The same is true, obviously, of a European businessman visiting the States. Many telephone providers encourage this use by offering customers a favourable or even local rate for overseas internet access time. The portable PC will also interface with every other benefit of the internet: the enormous global library of information is available the instant the connection is made. It is difficult to imagine a more potentially powerful communications tool.

The second level of internet portability is the opportunity to access the internet from a mobile telephone or from any hardware that connects to the internet via a modem. The limited screen size of a mobile telephone (even WAP phones, which many experts do not, in fact, believe are destined to become a dominating technology) means that satisfactory internet mobile connection is probably more likely to be achieved by devices which in effect combine the more useable screens of palmtop computers, palmtops with QWERTY-keyboards and laptops with a mobile telephone function that features built-in internet connection via a modem. We can expect manufacturers to use increasing ingenuity to develop devices here which are function-rich yet relatively lightweight and as compact as is compatible with an adequately large screen for viewing.

The significance of the internet as a means of interactive communications

The real importance of the internet in e-business lies in its ability to facilitate two-way communications.

These communications are increasingly likely to take place in **real time**, meaning that **the message sender and message receiver are both online simultaneously and aware of each other being online**. Communications may also take place as a non-live two-way communication process where a message is sent, left on the system and the recipient reads it and replies in due course, which may be a few minutes, hours, days or even weeks later. This, for example, is how e-mail works.

It is inevitable that some **internet retailers** – that is, **a retailer who operates exclusively via the internet or via the internet and also via physical channels** – will want to find ways of communicating with specially favoured customers while also maintaining a link to *any* interested persons. These specially favoured customers will be people or organizations who are either good business partners now, or will be in the future. As we shall see, a crucial element in maximizing the good faith and security of e-business is an organization's ability to create a hierarchy of users by means of offering different classes of users different levels of access privileges to its website. In particular, organizations try hard to create a user base of existing, known customers whose bona fides can more easily be proven than when the organization is dealing with complete strangers.

In practice, some organizations follow the terminology of regarding the **internet** as their delivery channel to 'any' people (that is, potentially the entire user base of the internet) while they serve specially favoured customers via what is often styled the **extranet**. From a purely technological perspective, the extranet is in fact the same as the internet; it is a special sector of it to which access is privileged.

Extranet customers, or web-browsers who want to initiate a relationship with the retailer, will want to see the same or similar type of information provided to anybody *but may wish to reply in an interactive way to the website provider*.

One way of arranging this is for the reply to be made by telephone or fax and consequently enabling the website provider to establish the bona fide nature of the caller. For example, a bank could trade foreign exchange (forex) over the internet by posting its prices for different currencies on the internet, but only permitting trading from bona fide persons whose credentials are established when they call in or fax and who, for example, will probably have left sums on deposit with the bank to cover transactions in which they participate. A particular customer can see the prices posted on the internet but she can't deal with the bank unless she has established her bona fides. However, restricting the interactive communications based around the internet to the telephone or fax is not really very good business, for the following reasons:

- It obliges users to go to the trouble of making a telephone call or sending a fax: something they might find too time-consuming to do. This is, one might add, especially the case in many financial applications, such as foreign exchange trading, where prevailing prices do not prevail for very long, and might even have changed by the time the fax lands on the trader's desk.
- It restricts users to interacting with the organization in real time during office hours. Outside office hours the user can still leave a message, but this would not be acted on until the counterparty's office opens.
- Use of a telephone or fax involves the user in additional charges which he or she might not wish to pay.
- Use of a telephone or fax necessitates relatively complex security authorization in any case and will tend to slow the process down even further.

Faced with these problems, it is hardly surprising that most website providers and most people with access to an internet will inevitably have given serious thought to the possibilities of conducting secure, private interactive communications over the internet.

There is a great deal to be said for the internet as an interactive **off-line** medium (that is, **when the two communicating parties are not simultaneously online to each other in real time**) communications medium. The breadth of information that can be communicated is very substantial: the speed of communications can be close to instantaneous, the screen interface provides considerable opportunities for displaying feedback, and the very nature of the PC makes the conversation private. Furthermore, a counterparty can be selected with enormous facility and speed.

Additionally, the interactive communications facility can be integrated into an existing desktop facility and can be triggered by simply clicking on an icon with a mouse or pressing a key. There is no need to shut down an application; the interactive communication via the internet can simply sit 'on top' of it. Furthermore, a complete and comprehensive record can readily be kept of the interactive conversation and can be provided as proof of anything agreed via the two counterparties.

The fact that the internet facilitates two-way communications in which relatively complex information can be communicated, which can be accessed at either party's convenience, and of which a permanent record can readily be made, naturally raises the question of how effectively the internet can be used to conduct useful business on an interactive basis. The answer is that the internet is a remarkably useful tool for this purpose. Its scope for facilitating business is not limited by any regulatory or practical constraints other than the following two factors:

- the need for the organization and its customer, counterparty or other associated entity to have internet access

■ the desire for organizations to conduct profitable business across the internet.

In practice the first constraint is trivial, internet access being so widely available and inexpensive. The real necessity is the straightforward one of the organization wanting to conduct profitable business across the internet, that is, e-business.

Types of e-business

Strictly speaking, there are as many types of e-business as there are types of business. It is, however, useful to identify some of the most important types of e-business. The following are particularly important:

■ e-Customer Relationship Management

■ e-procurement

■ internet-based supplier and counterparty relations

■ e-learning

■ the development of the 'web-enabled' organization

■ e-commerce.

These are now discussed in turn.

E-Customer Relationship Management (e-CRM)

This term is used to cover the entirety of an organization's dealing with its customers over the internet. The actual selling of goods and services to customers is strictly separate from the general provision of customer services. This would include the provision of information, billing information and dealing with customer queries.

> Organizations have more delivery channels available to them for interfacing with customers than they have had at any time in their history.

It is important to recognize that organizations have more delivery channels available to them for interfacing with customers than they have had at any time in their history. The delivery channels available include all the following:

■ face-to-face physical contact

■ telephone

■ e-mail

■ fax

■ post

■ Structured Message Service (SMS) (i.e. text message communication via mobile telephones)

- WAP phone browsers
- voice over IP (internet protocol)
- web-based chat
- interactive web communications.

Faced with this plethora of communications options, organizations need to decide exactly which ones they will use to communicate with customers. This is a complex decision. It is not merely a question of selecting one particular channel and sticking to it. Instead, organizations usually have to make available a 'menu' of delivery channels to customers and decide on what form of dialogue is appropriate for each type of customer relationship interaction. Sometimes, for example, a face-to-face meeting will be necessary to handle a particular aspect of the relationship. At other times this will not be the case and a more 'virtual' kind of dialogue will be appropriate. Naturally, the organization will always aim to make use of the most economical form of dialogue it can get away with.

For this reason the internet is an overwhelming popular choice for organizations as a principal means of interfacing with customers remotely. Substantially, this has to do with cost issues. As a delivery channel the internet is even less expensive to operate than the telephone. Even where the organization uses live operators to handle incoming traffic and answer queries (not all organizations actually do this), many of the queries will be about similar subjects and can sometimes be handled *en masse*. Furthermore, interactive real-time conversations via the web can be handled more easily than by using telephone call centres. It is perfectly possible that in time to come telephone call centres will be rendered largely obsolete as a consequence of the proliferation of internet service centres.

Internet-based customer service is a particularly potent resource for very large organizations, such as major financial institutions and utilities, which have millions of customers and are desperate to bring down the cost of communicating with these customers and handling their incoming enquiries. Such organizations cannot realistically expect that for the foreseeable future there will be more than a relatively modest proportion of their customers who will have access to the internet and also be prepared to interface with the organization through it. However, the cost benefits to the organization of handling its customer service responsibilities via the internet are so great that if even a small proportion of the customer base can indeed have service delivered to them in this way, the benefits to the organization's bottom line can be enormous.

Matthew Rees, a consultant with London-based e-business consultancy and solutions provider Charteris plc, made the following comments to me about the usefulness of the internet as a tool for a major utility's CRM.

> Winning and retaining customers are absolutely fundamental criteria for success as a retailer of utility services. This stems primarily from the need for a utility to have a substantial customer base to achieve competitive economies of scale, e.g. in the

running of IT systems and call centres. Furthermore, as margins tend to be very low in most utility sectors, profits can easily be eroded due to the high cost of acquiring new customers and servicing existing ones. Putting it bluntly, you can only make money if you can win, and retain, a seriously high number of customers.

If a utility uses conventional methods such as direct mail and telemarketing to communicate with its customers, there is no way that it can expect to provide a suitable personal service to millions of customers without risking a severe downward impact on its profits. These methods of communicating with customers are labour intensive, time-consuming, expensive and, in reality, not that personal.

Using the internet for customer service needs to be part of the solution to the customer retention problem because of its ability to provide a higher level of personalization and because it is a much cheaper channel per transaction. Typically an internet transaction costs 20 per cent of the equivalent telephone transaction, which, in turn, weighs in at about 70 per cent of the cost of a paper-based transaction.

Rees continues:

To date, few utility companies have managed to make much progress with implementing the internet as a powerful weapon for customer service. One reason for this is that they have other preoccupations: such as the challenges imposed by regulators and the market to reduce costs, improve service levels, implement new processes and business models, reducing leaks, etc. etc. With these pressures bearing down on utilities it is not surprising that customers are not always a top priority.

Utility companies can do better than this. They do not need to be intimidated by the idea of delivering a top-class level of service to customers. The internet now offers tremendous opportunities to maximize customer service quality at minimum cost. This is substantially because organizations in other commercial areas have paved the way for maximizing quality of internet-delivered service and consequently have made important discoveries about how the internet can be used as a customer service tool: discoveries from which utility companies can benefit enormously.

Rees quotes a justly famous example of a highly successful internet retailer which has achieved an enviable reputation for its quality of customer service.

Take the example of the highly popular internet retailer Amazon. In many respects, Amazon is the best example so far of how to deliver customer service over the internet. Maybe you have already bought books or CDs from Amazon yourself. If you have, you will know that the Amazon website is attractive, visually appealing and extremely user-friendly. You will know that the websites are open 24 hours a day, seven days a week. You will know that if you are an existing customer of Amazon, the organization remembers your name and knows what you have bought before. It will even make pertinent suggestions for what you might like to buy in the future. It updates its bestseller lists every hour and allows you to pre-order books, etc. whose publication is imminent. This is a quantum leap from the traditional bookshop, which is open for part of the day and has no idea whether you have been to the shop before let alone any idea of what you like to read.

The important point is that it is the business processes that have changed not just the technology. Charteris sees e-business as a fundamental change in the way business is done – aided, abetted, supported and enabled by technology.

A fundamental change in the way business is done: this is the hub of the whole thing. And what is more fundamental for utility companies than retaining customers through good, but affordable, customer service? Having established the need for utilities to provide good customer service at a reasonable cost and shown how the internet has been used by Amazon to do this, let's now look at some specific initiatives utilities can be taking to exploit the opportunities the internet offers.

Essentially there are three levels of sophistication in the creation of an e-CRM strategy for an organization which wishes to implement that strategy across the web.

- *Basic web publishing* can also be described as 'brochure ware'. It basically consists of promotional material that would otherwise be distributed in paper form. While not very inspiring, it does at least provide interested parties with basic information about an organization's products and services.
- *Putting business processes on the web* gives customers access to customer service functions twenty-four hours a day, seven days a week.
- *Building new processes around the web* enables organizations to provide completely new products and services to their customers. Perhaps the most promising example of this is the use of the internet as a means to deliver customers' bills and to facilitate payment. It seems inevitable that this method of distributing bills and collecting payment will become a principal way for organizations to undertake this chore – perhaps, indeed, *the* dominant way.

E-procurement

This is a catch-all term being used increasingly to describe the process whereby an organization or community of users makes available to all staff (who are authorized to make purchasing decisions) a customized 'catalogue' of goods and services. The goods and services will typically originate from a range of vendors and will have been approved by the organization for its own use. In many cases the vendors will have extended to the organization a special deal concerning the products available for procurement.

For a large organization, the e-procurement catalogue will represent a centralized list of approved, reliable, good-value items that can be accessed extremely rapidly via the internet, with the actual buying decision being actioned easily and quickly by the centre. The use of such a catalogue represents a huge improvement on a situation, familiar to almost anyone who has ever worked in a large organization, whereby someone who wants a particular item quickly knows perfectly well that the organization's purchase approval procedures are likely to prevent its rapid procurement and are thus likely to be tempted to buy the item from a high street shop and then submit an expense claim. The deal, credit terms and follow-up service offered by a high street retailer are unlikely to match those that the organization could obtain for itself. For these good reasons, e-procurement is becoming increasingly popular.

Internet-based supplier and counterparty relations

As a highly flexible new communications medium, the internet offers close to limitless scope for enabling organizations to communicate with suppliers and counterparties to mutual advantage. It is a particularly useful tool for large organizations which have numerous suppliers and can benefit considerably from keeping in regular, or permanent, online contact with them. For example, organizations which need to match their schedules for raw material delivery precisely with vendors in order to pursue Just in Time (JIT) logistical procedures can use the internet to great effect. Why the internet and not some other online system? Firstly, because the internet is much less expensive to set up and run than any other online communications network. Secondly, because the ready access to the internet which anybody can enjoy from a computer makes it easy for individual members of the organization's and supplier's staff (such as individuals running depots) to be part of the communications process. Furthermore, the real-time, instantly updatable nature of the internet means that changes to schedule – and all other time-critical information – can be instantly relayed to all participating parties, who can even access schedules from mobile internet interfaces such as WAP phones.

> The internet offers close to limitless scope for enabling organizations to communicate with suppliers and counterparties to mutual advantage.

As a business strategy, this process of dealing with suppliers is often known as supply-chain management. Many organizations nowadays make use of an extranet which will network together all relevant suppliers. As well as allowing the organization to communicate directly with its suppliers via this extranet, suppliers may also be permitted to communicate with one another if it is in the organization's interests to let them do so. Frequently it is: if, for example, one supplier is providing a component that will be used in conjunction with a component provided by another supplier, it is likely for logistical reasons that the organization will want to co-ordinate the delivery of one component with the other component. Today, the number of major extranets composed of major organization's suppliers is burgeoning.

Some organizations take the supply-chain management via an extranet an important stage further. In certain industries, arch-rivals are forming collaborative alliances that would have been unthinkable even a few years ago. For example, major British retailers including Kingfisher, Marks & Spencer and Tesco are collaborating in such an alliance. Another alliance involves car firms DaimlerChrysler, Ford, General Motors, Nissan and Renault. It would be difficult, perhaps, to imagine a more fiercely competitive group of organizations.

What are these alliances designed to do? The answer is that their purpose is to create e-marketplaces which connect numerous suppliers – sometimes thousands of them – and give all the participants in the alliance the chance to benefit from the keen pricing and volume discount expected of suppliers in return for gaining access to such a blue-chip client list. The e-marketplaces support spot trades, internet auctions and sophisticated supply-chain management solutions. There are already more than 3,000 such e-marketplaces around the world, with more coming online every day.

Marina Geri, managing principal for e-marketplaces in Europe, the Middle East and Africa at IBM Global Services in Paris told me: 'The benefits of e-marketplaces include significantly lower costs, greater choice and increased speed to market'. How much lower? Geri adds: 'Volkswagen and Audi are launching one of the largest private exchanges in Europe which targets most of their direct and indirect supply-chain needs. They expect the exchange will cut certain supply-chain costs by up to 50 per cent'. With savings like this available, it is no wonder that the Gartner Group predicts that e-marketplaces will handle $2.7 trillion in transactions by 2004 and account for around 37 per cent of all business-to-business e-commerce.

E-learning

Many believe this to be *the* 'killer application' for the internet. The concept is straightforward: the internet is used as the delivery channel for remote training and coaching programmes which can readily and inexpensively be delivered this way across the entire organization.

Internet-based training does not necessarily need to be fully interactive, but it can be made so if required. It brings with it all the internet's capability to handle full-colour images. The internet's other important capacity – to present information 'to an audience of one' – also means that personalizing the training to meet the needs of a specific individual is easy and inexpensive.

The development of the 'web-enabled' organization

This is a much more sophisticated internet base. It describes the phenomenon whereby an organization migrates *all* its internal processes and operation onto the internet. Such an organization is likely to take the need for a paperless office for granted and expect employees who are away from their desks to communicate exclusively via e-mail and via the extranet.

The classic example of a web-enabled organization is the phenomenally successful internet infrastructure supplier Cisco Systems. Cisco has developed something of an evangelizing approach in spreading the word about its belief that organizations can win enormous benefits from running themselves as complete e-businesses. Cisco accepts that as a vendor of networking hardware and software to customers who by definition are going to be sympathetic to the internet it is more obviously suited to complete internet operation than many of its clients themselves. But it points out that even those clients who operate in traditional industries are likely to be migrating many of their business processes to the web in the near future, and that almost every organization can benefit from the efficiencies and cost savings surrounding transforming internal administrative procedures to web enablement.

There are extensive efficiencies that Cisco has gained from this web enablement. They range from the obvious, such as the almost complete absence of paper at any of Cisco's offices around the world, to the 'invisible' and internal, such as the fact that, using the Cisco extranet, three staff members are able to handle all expense claims filed by any of the 34,000 worldwide Cisco staff, with refunds of expenses furnished within forty-eight hours.

Efficiencies like this naturally lead to significant cost savings, which Cisco has quantified. For example, in the fiscal year 2000, it achieved cost-savings throughout its entire global operation of the following order, and in the following areas, as a result of its web enablement.

- *customer care* – $506 million
- *e-commerce* – $65 million
- *supply-chain management* – $695 million (Cisco says that these savings derive from a 70 per cent cut in order time; a 45 per cent reduction in inventory, savings in annual operating costs, and savings in what it terms 'time-to-volume', that is, cost savings in the process that covers the process of planning a new product or service through to its launch and up to the point where it becomes a significant generator of sales revenue)
- *workforce optimization* – $86 million (Cisco explains this as consisting of improving internal resourcing and productivity).

Cisco's total cost savings, worldwide, for the fiscal year 2000 stemming from its web enablement amounted to $1,352,000,000.

E-commerce

In order to understand the importance of e-commerce and its remarkable rise to becoming – already – one of the world's most important ways for customers to buy and sell goods and services, it is helpful to start by thinking about what commerce actually *is* in the first place.

The *Oxford English Dictionary* defines commerce as 'the exchange of the products of nature and art; buying and selling together'. But in some respects this is a disappointing definition, because it is easily provable that the essence of commerce is not the buying or selling transaction itself, but the exchange of *information*.

There is no commerce without this exchange of information, and the exchange of information is at the core of commerce; the buying and selling at the end of it is merely a consequence of that exchange. No commercial transaction can take place without the buyer knowing what the seller has to offer. After all, all commerce is about meeting human needs (even the buying and selling of pet food is about meeting the needs of pet owners to feel they are looking after their pets), and until a buyer knows how his or her needs will be met – that is, until the buyer knows what is available for purchase – there can be no commercial activity.

It is necessary to emphasize the importance of focusing on the *information* side of the commercial transaction because there is no doubt that in the past the development of commerce has sometimes been inhibited by people imagining that the means by which buying and selling is effected (which, for many centuries, was simply a physical market where buyers and sellers could meet) is the essence of commerce. It isn't. Again, the essence of commerce is the exchange of *information*. This point can be shown by taking two examples which, while not directly related to internet commerce, cast important light on the subject.

Firstly, consider stock exchanges. Ever since their origin in the coffee-shops of Europe in the seventeenth century, stock exchanges were very much physical locations. Indeed, they tended to represent the classical economic model of a perfect market: there were many buyers and many sellers; it was easy for buyers to move from one seller to the next and vice versa; most buyers and sellers had access to the same information. The longer-established stock markets in Europe, the United States and Japan had – by the 1970s – acquired something of a mystique, with their membership rules and rituals regarded as written in stone and lying at the heart of capitalism. An observer of the world's major stock markets in the 1970s might have been forgiven for assuming that a stock market could actually be defined as a physical marketplace where buyers and sellers met.

With hindsight, we can of course see that that perspective is not valid. The stock market revolution of the 1980s transformed most of the world's stock exchanges into quote-driven or auction-driven exchanges conducted electronically. In the case of the London Stock Exchange's market, for example, many participants are located thousands of miles away from London, but receive exactly the same information and quality of service received by typical stockbrokers on Threadneedle Street. The migration from a physical market to an electronic market was not

> The essence of commerce is not the buying or selling transaction itself, but the exchange of *information*.

achieved painlessly; not least because some traditional players regarded the switch to electronic market activity as somewhat sacrilegious!

There is no need to go into the reasons for the migration here; it's enough to say that the success of the new electronic market proves conclusively that the physical, open outcry market was not at all what the essence of the London Stock Exchange was. The essence of the London Stock Exchange, like the essence of all stock markets, was the relaying of information, and electronic relaying of information is certain to be quicker, fairer, more accurate, more reliable and less expensive that physical transmission.

Another example, again from the somewhat archaic days of the City of London, is the insurance industry. The insurance business is much older than the stock market business and even more traditional. Partly because of Britain's former pre-eminence as a maritime nation, London was and is the centre of the world insurance industry.

Insurance was, until even the mid-1990s, almost absurdly old-fashioned and restrictive – or at least we can say so with hindsight. It was sold by grey men (rarely women) working in grey offices and being generally grey. Meanwhile, consumers were enjoying vast arrays of choice from such traditional industries as banking, estate agency and health. They could buy investments over the telephone, they could visit an estate agency at nine o'clock in the evening, they could ring around to find the best doctor for their purpose. But when they wanted to buy insurance, they had to deal with a grey-faced man in a grey office which closed its doors very firmly at five o'clock in the evening.

At least they did until Peter Wood, a British businessman, hit on the idea – which seems obvious now, but was provocatively revolutionary at the time – of selling insurance to consumers over the telephone. He started, sensibly enough, by selling the most popular type of insurance required by consumers: motor insurance, which has the inestimable advantage of being legally compulsory. The insurance company he founded, Direct Line, was not particularly subtle in its approach. Its business proposition was ultra-simple: you buy your insurance from us by making a phone call, and we give you a better deal because we pass on to you our cost savings from not having to operate physical offices. There was even a successful television advertising campaign featuring a little red telephone on wheels. Direct Line has been one of the sensational success stories of British commerce, and now sells a wide range of other insurance, as well as investments. It has, incidentally, made its founders multi-millionaires.

I have taken the time to present these two case studies because of their importance in demonstrating the central fact that is at the heart of the expansion of e-commerce: *commerce is about the dissemination of information, and there is absolutely no need for that information to be disseminated face-to-face in a physical location.* To take the point one step further: *the internet, with its easy*

interface, accurate and speedy communications, and inherent opportunity for
sellers to provide information about their products and services to hundreds of
millions of people around the world, is the most exciting commercial medium
there has ever been.

One reason why people have in the past confused a physical market with the
actual essence of commerce is that in the history of commerce there have been
very few major advances in the ability of buyers and sellers to exchange information with one another. Since prehistoric days until about 120 years ago, as we have
seen, the only means of exchanging information was face to face, in a physical
market. The telephone's invention eventually had a major impact on the nature of
commerce and indeed created a new way for information to be exchanged, as did
the development of electronic data communications. But the two examples we
have just quoted demonstrate how persistent the idea really is that the physical
market is the essence of commerce.

Even though the internet has now been part of the consciousness of the majority of people in developed countries for at least five years, commerce over the
internet is still a relatively minor – or in some cases non-existent – element in the
activities of most organizations. Again, this proves the persistence of the notion
that commerce is essentially a physical activity, perhaps aided by the telephone.
People tend to be conservative about commerce anyway; buying and selling is correctly regarded as an extremely important part of one's life, where not only one's
money, but also one's status and credibility as a person are at stake.

This is shown rather amusingly in the extremely emotional nature of buying and
selling in the markets of the world – such as the souks of the Arab world – where
haggling over prices is a feature of the commercial process. Anyone who has
visited such markets often comes away, purchase in hand, feeling emotionally
drained. In the Western world, the more formal nature of commerce tends to rule
out haggling, at least over retail transactions, but it is a mistake to assume that
buying and selling is necessarily any less emotionally draining. People get emotional about things that matter to them, and just as people with firm religious
beliefs, or firm opinions about personal matters such as sexuality, sex and eti-
quette, are likely to be slow to change, so people are also highly conservative
about how they buy and sell things.

However, even the most conservative person can hardly fail to recognize the
enormous advantages of e-commerce, which – as I suggested in the Introduction
to this book – should be formally defined as buying and selling goods and services
over the internet.

Note that this definition embraces *all types* of buying and selling over the internet: that is, both **business-to-consumer (B2C)** and **business-to-business (B2B)**
buying and selling.

From a commercial perspective, before the internet was widely available, organizations could basically use three channels for exchanging information with consumers, and vice versa. These channels were:

- face-to-face contact at a physical level, typically taking place in retail outlets and in people's homes (when a member of sales staff visited them)
- by post – via mail order catalogues
- by telephone, with the customer often gaining access to toll-free numbers or tele-sales.

Incidentally, it is interesting that even by the 1990s the telephone had not achieved the level of penetration as a sales tool that one would have expected. It might very well be asked why physical sales outlets were retained at all once the telephone became ubiquitous. It is certainly true that commercial telephone directories such as Yellow Pages achieved very considerable success, and of course an enormously important role of the telephone had from earliest days been to facilitate business and all kinds of buying and selling. However, the fact still remains that the telephone cannot really be said to have *replaced* physical sales outlets in the way it might have been expected to do. The only really exception here is the development of virtual banking during the late 1980s and 1990s, where the increasing popularity of telephone banking has certainly helped to reduce the number of physical branches of banks. Yet even here, many people still want to use a physical bank, and it is a fact that telephone banking for businesses has never really caught on to a significant extent.

So why exactly is it that the telephone, while its usefulness as a commercial tool cannot possibly be doubted, has not replaced physical sales outlets in the way one might have expected? The answer to this question goes a long way to explaining why the internet has become such an important commercial tool in such a short time.

A substantial part of the answer is that, immensely useful as the telephone is, it is more useful for comparatively short, uncomplicated conversations than for long and involved ones. Such conversations by telephone are not only stressful but also suffer from basic problems that no record can easily be kept of what was said. For these and other reasons the usefulness of the telephone as a medium for buying and selling is actually surprisingly limited. The only reason it is used so extensively for this purpose is that it is at least enormously more convenient than a physical visit by the buyer to see the vendor, or vice versa. Among the telephone's other disadvantages are the following:

- Most severe of all, it puts buyers under severe time pressure; it is certainly not a medium that lends itself to 'browsing'.
- It also enormously limits the amount of information that can be conveyed by the seller about what is for sale. All the seller can do is talk about what is for sale over the telephone, which is a very one-dimensional type of information flow.

- Its usefulness is also drastically limited by the fact that it is, by definition, a medium which only carries *sound*. It is, if one thinks about it, rather strange how we all take for granted that when we participate in a telephone conversation, we are not going to see the person we are talking to. Imagine if one went to meetings and closed one's eyes for the entire duration of the meeting. More seriously, we are basically visual creatures; we like to see what is available, and this is especially true of buying and selling. If video telephony had ever taken off to any significant extent, the telephone might have found another useful application, but this has not happened.

- The telephone also provides absolutely no facility for enabling the buyer to refresh his or her memory. Once you have been told something by telephone, you either remember it or forget it. There is no way of 'scrolling back' to information you have already received unless you ask the caller to stop talking about what he or she is talking about how, and remind you of what you have forgotten.

These features all add up to a medium which is actually far more limited in its usefulness for commercial transactions than one would imagine. Of course, the one enormous undisputed advantage of the telephone – that it lets you talk to people who are out of earshot – is so important that it more than explains why it has become by far the most important global communications medium. Modern life is, simply, impossible without the telephone. But being able to talk to people who are out of earshot is one thing; wanting to buy and sell products and services over the telephone is quite another.

Turning now to the internet, which is very reasonably described by e-commerce commentators as the 'fourth channel' for commercial activity, we see that all the disadvantages mentioned above of the telephone are actually advantages of the internet. The full advantages of this fourth channel for buying and selling are as follows:

- The internet does not put buyers under serious time pressure, or under much time pressure at all. Cost of internet access is relatively low, and buyers can easily 'browse' through not only what one particular seller is offering, but also what other sellers are offering. Furthermore, this browsing can cover sellers from around the world as much as from the buyer's own town or country. As always with the internet, the physical location of the buyer or seller is essentially irrelevant.

- There is no limitation to the amount of information that can be conveyed by the seller. The seller can convey as much information as they want, in a variety of media: graphic, text and sound, with video graphics also being available to buyers who have the requisite technology installed.

- Of course, in one sense, there is a practical limitation to the amount of information that can be conveyed: it's limited to how much the buyer is likely to want to read! But in principle there is no limitation, and as internet access speeds increase, and as the power of typical user terminals increases, the information that can be conveyed will also rise dramatically.

- It is both a visual and sound medium. The internet provides images that buyers can visually inspect.

- The internet readily allows buyers to refresh their memory by the simple expedient of moving back or forwards between different screens.

Moving on to other specific advantages of the internet, these are as follows:

- For a retailer, selling via the internet is *enormously* less expensive than any other sales channel. This single fact is perhaps the most important advantage which the internet enjoys from a commercial perspective. This cost advantage applies in any retail sectors, and – as one might expect – is especially pronounced when the delivery contains a significant service element. For example, according to the research organization Jupiter Communications, in the United States, today, it costs a bank $1.07 per retail banking transaction made physically via a branch outlet (we tend to think this figure is on the low side, and that a more realistic figure for a physical branch transaction would be at least $10 or even much more, depending on the quality of the bank's internal efficiency). Jupiter assesses the average cost of a banking transaction made by mail as 73 cents, the cost of one made by telephone as 54 cents, and the cost per automated teller machine (ATM) transaction as 27 cents. The cost per internet banking transaction, however, is estimated as being a mere *one cent!* Quite apart from the obvious profitability advantages which accrue to retailers who deliver via the internet, these cost savings can be partially passed on to customers in terms of lower prices, which attract new customers and retain existing ones, without denting profitability.

- There is no physical need for the buyer to handle a complex (and heavy) printed catalogue. All the information which can be placed in a catalogue can also be transmitted readily over the internet.

- There is no distribution cost to the seller of dispatching catalogues, nor any cost to the buyer of receiving them (not all sales catalogues are free of charge).

- The internet *provides individual attention* in the same way that a direct sales force does.

- The internet is not intrusive. The numerous jokes about the salesman 'putting his foot in the door' all demonstrate that buyers do often resent the visit by a member of a direct sales force. Quite apart from the fact that the visit always places the buyer under some emotional pressure, there is also the more practical consideration that the visit may not be convenient for the buyer even if an appointment has already been agreed. The internet, on the other hand, can be used at the buyer's complete convenience, and at times of the day (or night) when members of a sales force would not want to work anyway.

- Picking up from the previous point, the internet in effect represents a 'sales store' which the seller operates twenty-four hours a day, every day of the year.

- For organizations operating across national boundaries, the internet makes it easy for a seller to provide different language options on its website, thereby enabling buyers to see text written in a language with which they are familiar and to conduct business in that same language.

- One huge advantage of the internet which is rarely given the credit it deserves is the enormous facility it offers for the process of procurement. Customers who have ready access to a major town centre or major shopping mall are unlikely to worry that they have not seen all the sellers in the marketplace who offer goods they might be interested in. However, somebody living in a remote village is unlikely to feel the same confidence. The point is that *procurement* – the assembling of different sellers offering what one wants to buy and the process of selecting one seller out of these – is not difficult for shoppers who can visit major shopping centres, but it is difficult for shoppers who cannot do this, and almost always difficult for purchasers of business-to-business products or services. The internet solves this problem by the inspired method of allowing buyers to search not for the name of the seller or the brand they are selling, but for the item itself. This is particularly true where the item to be purchased is relatively esoteric or unusual. People wanting, for example, to buy a cable car system for a recreation and leisure park they are creating may be surprised to learn that there are far more manufacturers of this fairly unusual item than might be imagined. A buyer with little knowledge of the cable car industry would ordinarily find it extremely difficult to find potential sellers. However, using the internet, he could simply key in the words 'cable car' into the search engine, and the search would be likely to reveal all the major manufacturers in the world of cable car systems. When manufacturers of anything post details on the internet in their website, they will place key words in an index which is referred to by the search engines. This makes procurement by buyers extremely easy.

These points add up to a commercial medium of unrivalled power, flexibility and appeal. For retail customers, it is no exaggeration to say that the internet brings the world's retail stores into one's own home. For business-to-business customers, it enables very rapid comparisons to be made between different suppliers and lets buyers 'shop' at suppliers around the world. For sellers, even with the costs of physical despatch factored into the equation, e-commerce via the internet offers a remarkable potential for business expansion.

At the time of writing, the market capitalization of many new internet-based retailers and business-to-business suppliers has famously overtaken that of traditional, long-established organizations. No doubt, some of this valuation is based on hype, but even so, the hype may prove to be less ill founded than some detractors claim. The fact is that the internet is the buying and selling market of the future, and that future is already here.

Conclusion

The internet has triggered an enormously important revolution in one-way and two-way communications. Its use as a medium for facilitating business is especially important.

However, the achievement of the full potential of the internet as a medium for facilitating business is threatened by an extremely serious problem. It is this problem to which we now turn.

Note

1. Tim Berners-Lee (1999) *Weaving the Web*, Orion Business Books, London, pp. 1–2.

2

The challenge of e-business trust and security

The communications safety problem

The fulfilment of the internet's potential as a remarkably useful medium for conducting business is dependent, worldwide, on ensuring that communications sent across it are *safe*. At this point I prefer to use the word 'safe' rather than 'secure'. The reason is that there are in fact *two* fundamental communications safety problems relating to the internet. One of them is generally referred to as 'internet security', which is a reasonable and logical description, but the problem of security of the communication is in fact only a subset of the overall *safety* of the communication. There is another safety problem too, and in many respects it is more difficult to solve than the internet security problem.

All surveys of consumer and business attitudes to the internet prior to 1 January 2001 – the cut-off point for the preparation of material for this book – reveal that the safety of internet communication is the most serious concern people have with using the medium for e-business. The specific fears people have tend to consist of the following:

- that their communication may be read by someone who shouldn't read it
- that their communication may be modified by someone who shouldn't have any access to it
- that the confidentiality of valuable and personal information may be compromised; this is, for obvious reasons, a particular concern regarding personal financial information such as credit card details and details of bank accounts
- that the person's funds may be spirited away via the internet by an internet fraudster and will be lost irretrievably
- that breaches in the safety of internet communications may cause the person financial loss that cannot be reclaimed or retrieved from any third party
- that goods and services legitimately purchased and paid for by the person over the internet may be intercepted during the delivery process by someone who is not entitled to them.

There is no point condemning these fears as irrational and unreasonable. They are not. Let us revisit Tom Standage's comment quoted in the Introduction: 'Ever since people have invented things, other people have found ways to put those things to criminal use'. Because we *know* this is true, why would be expect that a major new communications system should not be welcomed with open arms by fraudsters and other criminals who will seek to maximize the illicit gain they can make from it? Especially as such people might conclude – correctly, as it happens – that a relatively recently created technology might be more vulnerable to safety breaches than one which has been used for many years and whose potential points of vulnerability are likely to be well known and well protected.

The cultural tendency to glamorize crime

Most crime is, in essence, a short cut to something desirable that is otherwise usually difficult or impossible to obtain except after long effort. In practice, there are always plenty of people in the world who are happy to take that short cut, either because they do not want to wait to acquire the desirable things in the full-ness of time or because they do not believe that they *would* ever acquire them.

At a purely objective, insensitive level crime is an energetic and quite possibly highly ingenious endeavour. Even in today's sophisticated societies with their complex economic and social frameworks and strong anti-criminal bias, the romance of criminal endeavour remains part of our culture. It explains, for example, why thugs who receive well-deserved lengthy prison sentences are some-times fêted on their eventual release as if they were popular heroes, especially if they come from fashionable districts of large cities. It explains how even mass mur-derers are sometimes seen as comic grotesques. (This may seem to be stretching the point until we consider thoroughly horrible people such as the British serial killer Fred West, who up until the time of his suicide while on remand in prison was regarded by many as a sort of national joke.) It explains the unending popu-larity of movies and books that seek in effect to make a criminal's crimes seem unimportant in comparison with the supposed fascination and charisma of the criminal's personality.

The enormous popularity of the book and movie *The Silence of the Lambs*, for example, was surely not so much due to the superbly documented forensic pro-cedures of the tale as to the appeal of the psychopathic cannibalistic murderer Hannibal Lecter. Lecter is perversely (though not unsuccessfully) cast as a villain who winds up becoming something very close to a hero. It is interesting in this context to observe that the novel's sequel, *Hannibal*, seems disgusting and absurd for the very reason that it panders too much and too openly to the aspect of our culture that glamorizes criminality. An audience might be happy to concede certain heroic attributes to a villain who tempers his love of eviscerating people and eating their inner organs with intelligence, a love of the arts and fine wine and an unwillingness to seek the death of the beautiful young woman investigator because doing so would be 'rude'. However, when Lecter is proposed as the only hero of the story (as he is in *Hannibal*) we feel uneasy because we know that at heart something very close to devious trickery is being played on us.

In practice, criminal endeavour may indeed seem exciting, glamorous and even romantic until one is the victim of it oneself. At that point the excitement, glamour and romance vanish in a puff of sulphurous smoke and we are left with nothing to contemplate but destruction, loss and misery.

Unfortunately, there are many criminals who are at this very moment seeking to inflict those very things on their victims by means of the internet. And while the deeds of thugs, serial killers and cannibals are likely to be only too evident, the deeds of those who seek short cuts to wealth or confidential information via the internet may not be evident until long after the criminal has carried out the crime and got away. In some cases the crime may not be readily evident at all. Internet criminals are perfectly aware that the best way never to be caught is if nobody has realized that a crime has been committed. Furthermore, the border between legitimate internet browsing and internet crime is a narrow one. It is sometimes the matter of the press of a keyboard or the click of a mouse. Similarly, it is frequently difficult to be certain where expert and resourceful use of a computer ends and computer crime begins.

> Internet criminals are perfectly aware that the best way never to be caught is if nobody has realized that a crime has been committed.

But just because defining an act of computer crime and showing where the crime begins is difficult, this does not mean that there is no point in seeking to do these things. Indeed, the safety of computer-based communications in general and internet communications specifically is of such enormous importance that a dedicated and highly specialized industry has sprung up over the past five or six years which seeks to assist all kinds of interested parties to maximize the safety of internet communications relevant to them. We now need to consider why exactly this industry has become so important, to examine the ideas and safety strategies generated by the industry, and finally we need to look at some of the most successful vendors themselves.

▰▰ The reality: computer criminal at work

One of the most popular and widely respected news feature programmes in British television is *Panorama*. The programme has a well-deserved reputation for investigative journalism at the leading edge. A recent *Panorama* programme focused dramatically and cogently on the threat posed by '**hackers**': **people who**

seek to make illicit use of computer systems for their own personal financial gain or – sometimes – merely to show that they are more clever than the people who built the systems.

An indication of the corrupting potential of the human personality is shown in how the very meaning of the word 'hacker' has changed since the term was first used in the 1970s. Initially, it simply meant anybody who was enthusiastic about using computers, and in many respects was at first a term of praise. Nowadays, however, that initial meaning has been eroded by the connotation of someone who has some malicious purpose in their enthusiasm. And it is indeed true that some of the most talented hackers in the current meaning of the word are extremely able computer enthusiasts. So much so that some are actually hired by commercial organizations to identify and cure potential security loopholes. These types of hackers – sometimes known as 'white hat' hackers – undoubtedly play an important role in increasing security in many computer systems. Yet it is difficult not to feel that there is something somewhat fragile and precarious about the relationship between white hat hackers and their employers: as if when hackers are playing the good guys, this really is only an act and they are not quite being true to their essential nature. Poachers may turn gamekeepers for the right wage, but many of them probably retain the potential to become poachers again, or indeed to do a little quiet poaching out of hours.

With very few exceptions, hackers are intelligent, articulate and technically extremely gifted people who are perfectly aware of what they are doing. The contrast between the computer criminals of today and the old-fashioned criminal who held up banks or committed any other type of robbery could not be more striking. Indeed, the very term '**computer criminal**', which I define here as **anybody who participates in any unauthorized access or use of a computer system**, is, strictly speaking, a misnomer, because unless there is actual legislation in place, the person cannot with entire accuracy be described as a 'criminal' at all. For the purposes of this book, I overlook this nicety, but it is important to point out that many countries do not have computer misuse legislation in place at all, and even those that do have often rushed into law inadequate legislation which leaves so many loopholes that it is doubtful whether it is effective.

For example, computer misuse legislation needs to make all illicit access to a computer system illegal, even if the user has not enjoyed any financial benefit from so doing. Even today, too many national legislations are based around the nineteenth-century principle that a crime involving property is only a crime if the property is physically removed from where it ought to be, and if the person moving it intends to deprive the owner of the property permanently. This conception of property crime simply does not work in today's information technology (IT) world, for the following reasons:

- Mere sight of a document that has been illicitly accessed can be enough to confer an unfair advantage on the computer criminal. Consider, for example, an oil exploration company which discovers a valuable new field. A computer criminal merely has to obtain illicit access to information about the latitude and longitude of that field in order to gain a potential advantage which might lose the exploration company billions of dollars in revenue and enable the hacker to sell the information to a rival company for an extremely large sum.

■ Interference with data on an unauthorized basis can also be extremely damaging to the owner of that data. To continue the example mentioned in the previous bullet, consider that the hacker is able to change a reading for latitude or longitude. He (hackers are invariably male) could record the original reading, sell it to the rival company and deliberately manipulate the information in the computer to send the exploration company drilling for oil where there is none.

■ Ownership of data in effect starts at the keyboard of any computer system which has access to the data. It should be recognized by any computer misuse legislation that with the first press of a key in the direction of accessing the information, the hacker has made his first illegal move.

A Welsh hacker interviewed in the *Panorama* report was pursued by police for downloading thousands of credit card numbers. He was only known by his online name of 'Curador'. As he explained to the *Panorama* reporter after he had been arrested, when the police came to his family's cottage in the early morning they woke him and challenged him:

> They said 'Are you Curador?' and I said 'Cura what?' You know, I tried to act innocent. But they said, 'If you're going to be funny with us, we'll have to arrest everyone in the house because it's definitely someone in this house.' They said, 'We'll have to arrest your mother and everyone.' And I said, 'OK, fine, I am Curador then.'

What was notable about this man was his youth – he was only 18 – intelligence, articulateness, ability with computers and clear understanding of the game he was playing – a game that also involved the FBI: a Bureau agent was there to witness his arrest. The man had created a relatively straightforward computer program which enabled him to target random security flaws in nine online databases where thousands of credit card numbers had been stored. He was then able to access the numbers on the retail sites.

What is *also* notable – and typical – is that even the young man in question was surprised at how easy it was to obtain the credit card details. Many computer criminals are in fact people who seem initially to be impelled by wanting to test their technical skills and find that they can access valuable information with laughable – even embarrassing – ease. As our hacker explains:

> I just chose one website at random. I just clicked on it, tried it, and that was only ten minutes after I'd had the idea, and I was already getting 5,500 credit card numbers. No password, nothing, just click, click, click and here they were.

In all, he was able to download the details of 26,000 credit cards. He says he sent a message warning some of the retailers that he had their customers' details and that they should lock their files. However, the retailers did not respond. So he decided to set up his own website and posted some of the card numbers there to advertise the security flaw he had found. Not surprisingly, these efforts soon came to the attention of the police.

Whether or not this particular act was indeed criminal is not really the point here. It is certainly true that many organizations are appallingly lax with their IT security provisions. They often rely on the police as if the latter, overworked as they are, were a sort of safety net who will run to ground anyone setting out on a career in hacking. But there are several reasons why such thinking is itself almost criminally irresponsible:

- Many hackers are never caught because they are highly adept at concealing their traces.

- Even when hackers are caught, it is often difficult to prove criminal intent if the hacker has derived no demonstrable financial benefit from his activities. Even where prevailing computer misuse legislation does include mere access as a criminal act, a jury will usually need to be shown evidence of definite criminal intent before it will convict. The defence that the access was accidental can almost always be used and may in some cases be a valid one anyway if the IT system was so unprotected that accessing it was extremely easy.

- Even where a hacker *has* displayed some clearly criminal intent and has benefited financially from the act, many organizations are reluctant to launch a criminal prosecution. This is because they fear – very reasonably, if past experience is anything to go by – the negative publicity which such a case would inevitably bring them. This is especially true of financial institutions. For example, if it is revealed that a bank has run its IT systems so insecurely that an outsider can readily access them, the damage caused can be immense and could easily run into millions of pounds of lost business from disenchanted existing or potential customers.

- Whatever the nature of the police investigation and the ensuing trial (if there is one), this is only a remedy – and an inadequate remedy at that – *after the event*. It does not remove the fact that the event has happened. A lesson one learns in IT security of all kinds is that prevention is always much more important than cure. For any organization, the best kind of news about its IT security is the absence of news.

This book devotes an entire chapter – Chapter 5 – to behavioural issues relating to the psychology of computer criminals and aims to suggest why they do what they do and how these insights might be used by organizations. However, some key points need to be made about computer criminals right away. Too often IT and internet security is discussed in the press in an abstract sense as if it were somehow divorced from the very people who commit breaches of security. In fact, just as it is people rather than guns that kill people, it is people, rather than computers, who commit computer security breaches.

Experience shows that most computer criminals are relatively young (40 is about the upper age limit, and many are younger than 25) and almost invariably gifted at using computers, and deeply interested in computer programming. Some commentators go so far as to say that the idea of a hacker being a socially inadequate, spotty teenager holed up in a bedsit or a gloomy attic bedroom with posters advertizing morbid movies on the walls is far-fetched. One IT security observer told me that most expert hackers break into computer systems for the intellectual challenge:

> To them it is a puzzle equivalent to a cryptic crossword, only more difficult. Chipping away at a corporation's electronic defences until they break can be a fascinating brainteaser. Studies of computer hackers have found two consistent factors: they are among the most intelligent people and they have a distorted sense of morality. To hackers, breaking into computers is a numbers game with no thought given to the possible consequences.

In 1996, Matthew Bevan, a computer technician from Cardiff, became one of the world's most notorious alleged hackers when he was arrested on suspicion of gaining access to computers belonging to the United States Air Force and the Lockheed company in California. Bevan, who was acquitted in 1997 and is now the head of an internet security firm, explained at the time of his acquittal that hacking was above all an intellectual challenge:

> You hack thousands of systems and the next challenge is 'what will be tougher?' You go from medium-sized corporations and universities to military systems and the Pentagon.

And as he also explained, the need to have prolonged internet access in order to undertake the hacking that is such a source of intellectual pleasure to its adherents may itself on occasion require illicit high-tech activity. Bevan admitted that his first successful hacking was when he altered his parents' phone bill, a practice known as phreaking:

> I was on the internet pretty much twenty-four hours a day calling the States. My parents would get very upset so I had to use my knowledge about telecommunications, how to eavesdrop and redirect at operator level.

He added that many hackers from his generation had become internet security experts.

▨▨▨▨ Hacking into Microsoft

In October 2000 a particularly spectacular example of successful hacking occurred when a computer hacker succeeded in accessing the main source code (also known as program code) for one of Microsoft's products that is currently still in preparation. Microsoft did not announce which product was the subject of the hacking. It seems likely that the hacker involved in the Microsoft incident broke in via a computer being used by an employee at a remote site and which may not have been as adequately protected as Microsoft's office systems.

Microsoft called the hack 'a deplorable act of industrial espionage'. However, this is considered by many to have been corporate spin on what was fundamentally a deeply embarrassing matter. The fact was that the world's largest, richest and most powerful computer organization had been hacked by a relatively straightforward technique using a hacking program known as a Trojan horse, which seeks to induce a program to accept the hacking element in order that the hack can be completed.

Commentators writing about the hack in October 2000 speculated that this would not be the last time that Microsoft would be hitting the headlines because it had suffered a security breach of its product or its systems. The organization has been at the centre of many major internet, e-mail and virus security breaches in recent years. The reason for Microsoft's frequent victim status on the security breach front is simply that its software is so ubiquitous due to its dominating share of so many key markets. As far as this particular hacking event is concerned, it is at least to Microsoft's credit that it detected it.

Was there a benefit that the hack could have brought to a Microsoft rival – inasmuch as an organization of Microsoft's size and calibre has any real rivals? In practice, it seems unlikely that any competitor could gain anything from the hack. Even more to the point, it seems unlikely that *anyone* could win any benefit from such a hack. According to security experts, there is little of industrial espionage value in Microsoft source code to a hacker or, indeed, to most of Microsoft's rivals.

The source code would reveal how some of Microsoft products work, but the secret would be hidden within millions of lines of computer code. It would be a huge undertaking to sift through all the code and then try to work out how various parts of it interact. This seems to suggest that the claim made by Microsoft that the hacking was the result of industrial espionage cannot be sustained.

A more likely explanation is that the source code was removed by the hacker simply because the hacker found that he (or she) *was able to do this*. It was, perhaps, the hacking equivalent of a mountaineer explaining that he scales Everest 'because it's there'. Certainly, as far as hacker trophies go, Microsoft source code is hard to beat. What is incontestable is that Microsoft's admission that the security of its computer system had been breached and that hackers had obtained early sight of unannounced products sent chills down the collective spines of IT and internet channel managers worldwide.

The first cause for alarm was the apparent ease with which the miscreants using, it seems, a readily available and not too sophisticated program called QAZ Trojan were able to break through the defences of the world's mightiest software organization. 'If this could happen to Microsoft then no company is safe', was a typical view from a high-tech security consultant. The weakness was a system being used off-site, possibly at home, raising the likelihood that companies will have to screen employees more rigorously.

The second cause for alarm was the growing realization that if Microsoft owns up to having a cold, then the rest of the world is suffering from raging influenza. Security experts agree unanimously that the Microsoft attack was merely the tip

> Microsoft's admission that the security of its computer system had been breached sent chills down the collective spines of IT and internet channel managers worldwide.

of an iceberg threatening all the world's leading intellectual property companies. The level of the threat has been camouflaged by the reluctance of most companies to admit either that their security has been compromised or that they have the means to track a break-in. Consultants who try to draw attention to the scale of the problem are frequently accused of scare-mongering with a view to generating more business. Scott Charney, a former chief of the US Department of Justice computer crime division, told me most companies are simply unaware that 'virtual' intruders have made off with their intellectual property. 'If I break in and copy your customer list, how do you know?' he asks, adding that most computer crimes are not reported.

Charney, now a principal consultant at PriceWaterhouseCoopers, pointed to a test carried out by his staff on US Defence Department computer systems. They tried secretly to break into 38,000 Defence Department computers and were successful in penetrating 24,700 of them. A security audit later showed that the department's system administrator had spotted only 988 successful attacks, or 4 per cent of the intrusions. More important, he had reported only 267 of the incidents to his superiors. 'And that was in an agency with mandatory reporting and some pretty tough security measures', Charney told me.

Experts also agree that the spread of computer viruses is woefully under-reported. Srivats Sampath, the chief executive officer of McAfee, the computer security software group, told me the company had spotted more that 2.8 million files infected with the infamous Love Bug virus on its North American customers' computers during October 2000. The implication is that the virus, which paralyzed corporate e-mail systems in 2000, is still out there and multiplying. But very few people had come forward to report it Sampath told me. 'Maybe people are just keeping quiet about these things' he added.

Security experts say that the majority of break-ins are not identified because hackers have become more sophisticated in their mode of attack and because management still refuses to devote adequate resources to basic risk management. Once a break-in had been spotted it was frequently not reported, often because the tools were not available to gauge the seriousness of the intrusion. News of break-ins rarely reaches the public as companies fear losing the confidence of their customers and investors.

The growth of the internet has made intrusion significantly easier than in earlier times, when hackers frequently depended on company insiders to provide both telephone numbers to make it possible to dial-up a firm's network and passwords to smooth their way inside. Unlike proprietary networks, however, the internet is designed to make communications easy.

Scott Charney told me companies have first to acknowledge that they were at risk: 'It's a risk but it's a manageable risk'. He advised companies to make a thorough assessment of their networks, identifying assets that they wanted to protect and working out the potential threats to those assets. 'Sometimes that's not so difficult: a recent joint venture could bring outsiders into your operation'. Companies also needed to form an emergency response team to tackle intrusions. No security systems were foolproof. 'But its like having a club lock on your steering wheel. Any security measures are going to make hackers stop and think whether their time would be better spent looking for easier prey'.

A source at Microsoft told me that the October 2000 break-in was only the latest in a string of attacks on its network: 'Microsoft is a frequent target of network-based attacks and corporate security actively works to protect the network against them'.

The complex motivation of hackers

The importance of this aspect of hacker motivation – that they want to solve complex problems to show the world, and perhaps also themselves, how clever they are – can hardly be overstated.

Generally, many hackers all seem to share a feeling of being insufficiently highly regarded by the society in which they live. Admittedly, most people feel this at some time, from presidents and kings down to the humblest members of society. The difference is that hackers appear to feel it particularly keenly, and also, by the fact of their conditions of their lives, are continually frustrated by it. The importance of this aspect of hacker psychology is seen in that what 'cures' many hackers of their vice is not moral exhortation but when they find they can enjoy status and wealth from selling their skills to internet security firms on the open market. When they do this, the need to show the world how clever they are by engaging in hacking is likely to vanish abruptly because they win that status through their talent and ability to show their smarts to the world in a more legitimate way.

Another observation that it is important to make here is that the very nature of computers makes them appeal to solitary people engaged in pursuing private fantasies and private motives. Computers have brought untold benefits to human society, perhaps particularly in terms of simply making life more *interesting*. One serious problem, however, is that almost by definition they are indeed a tool which is above all designed to be used by one person at a time. Even when teenagers get together in someone's bedroom to play computer games, the games are usually played by one teenager at a time rather than in any social framework. This drawback of computers would be relatively trivial were it not for the fact that it clearly ministers to disaffected or socially inexperienced people who find interacting with a computer much easier than interacting with another person. Young men, who, as is well known, frequently lack social skills compared with young women of their own age, are frequently drawn to computers and spend more time using them than is good for either the user or the computer. Such people may be exquisitely delighted at discovering the extraordinary amount of power which their mastery of computers can give them.

It is a power which all too often has had practical repercussions in breaches of what are often extremely important and confidential databases. An alarming number of high-profile and crucially important databases have been successfully accessed by computer criminals, from banks' databases of customer details to air traffic control systems, computer systems used by national departments of defence, hospital databases and many others. The point is that if a database is not properly protected against illicit access there is a strong likelihood that someone, somewhere, using some computer will seek to access it illicitly sooner rather than later. Many hackers actually engage in a form of random hacking attempts rather as people flick between channels using a TV remote control. These hackers will use a variety of random dialling systems to see what they can access, and when they do, they will make use of similarly sophisticated tools to try to crack passwords and other elementary types of security protection. For example, a number of dictionaries are now available to hackers and the power of modern computers is such that hackers can easily try every word in the dictionary in a few minutes (or even seconds) until they find the password that fits.

> If a database is not properly protected against illicit access someone, somewhere, using some computer will seek to access it illicitly sooner rather than later.

Facing up to the reality of the IT security challenge

Understanding what kinds of people commit computer crime does not of itself help one to protect against that crime. But a good understanding of why people commit such crimes and what kind of people do so can play an extremely important role in encouraging an organization to be on guard and above all to take positive steps to make its computer systems secure.

In this context, the following points should be taken on board:

- If a computer system does have an area of vulnerability from a security perspective, someone is probably going to exploit that vulnerability, and probably sooner rather than later.

- Computer studies are increasingly popular in schools. Indeed, they are part of the curriculum of most schools nowadays. The result of this is that an endless supply of talented individuals with knowledge of computers and computer systems is being produced by the production line of education. Of course, there is every reason why this should happen, because career opportunities in computing are immense. But just as many good people learn to use computers, many bad people do so as well. Ironically, computer studies are even particularly popular on the curricula of prisons and penitentiaries. As Alan Brill, senior managing director of the highly successful private investigation organization Kroll Associates, told me in New York:

  A horrifying statistic is that the United States currently spends more money on training and teaching prison inmates how to use computers than it does on training law enforcement officials in how to prosecute computer crime. ... The truth is that when it comes to computer crime, the deck is stacked against the good guys.

- Any technological resource that is available to – using Brill's term – 'the good guys' is also available to the bad guys. This is, perhaps sadly, a fundamental feature of technology: it is available to everyone. There are some exceptions, but not many. For example, the US Department of Defense restricts access and sharing of some of its more advanced technology. Its global positioning system (GPS), for instance, is only available to the general public at a lower level of accuracy than it is available to the Department itself. Furthermore, some types of technology have a *de facto* access restriction built into them by virtue of their high cost. This, for example, is how banknote manufacturers seek to keep one step ahead of counterfeiters. They know that they, as manufacturers, cannot in principle expect to have access to technology to which counterfeiters do not have access. On the other hand, they also know that there are certain methods of printing banknotes which require considerable capital, and that if the capital required is sufficiently large, counterfeiters may decide it is not worth their while to use it. Hence the development of such special indicators in banknotes as the watermark (which requires a complex manufacturing process that introduces the mark onto the paper while it is still in an intermediate stage of manufacture), the metallic strip (which also requires a complex manufacturing process, and which is nowadays made even more difficult to imitate by the use of a broken strip on one side of the note, and the use of a hologram). The final attempt at safe-guarding banknotes is that they are printed on special paper with a high rag content. The production of this paper is rigidly controlled and every sheet produced is accounted for. The high rag content means that the paper will glow differently under an ultraviolet light and explains why this method is an effective detection system of forged banknotes.

Despite the exceptions, it is generally true that a bona fide user of technology cannot expect illicit users to have access to any lower grade of technology than they have themselves. Furthermore, the banknote principle, whereby manufacturers hope that counterfeiters will be dissuaded from investing in extremely expensive manufacturing processes to copy banknotes whose intrinsic worth is not necessarily going to be great, does not work where illicit use of IT is concerned. No doubt a counterfeiter may be dissuaded from investing, say, $1 million in a complex manufacturing plant to produce banknotes which, to avoid detection, can only be released slowly into the banking system, and which may have an intrinsic face value that is quite small. However, it is usually worthwhile for almost any amount of money to be spent on technology by a committed computer criminal because the rewards can be so great. Ironically, while manufacturing banknotes is likely to become more expensive all the time, IT becomes less expensive all the time, and this trend is set to continue.

- Even when the 'front-end' of the computer crime is being carried out by a disaffected teenager with more IT knowledge, and less sense of social responsibility, than is good for him, it is naïve to assume that he will be the only player involved in the crime. In fact, organized crime has for some years been moving more and more heavily into computer crime for the very good reason that it is comparatively easy for organized criminals to remain undetected, and even easier for them to hire some naïve, disaffected person who can be left to take the blame if things go wrong. It is sometimes difficult for law-abiding people to realize that the world is full of career criminals for whom life is relatively cheap and who are more than ready to injure and kill in pursuit of their illicit financial gains. For such people, the idea of stealing prodigious sums of money by transferring funds illicitly or obtaining enormous financial benefits by gaining access to valuable information is fantastically attractive. The fact that so few instances of this kind of crime become public should probably be seen simply as proof that such criminal ventures are often extremely successful at obtaining the funds they seek and at remaining undetected.

- The idea of the external hacker devoting his energies to trying to access computer systems he has no business accessing is to some extent a romantic one. Plenty of such people do exist, and the threat they present is an extremely real one. However, an even more potent threat to any organization is provided by *insiders*. These are people either who work for an organization now, and consequently enjoy various access privileges in terms of using the organization's IT resources and being allowed to enter computer rooms, or who have left the employment of the organization, but have not yet had these privileges removed from them. In practice, most truly serious instances of computer fraud or other computer crime are caused by insiders. There is no easy way to deal with this problem because, by definition, an organization is going to have to make its IT resources available to some employees if the resources are to be used for profitable activity. This book considers the issue of security problems stemming from illicit actions from insiders in more detail later. For the time being, the problem insiders present is merely flagged here as an initial, and grave, warning.

Important terms of reference

Computer security, or IT security, is an exact science. It is not possible to discuss it usefully without first defining the terms of reference we need to use. Unfortunately, as is often the case when discussing specialized applications of technology, there is less general agreement on the definition of certain key terms and definitions than is desirable. For the purposes of this book it is consequently necessary to formulate precise definitions for such terms and concepts before proceeding.

The first point to make is that this book is grounded on the fundamental concept that *the problem of e-business trust and security is essentially a subset of the broader problem of IT security* generally. In practical terms, an understanding of the challenge of IT security as a whole is necessary before the particular requirements of e-business trust and security can be addressed.

I mentioned in the Introduction that this is a general book that is intended for all industrial and commercial sectors, but that it is particularly targeted towards those sectors – such as the financial sector – where computer-held information is likely to be especially valuable. It is also important to mention that type of job titles to which the book is targeted. These include:

- chief executives
- financial directors
- accounts managers
- IT directors/IT managers
- security officers
- compliance officers.

In practical terms, however, *everybody* at an organization needs to be concerned about IT security in general and e-business trust and security in particular. It is naïve to assume that only people with specific job responsibilities need to be concerned about security. In practice, security breaches of all kinds are perhaps *more* likely to involve staff other than senior staff, partly because computer criminals naturally tend to choose inconspicuous, low-profile points of entry to an organization, and partly because – as we shall see – physical access points must be rigorously controlled if IT security is to be maximized, and these physical access points are normally manned by non-senior staff.

Relevant definitions used in this book are as follows:

A **computer criminal** has already been defined, but the definition can again be included for completeness here: **anybody who participates in any unauthorized access or use of a computer system**.

Generally, the concept of **IT security** (which can be regarded as interchangeable with **computer security**) means **any activity directed at affording maximum protection to any kind of IT system or installation against wilful or accidental loss of function, reduced efficiency or compromise to the data held or the confidentiality or integrity of those data**.

An **IT security breach** can be defined **as any breach of IT security whatsoever**. The breach is still a breach even if no money or information is stolen; the breach is still a breach even if the organization suffers no loss at all as a result of it; and, it might be added, the breach is still a breach even if the organization has not detected it.

An **IT security hazard**, frequently abbreviated to 'hazard', can be defined as **any threat to IT security**.

An **IT security measure** is **any implementation of activity, whether procedural, operational, technical or related to management policy or personnel, directed at increasing the level of computer security**.

Narrowing the field of inquiry to focus on the e-business area that is the main topic covered by this book, we need to define the twin concepts of e-business trust and e-business security. These are related but strictly separate. The importance of focusing on them and identifying them as special areas of IT security which need attending to stems from the fundamental virtual nature of the internet, which was discussed in the previous chapter.

▨▨▨▨ The internet trust challenge

The most serious security challenge arising from the fundamental nature of the internet as a virtual medium is the problem of internet trust. **Internet trust** can be defined as **the challenge of verifying bona fide identity across the internet**. It is a problem whose definition is much simpler than its solution. Similarly, **e-business trust** can be defined as **the challenge facing an organization and its customers of verifying each other's bona fide identity across the internet**.

Both these problems are at heart the problem of **authentication**: that is, **the confident establishment of the truth or genuineness of a person or organization**.

At a practical, day-to-day level, an example of where authentication will be required across the internet would be where an internet retailer wants to ensure that the customer who is receiving goods is the customer the retailer thinks they are. Similarly, an individual who is communicating confidential information (such as details of his or her credit card) wants to be certain that the retailer receiving this confidential information is the retailer whom the customer has, in effect, chosen as a trustworthy supplier. Inherent in this trust relationship is the retailer's confidence that the genuine customer will pay for the goods or services received. Inherent in the customer's confidence is the customer's belief that sending confidential details across the internet does not involve any risk arising from the recipient, because the recipient is a reliable and trustworthy party to become privy to that information.

In practice, the problem of establishing authentication over the internet is a difficult and unique one. Why should this be?

The best way of answering this enormously important question is for us to consider how authentication is established in a face-to-face situation. After all, it is only relatively recently that people and organizations have had to worry about authentication in a situation where they cannot see the other party or have any direct physical contact with them.

The first time this problem reared its head was in the 1970s, when banks and other financial institutions started to realize that they could cut down enormously on costs – and deliver a better service into the bargain – if they delivered some routine banking services remotely, via automated teller machine (ATM) networks. And it is only during the past few years that the internet presented particular authentication challenges: with this new communications system creating a serious authentication problem by virtue of its completely virtual operation.

Clearly, compared with the history of the human race, the development of ATM networks and the internet are extremely recent events. This does not, however, mean that authentication is a recent problem. It has always been necessary to authenticate people, from our earliest days in primitive tribes. In essence, there have always been three principal ways of authenticating an individual.

Firstly, a person can be authenticated by attention being given to **what they are**. In this type of authentication, the individual in effect proves his or her genuineness (or is revealed to be fake) by virtue of what he or she is. This has undoubtedly been the most important authentication system, and in any physical meeting between people it is as important today as it ever was. Psychologists studying human perception have found that the human brain has evolved a particularly effective perceptual mechanism for allowing us to recognize people we know, even among a vast sea of faces. In practice, the thought process behind this identification is so rapid that we hardly notice it. It is, however, remarkable that we are able to identify friends and loved ones so effectively and so rapidly. Incidentally, this ability seems to be more effective when applied to people of our own racial type. It is easy to see how evolution, acting during thousands of years when people only ever met other members of their own racial type, did not find it necessary to develop a faculty for cross-identification of other racial types.

Identification of faces is not, of course, the only type of identification that relies on us assessing the physical nature of somebody. Build, height and other features are also relevant in this type of authentication. Eyes are particularly important: it is a well-known fact that eyes contain a large element of the facial identification process. In some circumstances (though presumably more in the past than in these hygiene-conscious days) smell was presumably also an important physical identification method. However, faces were always the most important, and will no doubt continue to be so.

Secondly, a person can be authenticated by **what they know**. On the face of it, this seems like a more modern type of authentication process, but we can readily imagine our forebears requiring this secondary authentication method during dark nights, when it was simply impossible to assess the genuineness, or otherwise, of somebody by his face before he got so close that, if he were hostile, he might have delivered a fatal blow. It is impossible to know exactly when passwords were first used, but very likely they – like language itself – evolved with the rise in intelligence which marked humans from mere primates. Some linguists believe that the very evolution of language came about because our distant forebears wanted to comfort each other with intelligible sound during dark nights when they could not see each other, and that language proved so useful that it was eventually used during the day as well.

In the Bible, in Judges 12.5–6, we read that the genuineness of men claiming to be from Gilead was tested by the genuine Gileadites asking them whether they were Gileadites or Ephraimites. If the man claimed to be from Gilead, he was told to say the word 'shibboleth' (the Hebrew word for an ear of corn). Unfortunately, Ephraimites could not pronounce the first consonant and said 'sibboleth' instead. As the Bible explains, the Gileadites took each man who failed the test 'and slew him at the passages of Jordan, and there fell at that time of the Ephraimites forty and two thousand'.

This violent, dramatic and intriguing story has given a word to the language. A 'shibboleth' means a custom, doctrine or phrase which distinguishes a particular class or group of people. If you think passwords are a modern invention, think again.

In the case of the shibboleth, one might see this password as a kind of test which incorporates both **what one is** and **what one knows**. A password like that is particularly effective. One might even go so far as to maintain that language itself is, in a sense, a kind of elaborate password. We recognize that someone who speaks our language correctly is at least one of us, even though this is only very much a preliminary authentication test. In modern usage, passwords are employed in an extremely subtle way to indicate that a particular person has the privileges associated with a particular status, such as that enjoyed by a customer of a particular bank. In practice, although passwords are still widely used as authentication devices, secret numbers are more practical, partly because they can be more readily digitized, and also because they can be changed more easily.

The third way to authenticate someone is to focus on **what they have**. Again, this is far from being a modern technique. The classical world made considerable use of special seals and other tokens which indicated the genuineness of the bearer. In modern usage, tokens such as bank cards are so widespread that there are few people in the developed world who do not have at least one, and many people have several. It is interesting that all these authentication devices, while useful in themselves, only become really effective when used in conjunction with another one, and ideally when all three are used. For example, you might make a mistake in identifying someone's face in the dusk, especially if you only have a brief glance at her, but if she also knows the password, you are likely to be more inclined to confirm the authentication, and if she brings with her the broken half of a seal which you gave her the previous week and which matches your own seal perfectly down the crack, you are hardly likely to disbelieve that she is who she says she is.

This principle of authentication requiring two indicators rather than one is at the heart of most authentication in business today. The core of the ATM authentication process, for example, is the use of two indicators: the personal identification number (PIN) and the relevant bank card, which is basically a special token designed to provide part of the authentication process because, in principle, it should only be used by the bona fide person to whom it is issued. Most PINs are four-digit numbers which are designed to be easy to memorize: an attribute furthered by customers having the opportunity to change the PIN they are issued with to something more readily memorable. Some customers have different PINs for different cards; others prefer to have the same PIN for all their cards. In any event, the PIN/card system is extremely effective, at least if the following procedures are adhered to:

- The card must be issued to the recipient in such a way that it is difficult, and ideally impossible, for an impostor to use it. This is increasingly often achieved by the individual being invited into the branch to pick up the card, in which case physical identification by the branch staff will confirm the genuineness of the recipient.

- The PIN must also be issued in a confidential way. Today, this is usually achieved by the recipient only being issued with the PIN after he or she has signed and posted an acknowledgement of having received the card. The PIN itself is issued automatically, by a special machine which prints PINs on a slip of paper without any human intervention. The PIN is held in encrypted form inside the computer system (e.g. the computer operating the ATM network) and never appears 'in the clear' to anybody but the bona fide user.

■ The PIN must be memorized by the user and not written down. Unfortunately, this rule is often not obeyed, because people often find memorizing a four-digit PIN more difficult than they expected, especially since they are urged by the card-issuing organization not to choose an obvious PIN such as 1111.

■ The PIN must not be disclosed to any other party, nor must the user allow anybody else to use the card.

We have seen how these three authentication methods use in face-to-face situations and also in the much more recent development of the ATM network. Let's now look at how they work in connection with the internet.

The internet, like the ATM network, is a virtual delivery system. However, there is a big difference: the internet tends to work on what are essentially open telephone lines, while the ATM network almost always uses a financial institution's proprietary lines.

The fundamental problem facing any retailer or other organization seeking to use any of these three authentication methods is unpleasantly straightforward: *there is a danger that the authentication process may be intercepted by an internet criminal*. This problem casts each of the three methods in a somewhat questionable light.

The first, 'what they are', is interpreted by modern authentication methods as the **biometric** type of authentication. The literal definition of biometrics is **the application of statistical analysis to biological data**. The specific use of biometrics in authentication involves the physical identity of the bona fide person being evaluated and stored in some form, and 'sample' authentications being presented and tested against it.

For example, an individual's fingerprint or thumbprint may be used in a biometric identification system to permit or deny him access to a physical location. In this case, the individual would press his fingerprint or thumbprint against a pad, which will then assess the sample either by an analogue method or digitally. Retina scanning is also an important biometric authentication technique, although its relatively low acceptability to customers means that it is only usually employed in extreme high-security systems where bona fide persons do not object to having their retina scanned.

How useful are biometrics in internet authentication? The answer is that they are less so than might be imagined.

The problem is that the very nature of the internet means that the sample can only be assessed digitally at a distance, and this is a vulnerability which makes the whole authentication method of dubious value. It is comparatively easy for an internet criminal to intercept the authentication (which, again, is only being sent in digitized form) and to imitate it, thereby providing an authentication of the internet criminal.

As far as the internet is concerned, the very *sameness* and *constant nature* of the genuine biometric sample restricts its usefulness. It means that the digitized version of the sample will always be the same, so that in effect the biometric is simply a complex digitized value sent across the internet.

What about passwords sent via the internet? Here there is a similar problem of the password being essentially a constant, at least throughout its duration of acceptability. Even if, in a highly secure application, passwords were changed every day, they could still be intercepted by internet criminals who would then be able to use them and authenticate themselves. The password also creates the problem that it is difficult to distribute to genuine users without its security being compromised. Furthermore, apart from special applications, customers are unlikely to accept the inconvenience of having a new passport issued more than very rarely.

As far as tokens are concerned, these are easy to distribute, and once distributed to a user can be employed for considerable periods. Furthermore, the use of **smart cards**, that is, **plastic cards which incorporate a computer chip** (whose memory capacity and speed of retrieval will vary from one model of card to the other, but which is continually increasing), means that a considerable amount of information about the user can be embodied on the card, and also – which is even more exciting from an authentication perspective – the chip can be programmed to generate many essential elements of the authentication technique, particularly the password. For example, one vendor, the US-based international internet security organization ActivCard, has pioneered the use of internet authentication based around the use of a smart card and what ActivCard calls a 'dynamic' password. The dynamic password is a password or number that is continually changing, but which is recognized by the sender card and the recipient computer system because both card and computer system make use of the same password encryption system. This encryption system is based around a number of factors, including the time when the transaction is made, so it is comparatively straightforward for both card and recipient system to generate the same password. Straightforward for the bona fide authentication system; but almost impossible for an internet criminal to crack.

It will be clear from the above that the virtual nature of the internet means that what one might term 'conventional' authentication techniques requiring a physical interaction of some sort with the candidate individual or candidate organization are not available. Of course, physical authentication is itself often unreliable. Anyone who has been taken in by a confidence trickster or even by some businessperson (or customer) who is not as solvent, reliable, honest or successful as he or she makes out to be will testify to that. People can be bona fide in the sense of being who they say they are from a purely identification perspective but can still turn out to be disastrous people with whom to interact.

But the *complete absence* of any physical interaction process over the internet means that the user has no alternative but to find completely different ways to support trust across the network. I have never flown an aeroplane, but I imagine that the problem of extending trust to someone or some organization across the internet is not unlike landing an aeroplane by instruments only during severely bad visibility. With no physical visibility to go on, there is no alternative for the pilot but to rely on the technology that provides him or her with dials detailing the plane's speed, altitude, attitude, position and the horizontal positioning shown on the artificial horizon. These *must* be reliable, and the pilot can only land the plane safely if they are. Likewise, when you seek to extend trust across the internet, there is no choice but to rely on the technology that you are using to support that trust. There is simply no physical interface available.

> The problem of extending trust to someone or some organization across the internet is not unlike landing an aeroplane by instruments only during severely bad visibility.

There are remedies available to the challenge of internet trust, and they are powerful, but the fact must be faced that the challenge is such that it can never be *completely* solved, and more than an instrument-only landing is ever going to offer a pilot the same 'comfort' as a landing made in perfect visibility. The remedies to the challenge of internet trust are considered later in this book.

The internet security challenge

Internet security is the second major subset of the safety of internet communications. It can be defined as **the ideal state where all information can be communicated across the internet secure from unauthorized persons being able to read it and/or manipulate it**.

Note that unauthorized manipulation can be as harmful as unauthorized reading. A message sent across the internet might be safe from being read by any unauthorized person, but if it can be manipulated somehow by, for example, the sequence in which the message is sent being changed, the damage to the bona fide sender and recipient may be considerable.

Perhaps the most dangerous form of manipulation is *delay*. The consequences if any unauthorized person is able to delay a message could be disastrous. In the case of some messages, particularly those relating to financial transactions, a delay of even a few seconds could mean the difference between money made and money lost. It is not difficult to imagine how some unscrupulous person could exploit this situation for gain.

Having defined internet security, we can now usefully define **e-business security**. This can be seen as **security of the internet communications relating to the totality of an organization's internet activities, including its internet-based relationships with its customers, suppliers, business partners and other associates**.

Throughout this book, the term **e-business communications safety** is used to describe **the ideal state where an internet communication for the purposes of e-business is being made on a secure and trustworthy basis**. E-business communications safety does indeed embrace both the internet trust and internet security challenges, and viewing the issue of safety as the overall problem of which trust and security are two subsets avoids considerable problems with terminology. In particular, it avoids the problem of the challenge of internet trust being de-emphasized.

Overview of e-business safety

What is the current state of play of e-business communications safety? This section answers this question in detail.

First, some general points. The first general point to make is that there is a general consensus within the e-business industry that safety of communications and transactions is an absolutely essential requirement if e-business is to fulfil its potential. Safety brings opportunities for developing an e-business enterprise because it provides confidence to those who back the enterprise and also to those who will be customers of the enterprise that the entire way the enterprise uses the internet will be successful and secure in every sense. Above all, e-business security is very far from being a merely a technological issue. It is in fact a business issue because inadequate security can affect very seriously the legal and financial status of any organization that is trading across the internet, from a dedicated dotcom organization to a traditional player that wants to create an e-business or e-commerce resource.

It is also generally agreed that the key to successful safety is planning and assessment, and that despite the daunting nature of the communications and transaction safety problem, many of the most effective steps that can be taken do not, in fact, require expensive products, although it is true that the products usually need to be implemented within a complex and comprehensive strategy to maximize safety.

At the time of writing, the e-business security industry is characterized by solutions which have comparatively little interoperability and integration between them. Many of the leading vendors are technology-led companies that have only been in existence for a short time. How viable these organizations will be even a year from now let alone five or ten years is open to question, although generally if the technology is really effective the market for it will be so substantial that the solution is likely to be available for a long time. Certainly, at present mergers and acquisitions between internet safety vendors are widespread. Incidentally, it is a mistake to assume that borrowing everything from one vendor will guarantee an integrated solution.

Now onto specific key issues. Much of the material in this section is adapted from the excellent and highly recommended consultancy report *E-Business Security: New Directions and Successful Strategies*, published by the London research group Ovum Limited in June 2000. (Note, however, that Ovum uses the terminology 'security' where I prefer to use 'safety' to describe the totality of the problem. I have replaced the Ovum term 'security' with 'safety' where appropriate in what follows, although not in the author's quotations below.

In publishing the report, Ovum announced its main findings. The organization pointed out that the traditional hierarchy of trust adopted by organizations does not fit the e-business model, meaning that new access channels – such as mobile devices – could pose a major security threat.

Graham Titterington, senior Ovum analyst and lead author of the report, told me:

> The old security model tends to rely on perimeter security – protecting the outer boundaries of the organization. But that is based on a hierarchy of trust which places 'internal' users at the top, and 'external' users at the bottom. This is plainly wrong for e-businesses, which need to allow customers and suppliers into the heart of their systems. And as we all know, the biggest security threats can lurk well within the boundaries of organizations, whatever their size.

Another flaw of the perimeter approach, he argued, is that it does not distinguish between different applications and systems, which may have radically different security needs according to how mission-critical or sensitive their contents are. This can mean that technical differences between access methods are ignored, which could pose a major danger when it comes to the new breed of mobile devices. As Titterington explained, these devices – whether smart phone or handheld PC – have too many vulnerabilities today to be afforded high levels of trust, even if the users themselves are trusted.

> There is no standardized security infrastructure in the form of end-to-end protocols, it is too easy to steal or tamper with the devices, and digital keys are stored at gateways rather than on the device. Organizations should restrict their access rights until such time as when there are better prospects of a standardized security infrastructure.

Ovum's solution is a model it calls 'ubiquitous security', where security measures are applied flexibly to specific parts of the e-business environment. This relies on access control measures to grant user access selectively, depending on the level of trust placed in the user (and the access device). Different applications would be afforded different levels of protection, according to how mission-critical or sensitive they were judged to be, allowing time and cost to be spent on developing defences where they are most appropriate. Titterington told me:

> Many organizations see security as a negative cost that has to be borne, but in fact it is a positive asset. The e-business that can demonstrate effective security has a huge competitive advantage. It is capable of building trust with partners and customers, because it can protect the confidentiality and integrity of business information shared with them. Trusted status means more business opportunities. It also makes it easier to satisfy data privacy requirements.

According to the Ovum report, the first priority for user organizations is a comprehensive and well-documented security policy. These are not available 'off the shelf' – requirements differ drastically according to the organizational structure. Dotcoms with IT infrastructures created from scratch have the greatest opportunity to get security right, whilst 'bricks and mortar' companies will often need to make substantial investment in re-engineering existing infrastructure and policies.

Tight internal control over the security environment is made all the more vital by the lack of legislative support and industry agreement, which for the time being is placing extra burdens on organizations wanting to do e-business.

Most countries, Ovum's report points out, have not only failed to legislate for digital signatures, but also keep strict control over the production and applications of cryptography in their territories. There are still no widely accepted accreditation standards, which means that organizations need to evaluate e-business partners using their own criteria. Similarly, the different certification authorities which issue security certificates use different standards of vetting customers.

The lack of interoperability between vendors is also a cause for concern. Titterington commented:

> The industry standards that most vendors claim to support are incomplete, and many vendors embellish the standards with proprietary extensions. The best advice is to assume that products do not interoperate unless the vendor can demonstrate that they do in fact work together.

He also pointed out that there is no integrated security management interface that co-ordinates the implementation of a security policy across an e-business. Despite these challenges, Titterington said he believed that organizations were moving in the right direction.

> Users are starting to appreciate the essential role of security in e-business operations. They are also increasingly seeing security as a means of raising efficiency, by allowing more people greater access to the information and functionality they need.

▮▮ The case for e-business safety

It should be clear from the earlier material in this book that e-business without communications or transactions safety is not realistically an option. Organizations that embark on e-business face numerous threats that have the potential drastically to compromise or even destroy their business unless adequate countermeasures are put in place and remain in place. However, with the right safety precautions in place, organizations can take advantage of the important and exciting opportunities to expand their markets, offer improved services to their customers and operate more efficiently. As I have already intimated, the glittering prizes of the internet revolution are only available to organizations which have truly got their house in order from the standpoint of internet safety.

There is an almost limitless range of different people and organizations who may need to access a website or other internet facility. For instance, employees working remotely away from an office, as well as suppliers, customers and potential customers and business partners can be permitted to run processes and access data. Customers can find out when the organization will be able to deliver an order to them, just as suppliers can find out when the organization needs to be restocked with some supplied goods. Employees of the organization can obtain the information they need and when they need it, and business partners can work on collaborative projects. By permitting direct access to internet systems, an organization can avoid the need for expensive call centres to act as nodes for filtering enquiries and problems. Organizations can generally offer a much faster and better service by offering a channel over the internet. Even if the organization persists in seeing the internet merely as yet another delivery channel (increasingly this belief is being revealed to be an ill-advised and shortsighted one), the benefits to the organization of offering safe communications over the internet are enormous. When computers interact directly with computers in other organizations, entire processes can be automated. However, much of this information is extremely confidential and must be made available in such a way that only those with genuine access to it can read or handle it. If this information gets into the wrong hands the results can be extremely damaging. Safety is needed to ensure that users only get to see – and modify – information, when authorized to do so.

The safety problem is generally recognized as being especially acute in the case of mobile internet access devices. Whether these are mobile phones, specially designed internet access phones or personal digital assistants (PDAs), they currently only offer a limited capability as access devices for e-business systems because of the limited bandwidth available and the slow switching speeds on the mobile network. Mobile technologies do not yet offer secure communications with these devices. Current levels of security might be seen as appropriate for low-value business-to-consumer transactions, or for passing messages to and from mobile employees, but it is unlikely that they would be seen as adequate for providing general access to corporate information technology systems.

Overall, the risks facing e-business from a safety perspective can be categorized under three headings: operational, legal and financial.

- *Operational* risks include attacks directed at denying service. They also include loss or corruption of important data.

- *Legal* risks include the impersonation of messages, the vandalism of websites with offensive material, attacks.

- *Financial* risks include fraud, corruption of financial data and theft of bank accounts or credit-card details.

An important part of e-business safety, as we have seen, is the trust angle. An organization operating through the internet may not previously know its users, and even if a user purports to be someone who is known to the organization, it is still necessary to verify that they are who they say they are.

Outsourcing and other measures that cause an organization to rely on business partners are a potential vulnerability – particularly if the supporting organization does not have adequate safety itself.

Trust, like security of transactions, is a foundation of e-business. E-business requires an organization to trust people it does not know. E-business safety raises confidence in business associates to the level of confidence in partners found in traditional businesses, and imposes safeguards to limit and control the damage that impostors can do to the organization's information assets and IT systems.

E-business is growing in complexity. For example, as we noted in Chapter 1, large organizations are using e-business systems to run their supply chains, often with thousands of suppliers. In some industries (such as in the US automotive industry) large corporations are coming together to share a combined supply-chain management system. Across industries, organizations that entered into e-business by web-enabling a few applications are now moving towards putting all their IT assets into a web-based infrastructure. These moves are both increasing the level of risk associated with web enablement and producing environments that are much more complex to protect.

Single e-business applications often involve customers, partners, suppliers and employees. Many of these have their own networks and so their network becomes part of the e-business environment.

Perimeter safety, which is focused on protecting the outer boundary of the e-business environment, is outmoded in this scenario. It is hard to define the boundary, and in most cases it is so wide that many threats already lurk within it. There is often no common safety policy across the entire e-business environment when this crosses enterprise boundaries. Zonal safety, in which critical parts of the network are protected at their boundaries, is the next strategy. However, this is too inflexible for the needs of e-business. Organizations therefore need ubiquitous safety, where safety measures are applied flexibly to specific parts of the e-business environment.

Organizations face different challenges depending upon how far they have gone along the road to becoming an e-business. However, most organizations will eventually evolve into a 'clicks and mortar' architecture. It is therefore wise to start by planning safety with a model that can evolve to meet the needs of this kind of enterprise.

It is necessary to face up to the fact that e-business safety has a cost, although organizations are often pleased to find that it actually costs less than they anticipate. There is, however, no avoiding the fact that safety is part of the cost of entry into e-business – it is not an optional extra. However, organizations can tailor the level of safety to their specific needs and situation. They can start by implementing the types of measures that will give them maximum return on investment. They have implementation options that include true in-house, insourcing and outsourcing solutions. Users with high levels of in-house expertise can make use of open source products. Many important safety countermeasures do not require any immediate investment: for example, reconfiguration of operating systems to close loopholes that can be exploited by hackers.

> There is no avoiding the fact that safety is part of the cost of entry into e-business – it is not an optional extra.

Safety gives you a competitive advantage, protection of your assets and control over your own situation. Safety enables new business processes and greater efficiency and automation. Safety is not just an insurance policy (important though this is) – there are real benefits that can offset part of the cost of implementation. Be selective, maximize the benefits and minimize the costs – but do not go without e-business safety.

Critical steps in e-business safety

How to set up safety

Organizations have to decide what the appropriate level of safety is for them. The starting point is therefore to examine the business and its IT systems to determine the assets that are most important and the threats that the organization faces.

Almost every IT security professional has different ideas on what he or she considers to be the most important steps in e-business safety. Ovum, which has considerable experience of consulting in this area, believes that an organization can only expect to maximize this safety if it first undertakes an enterprise-wide audit of its e-business safety provisions, and that the audit needs to take in all of the following matters:

- the business issues
- the legal framework in which the organization operates
- the operational implications of an attack

- the organization's business profile and political prominence
- the needs of its partners and/or directors.

After an e-business safety system has been implemented, risk assessment has to be performed regularly. Threats faced by the organization are continually changing. Inherent vulnerabilities of the e-business applications change as systems, and their usage, evolve. Therefore risks are continually changing and have to be monitored. Countermeasures include detection, monitoring, prevention and damage limitation.

Two points here are particularly important. First, the safety infrastructure will have to support a wide range of access devices, including the increasing use – possibly dramatically increasing use – of mobile devices between 2001 and 2005. The utility of mobile internet-compatible PDAs cannot be realistically doubted, even though the inevitable trade-off between portability and functionality means that these devices are for the time being only going to have limited keyboard and screen sizes compared to desktop computers.

Second – and this is an especially important point for financial institutions – automated e-transactions need special attention from the safety standpoint, because they work at electronic speeds, devoid of any form of what Ovum aptly summarizes as a 'human sanity check'. Furthermore, Ovum also points out quite rightly that electronic transactions are usually much larger than manually driven ones.

The authentication issue

As we have seen, determining the identity of a user (i.e. authenticating the user) is fundamental to all stages of an e-business transaction. Apart from direct use in authorization and authentication of users, the non-repudiation mechanisms for establishing whether transactions are completed are dependent on being able to prove who performed a transaction, and when. Proof of identity for a user in e-business is usually based on a two-stage process involving something the user knows (which could be a PIN, a password or a piece of confidential information), and something he or she has (usually a digital key that is stored on a smart card or on a SIM card in a mobile phone). Both of these can be stolen, and greater safety requires something more directly connected with the person, such as voice recognition or a biometric quantity. These technologies are still too costly for general use, but will become more commonplace over the next few years. Thus in the e-business world, cryptography is the root technology for proving identity, as well as for maintaining secrecy.

E-business is about co-operating networks of computers, and so it is just as important to establish the identity of a computer that seeks to participate in an e-business transaction as it is to establish the identity of a human user.

The safety policy

The safety policy implemented by an organization is the essential foundation of e-business safety. Appendix II of this book provides comprehensive details of a safety policy. In the meantime, some fundamental points about the safety policy can usefully be given here.

Generally, the safety policy needs to comprise, as a minimum, all the following elements:

- the analysis and assessment of the safety needs
- the design of the safety countermeasures that are to be implemented
- the definition of the working practices that are to be employed as part of these countermeasures.

The traditional approach to IT safety was to keep unwanted users *out* of an IT system. This was reasonable enough when IT systems were essentially in-house administrative and management support systems that could generally be self-contained and whose privacy and inaccessibility to other than bona fide employees made commercial sense. Such an approach also made sense when the in-house system was, in effect, extended to become a Wide Area Network (WAN) which might encompass one or more external offices of the organization, and even some external counterparties.

However, the general approach of exclusion is not appropriate for an e-business safety system, where the whole idea is to grant – and, indeed, *encourage* – bona fide customers and counterparties to use the website. Consequently a much more subtle approach to safety is needed where the maximum encouragement can be extended to those bona fide customers and counterparties but also where internet criminals will not only be discouraged from using the system but will absolutely be prevented from doing so.

As Ovum emphasizes, the focus of e-business safety has to be on securing critical applications and the data that they use. This requires ubiquitous safety measures that can be applied selectively to information held on the system, programs running on the system, or to critical hardware components in the network. This new approach allows safety to be tailored to specific needs within the environment, and for the avoidance of heavy safety that would impede business processes or impair operational efficiency.

Types of e-business safety products

Some tools are an essential part of e-business safety. Threats strike at electronic processing speeds and so only an automated response can prevent these attacks. For example, a tool is essential to detect a virus in a message.

Safety audit and assessment are tasks that could be done manually, but in practice are so complex that they are best automated. For example, the audit needs to consider the exact version of all the software products employed within the environment.

It is generally agreed that there are four principal categories of e-business safety tool:

- access safety products
- communication safety products
- content safety products
- safety management products.

Access safety will be the most fertile ground for competitive products over the next two years, as the enabling technology develops rapidly within a profitable market. Organizations need fine-grained access safety to control who can do what down to an adequate level of detail.

Major issues in e-business safety

Mobile communications

As matters stand at present, WAP-enabled phones are currently the state-of-the-art technology in mobile e-business. However, their value is not yet proven and they face tough competition in the mid-term future as the mobile network capacity increases rapidly. Their prospects are further diminished by political factors. The WAP Forum is a large and unwieldy organization in which several members are intent on pursuing their own agendas. It is perfectly possible that in time to come WAP phones will become an obsolete standard and be replaced by something with a wider range of functionality. Mobile phones are already adequately secure for low-value business-to-consumer transactions, but not for mainstream business-to-business applications. According to Ovum, vulnerabilities arise owing to the following factors:

- the discontinuity of protocols through the gateways, which requires decryption and reformatting of messages
- the theft of the device
- the storage of digital keys at gateways rather than on the device
- the possibility of rogue software being loaded onto the device
- although encrypted messages can be encoded within a Standard Message Set (SMS – check the longer term) message, these are too small to carry general business communications – single end-to-end protocols are needed.

Apart from its communications and transactions safety limitations, mobile technology is still limited in its usefulness to e-business because of the limited available bandwidth and slow switching speeds on networks. These limitations will restrict its use in the short term to such an extent that the safety aspects will not become critical. However, these limitations will rapidly roll back over the next two years and it is essential that safety is expanded in step with the increasing use of mobile devices for means of e-business access.

As e-business functionality becomes more widely available on mobile devices, we expect to see them becoming more elaborate and combining the functionality of a PDA and of a phone within a single device.

Legislation

Chapter 7 of this book provides a comprehensive account of the current state of play of e-business security. It is, however, useful to preface that material with an overview of the subject, which is provided here.

The legislative environment surrounding e-business is immature. Most countries have not legislated for the recognition of digital signatures. Many countries still have laws governing the export of cryptographic products, the use of strong encryption, and even the passage of encrypted communications across their territory. Legal issues are holding back e-business deployment. The lack of a legal framework is another reason why organizations must ensure the safety of their e-business systems, as it is difficult to obtain legal redress for any losses that are incurred. Most e-crime operates on an international basis.

Interoperability and manageability

Interoperability means that different trust and security systems are used by an organization to maximize the complete safety of its e-business resources. Unfortunately, as the technology stands at present, interoperability is limited to particular product groupings in e-business safety. As we have seen, it does not even follow that all the products supplied by a particular vendor will be interoperable. They may be, but this is not an automatic consequence of the same vendor supplying all of them. Interoperability of security and trust products does not exist at an industry-wide level.

Ideally, interoperability is needed at three levels:

- the trust level
- the tool interaction level
- the information representation level.

At the trust level, e-business needs to be able to establish what level of trust can be associated with a digital certificate, from whichever certificate authority it came from. At the two technical levels, the industry standards that most vendors claim to support are incomplete, particularly in the areas of data representation (which is essential for inter-product communication) and of how to handle errors. Many vendors embellish the standards with proprietary extensions. The best advice is to assume that products do not interoperate unless the vendor can demonstrate that they do in fact work together.

There is no integrated safety management interface that co-ordinates the implementation of a safety policy across an e-business. Many tools have a central control point for managing those aspects of the safety policy that relate to the particular tool, and for implementing them across the corporate network. However, where a requirement in a safety policy is implemented by more than one tool, the item of policy will have to be administered separately in each of the tool's management interfaces. We are starting to see progress in the frameworks from Tivoli (IBM) and Hewlett-Packard, but a real integrated solution is still some years away.

E-business trust and recognition of certification authorities

As a preliminary to the detailed discussion of the challenges of e-business trust later in this book, it is useful at this stage to make some important points about how e-business trust is furthered.

Essentially the establishment of e-business trust depends upon satisfactory authentication of the individual or organization concerned, with each successive use of the internet by the individual or organization requiring their identity to be verified before they are permitted to use the internet for the communication or transaction in question.

Because the authentication and verification process will itself inevitably always be virtual, the usual method of managing it at present is to tie the individual's or organization's communication or transaction to a 'digital signature', which is a unique 'marker' that only the individual or organization can use. The technology already exists to handle this process, with the digital signature being sent via a highly complex encryption system that is unbreakable for all practical purposes. This encryption system is known as public key infrastructure (PKI). It is discussed in more detail in Chapter 10 of this book.

However, a crucial element of vulnerability exists in this configuration. This point of vulnerability is the actual *issuing* of the digital signature to the individual or organization concerned. The issuing is based upon the possession by the individual or organization of a 'digital certificate' which testifies that they are who they say they are. The digital certificate issued by an organization is known as a 'certification authority'. The effectiveness of this digital certificate, which is a kind of electronic password, is in turn dependent on the rigorousness with which the identity of the party seeking to obtain a certificate is established.

Some certification authorities offer digital certificates over the internet itself. Others require the party to make a personal visit to the certification authority and to bring documents, such as a passport, to establish the initial authentication.

Just as physical identity authentication varies in quality, from a properly issued passport at one end of the spectrum down to a fraudulently issued card to 'testify' that a teenager is above the legal age to drink in a bar at the other end, virtual identification also varies dramatically in quality. A well-established certification authority which requires a physical visit with documentation should, other things being equal, offer top-quality identity authentication potential. On the other hand, as Ovum quite rightly points out:

> Unknown certification authorities are not effective. An e-business has to know all the certification authorities whose certificates it accepts. Since each certification authority has its own standards of vetting customers before issuing a certificate, organizations have to know what level of trust can be placed in certificates issued by each certification authority.
>
> Lax verification of users when issuing certificates is the weakest part of the process defined in the PKI-based Internet Trust Model.

Other points to make about the importance of trust are as follows:

- Trust is extremely important in all areas of e-business and e-commerce, but it is especially important when non-core services are being brought in from service providers on an outsourcing basis. This increasingly popular way of doing business makes it of crucial importance that organizations can trust their service providers on a day-by-day, and indeed even hour-by-hour or minute-by-minute, basis. Service providers have to be able to demonstrate and prove that they are trustworthy.

- An interesting and useful observation is that the need for trust gives well-known organizations an advantage over start-up companies. For example, utilities, governments and banks are in the best position to authenticate individuals, because they have a long-term relationship with these people that in most cases includes corresponding with the person at his or her home address. They also enjoy a trusted status and a high profile in their respective communities. The need for trusted products favours established vendors such as Hewlett-Packard or IBM over niche safety companies. Against this, though, must be set the fact that it is often niche e-business safety companies which develop and market the most ingenious and useful solutions. This trade-off between utility of solution and potential longevity of vendor is one which has confronted most organizations at some time or another in terms of their IT expenditure, and no doubt will continue to do so.

Lack of widely accepted accreditation standards for e-business safety

Closely related to the problem of the quality of initial identity verification on which the issuing of a digital certificate is based is the lack of widely accepted accreditation standards for e-business security.

There are some emerging standards in the area, such as BS7799 or the US/Canadian CPA Web Trust scheme. However, these do not guarantee safety. They recommend good practice for implementing e-business safety, but they need an accreditation framework built on top of them to monitor the execution of their recommendations. The business insurance companies are likely to encourage moves in this direction by offering lower premiums to e-businesses that can demonstrate that they have taken reasonable precautions to safeguard themselves.

The size of the market for e-business safety products and services

The total market for e-business safety products and services will be worth over $58 billion by 2005. The e-business safety market is growing very fast: Ovum expects growth of more than 100 per cent between 2000 and 2001, and annual growth rates of more than 30 per cent through to 2005.

Ovum's perspective:

> This explosive growth will be fuelled by the rapid spread of e-business across the world, and by a greater awareness of the importance of safety among e-businesses.
>
> Some vendors whose products are sold in wider markets, such as anti-virus tool suppliers, will not see such large percentage growth rates for their products because their other markets are more stable.
>
> The most visible aspect of the spread of e-business safety will be that electronic credentials will become as common as plastic identity cards are today.

Geographical factors in the development of the market for e-business products and services

Ovum, which is a specialist in the analysis of key commercial markets, believes that geographically the market for e-business safety products and services will follow the established pattern for the spread of IT systems. It will be led by technological take-up in the North American market, with Europe and Asia-Pacific approximately two years behind.

The geographical spread of the e-businesses will not be mirrored by the development of e-business safety tool suppliers. European suppliers have built a strong position in the market, helped by the US government restrictions on the export of cryptographic products. They will try to defend their position as these restrictions are dismantled.

The e-business safety services market

Ovum believes that within the e-business safety market as a whole, services will enjoy a more rapid rise than product revenues.

> The increasing use of e-business safety by smaller organizations, and the scarcity of specialist staff, will fuel an increase in outsourcing. Services will account for approximately twelve per cent of the market in 2000, and rise to about twenty-five per cent in 2005.

Value for money

Another matter which Ovum considered in detail was the extent to which, as the market for e-business services matures, there will be pressure on the unit prices of products. As Ovum explains:

> Products in the communication safety and content safety categories of our model will increasingly come to be seen as commodities and be sold at reduced prices or bundled with other products. For example, content safety products may be sold packaged with operating system software if the anti-trust political environment does not prevent this.

Ovum adds:

> However, the current product offerings in the access safety and safety management categories are typical of products in an early stage of their development. There is a big opportunity for vendors to produce products that are easier to use and that better satisfy the needs of their customers. These products will be sold at premium prices for several years. In these categories the next five years will see competition focused on product differentiation, rather than on price, and margins will hold up. In 2005 customer organizations will be getting more for their money, rather than buying cheaper products.

It is true that in a market as volatile as e-business security, one might not unreasonably wonder whether it is realistic to make projections to 2005. But that is precisely the time period within which this book aspires to be current, and ultimately it is perhaps better to attempt a projection of this type than not to bother trying to make such a projection at all. Trust is the vital foundation of e-business.

Mergers and acquisitions among e-business suppliers

This point follows naturally from the above one. Ovum says:

As a consequence of this need for an established reputation, small innovative product vendors will be acquired by larger companies that are building up their presence in the e-business safety products market generally, and particularly in those product category segments with the greatest growth potential.

The e-business safety market is already in a phase of rapid consolidation. The more mature sectors, such as firewall vendors, have been reduced from approximately 100 vendors to about 12 vendors – of which about four dominate the market. Approximately one major e-business safety vendor per month is merging with another company. For example, in April 2000 Entrust bought enCommerce to strengthen its access safety product range and bolster its services arm.

Winners and losers

Ovum forecasts that increasing competition between products that are becoming commodity items will put pressure on profit margins in these sectors, although even these markets have substantial potential for further growth in terms of the volume of sales. Greater profits will be earned in the still emerging markets for access safety and safety management products.

Profit margins will be higher in the services sector than in the products sector. Therefore those vendors with strong services divisions will be better placed to prosper from the next phase in the evolution of the market.

The short-term winners will include:

- service providers that can exploit their safety background to amplify the trust the market has in their services
- systems integrators that can use their safety experience to build and operate trusted managed applications.

In the long term, application providers that come from the real business world will have advantages over the ones that are technology-led. The technology-led companies will provide attractive take-over targets for these established players, as they try to build up a comprehensive and convincing presence in the market.

There are good opportunities for vendors of related technologies to move into safety by selling the new commodity-type safety products. For example, network vendors (such as Cisco) and operating system vendors (if they are permitted to do so) have opportunities to include basic safety products in their mainstream offerings.

Vendors to watch

Ovum believes that systems integrators, including Hewlett-Packard, IBM and the world's major consulting organizations, will become especially prominent in the market. It adds:

Cisco is in a strong position because of its established status in the network industry.

Linux vendors have an opportunity to gain a profitable supplementary business, and are less likely to suffer anti-trust hurdles than Microsoft because of the fragmented nature of the Linux/Unix supplier community.

Industry-focused organizations (such as the banking industry's Identrus) will play a major role in the development of e-business safety, at least as 'king makers', if not in their own capacity.

Some of the major players in the industry (such as Check Point and RSA Safety) will continue to play a prominent role, because they are already in a strong position, and because of their close links to other large companies.

Box 2.1 provides a useful summary of Ovum's predictions for the evolution of the e-business security safety market to 2005.

Box 2.1 Ovum's e-business security market scenario

2000–2001:
- Market characterized by integration of point tools for perimeter defence.
- Growing uptake of trusted application services leads to demand for certification at corporate e-business level.
- First Internet enabled mobile devices appear on market (e.g. WAP-enabled phones).

2002–2003:
- Proprietary security infrastructures securing the enterprise in use by large e-businesses and TASPs*.
- Packet filtering embedded in network; first access security sites with gateway-to-application control emerge.
- Security management products absorb content management functions.
- Development of business-to-business electronic marketplaces and supply-chain applications drives certification at finer-grained levels within e-businesses.
- Rapid market uptake of mobile e-commerce services (business-to-business and business-to-consumer) driving demand for security extensions over mobile networks.

* A TASP (Trusted Application Service Provider) is a service provider which has undergone security auditing and provides certification services.

2004–2005:

Suites of interoperable enterprise security tools more widely available to the market, following the model of network management tools.

- Security and networks (intranets) secured using VPNs†; increasing shift to managed VPN services.

- Mobile e-commerce portals extend certification to business-to consumer market; large e-businesses with brand stretch, and organizations inheriting real-world trust, take on certificate authority role.

- Support for secure mobile e-commerce applications embedded in security infra-structure.

† VPN is a Virtual Private Network.

Conclusion

At the end of its major study, Ovum offers the following guidelines:

For users

- Think positively.

- Focus on the benefits of implementing an effective e-business safety policy. Remember that safety allows you to exploit e-business opportunities and raise efficiency by speeding processes and eliminating middlemen.

- Build trust by protecting confidential information about your business, your customers and your partners.

- Find the most appropriate safety measures for your business. Safety can be a bottomless pit for your time and resources, so you have to be selective and focus on the areas where the cost/benefit balance is most favourable.

- Exercise caution before embracing mobile devices. Ovum recommends that organizations restrict their implementation of mobile devices within e-busi-ness systems to the minimum level needed for efficient working practices, until at least 2001. By then it will be clearer which technologies are likely to gain widespread acceptance, and will allow time for better safety measures to become available for use with these devices.

- Respect your customers' and partners' privacy. Organizations operating in EU countries have to observe strict data privacy legislation. Failing to apply ade-quate safety to personal data held in the e-business systems could be a breach of this law. Even outside the EU, there is increasing public concern about the use that is made of personal data, and this concern could become an impediment to the success of an e-business that does not address this issue. Most e-businesses currently concentrate on the relatively trivial issues such as credit-card details, whereas information about personal habits and likes and dislikes can be much more damaging to the individual. Customers and partners want assurance that their secrets are safe with you.

■ Find your own solution. Ovum explains:

Designing your safety strategy is vital to the success of your organization. Choosing safety products can be time-consuming, as the market is currently populated by niche players, rather than by integrated solutions. Choose an appropriate balance of tools and other measures, with an emphasis on cost-effectiveness.

Once you have identified your safety needs you can start planning how to scope your safety infrastructure. The safety market is currently fragmented. There are various tools available that can counter different types of threats and attacks. These products may not be compatible when installed on the same system, therefore a lot of integration is needed in order to have a fully functional safety infrastructure in place.

Every organization has different safety requirements according to its structure. For example:

■ a 'dot com' company is focused on the need to get to market as quickly as possible. Overlooking safety is a major risk. On the other hand, 'dot coms' have a great opportunity to get their safety right, because their whole IT infrastructure is created from scratch.

■ a 'bricks and mortar' company has to re-engineer its existing safety and IT infrastructure to allow greater access and restructure its policies to cater for thousands or millions of users. Because it is a traditional type of business, the safety investment required to automate and e-enable its processes can be substantial.

■ a 'clicks and mortar' organization is a fully developed e-business that needs the most sophisticated safety infrastructure to enable the smooth running of transactions and processes over wired networks and mobile devices. The technologies deployed here are disparate and have to integrate seamlessly.

Access control and safety is vital to all e-businesses. This needs to be fine-grained to protect information held on the systems. PKI-based user authentication is one of the technologies that many e-businesses will find is too expensive for their current needs, but this situation may change as unit costs fall. However, without fine-grained access control, PKI is a waste of money.

Ovum also offers conclusions about the e-business safety market generally, as follows:

■■■■ The market needs educating

Ovum argues that there is considerable ignorance about the need for e-business safety, and what products can actually do for e-businesses.

In the course of our research we have forecast the rate of take-up for these products over the next five years to 2005, but vendors can create opportunities for themselves by speeding up this process. Vendors must address the total needs of their potential customers, even if this means that part of the solution has to be supplied by a third party. Customers also need help in getting their chosen products to work together to yield maximum benefit.

Product opportunities

Ovum believes that all categories of e-business products have substantial opportunity to increase sales volume as e-business grows and more organizations understand the need for e-business safety. However, there will be price pressures on content safety and communication safety products, as these become commodities that are bundled with operating systems, networks or other safety products. Vendors of these commodity products should seek to form alliances with suppliers of the associated products, or with hardware suppliers.

Services will be the fastest area of growth

Ovum believes that as the need for e-business safety is accepted by small to medium-sized e-businesses, there will be an increasing demand for outsourcing safety, and particularly trust-providing services. Service providers can offer rapid solutions, and this is often more important than the cost of the service to an emerging e-business. Few e-businesses have much safety expertise in-house and their executives want to concentrate on the business rather than on the technology. It is also important to provide a pricing structure that reflects the financial priorities and constraints of the e-business customer. There is a role for validation authorities to broker trust between trusted application service providers. A validation authority is most likely to be successful if it can align itself with a specific industry sector.

E-business trust and security consulting in action

3

Introduction

The forward thrust of a business as relatively new and thoroughly state-of-the-art as the e-business trust and security industry is naturally highly dependent on its practitioners, just as in the Industrial Revolution of the late eighteenth century it was the technological pioneers such as James Watt and Richard Arkwright who spearheaded the revolution.

The modern counterparts in the internet revolution of people such as Watt and Arkwright are the consultants who provide consulting advice to all types of organizations which want to ensure the safety of their e-business transactions and communications and also the vendors who actually develop and market e-business trust and security solutions. In this book, some leading vendors are profiled in Chapter 11. This chapter looks at the approaches and attitudes to e-business trust and security taken by some of the world's leading specialized consultants.

In order to allow their voice to come through, the discussions are presented in order as far as feasible to re-create the tone of the interviews I held with the consultants. The interviews took place in July 2000 at the consultants' offices.

Arthur Andersen – Simon Owen

Simon Owen is a Director with Arthur Andersen's Technology Risk Consulting practice in London. Arthur Andersen is one of the world's largest consulting and professional services organizations and provides security assurance and consulting services for many organizations globally.

There is no doubt that security has become a major agenda item for the board and committees of private and public sector bodies. Nobody wants to get security wrong and whereas in the past, it had generally been accepted that some things do go wrong with security, more recently, failure to address this operational risk has been seen as a major management weakness.

There are some obvious commercial pressures in favour of getting security right first time. For one thing, customers are not prepared to conduct business with organizations they regard as being insecure and where they cannot feel confident about the safety and integrity of their transactional and personal data. Secondly, building security into an operation at the design stage is cheaper than 'bolt-on' applications at a later date. And finally, weak security presents a considerable threat to a company's brand image. One mistake is enough to damage a reputation or brand that might previously have seemed impeccable.

Unfortunately, too many organizations are complacent about the security of their IT systems generally and their e-business resources in particular. These organizations may, for example, have strong front doors but have forgotten about the need for security among network-connected partners and alliances, and neglected PCs with dial-up ISP access. I've personally lost count of how many times a CIT or COO has stated 'we're secure ... we have installed a firewall'. Using this technology as an example, a firewall is much like a TV purchased from a high-street retailer – it needs to be tuned before it becomes effective and requires constant review to ensure it provides adequate service. The weakest link scenario applies to security whereby the weakest part of the network defines the strength of the overall system.

The internet was designed to be an open network and is inherently unregulated and lacks a police force or global regulation in the e-business arena. Although there are various legal measures and regulatory bodies which consider risk issues – in the UK, for example, the Financial Services Authority (FSA) has a team that looks at such matters – there are fewer concerted global efforts than one might imagine. This means direct action against internet crime is difficult. Another hurdle is that the negative publicity arising from taking an attacker to court is a severe disincentive for any organization. The very act of being publicized as a company with poor security is a serious problem for most organizations and makes it hardly surprising that they are usually unwilling to take the matter further in a court of law.

So who are the attackers? All types of people who want to compromise IT and e-business security systems represent a serious threat to organizations. Hackers, as they are often termed, operate with malicious intent and often have very few moral qualms about what they do. Their motivation is complex but may consist of a desire to compete for recognition with other hackers or arise from political and social beliefs. What is clear is that hackers are frequently highly skilled and will have detailed knowledge in subjects such as computer science and engineering and are likely to be aware of the vulnerabilities inherent within much of today's e-commerce technology such as operating systems, application and network infrastructure.

Despite the 'doom and gloom' picture, the fact remains that security technology exists nowadays to make e-business almost totally secure. On the assumption that a company cannot achieve 100% security (unless of course you unplug the system!), the trick is to recognize and manage the risk, and maximizing security while still allowing all bona fide people access to the system. Use security to your advantage – remember your competitors face the same challenges and getting it right first time is not only more cost-effective but can provide competitive advantage.

As for the cost/benefit equation: it is a difficult one to answer. Maximizing e-business trust and security need not be fantastically expensive with the average cost being about £250,000 for a major operation. This figure would probably be less for a smaller operation. But remember the cost of *not* maximizing security can be dire, especially for financial institutions and other organizations that do business with inherently valuable information.

So what should be the first steps to improving security? Andersen recommends that, before you write a large cheque for cutting-edge security software, consider the softer aspects and easy wins. Remember humans are often 'the weakest links' in security, therefore instigate an education and awareness programme for your staff and business partners. Develop a security policy or set of rules that are practical, easy to read and understandable. Where's the value of a security policy that resides on everyone's desk and is never read? The policy should cover all eventualities, giving sensible advice on security threats, manual and system controls. It should consider not only how to prevent security breaches in the first place, but also offer guidance if a security breach is experienced.

Once education and awareness have been addressed, only then consider technology. Trust and security solutions are still evolving with vendors striving to create one-stop solution that work both internally and externally (after all, who wants to be a secure 'island' with no connectivity?). Let's consider Public Key Infrastructure (PKI). This solution has long been deemed the messiah in the world of security and trust yet, to date, very few organizations have taken the plunge and implemented the solution. Why? Many organizations cite cost, standard compatibility, on-going support/operation and a lack of understanding as part of their reluctance to implement. Maybe the vendors could do more to address any lack of clarity – nevertheless, there is no doubting the reluctance to implement cutting-edge security solutions.

If your company tends to exhibit the 'close second' approach to security innovations, why not consider more mature technologies? Are your logical access controls robust? How do you authenticate users? Are passwords sufficient? Are application and infrastructure access rights appropriate? Have you disabled unnecessary network and operating system services? Are test and dormant user accounts disabled? Do you have comprehensive audit trails or intrusion detection software in place to highlight a breach? Have you got the necessary technical knowledge in house to deal with security?

And finally, when you've finished addressing the soft aspects and the technology controls, don't neglect the speed of change. The risk posed by security is moving at the same pace as that of changes to internet technology. Securing an organization cannot be addressed one day and then forgotten for months. There are new problems that will continue to challenge security such as home working, increased business trading communities, broader network connectivity and a deeper awareness of technology (hackers too!). Management will need to be alert to this fact and ensure their risk management approach provides a secure architecture that is flexible, cost effective, practical, scaleable and, above all, sensible.

██████ Charteris plc – Alan Woodward

Alan Woodward is the director of e-business service at Charteris plc, a leading London-based e-business consultancy and solution provider.

Trust and security do need to be considered under separate headings even though the totality of the safety solution they represent draws on them both.

Addressing trust first, this is clearly a matter of enormous importance for e-business. If trust is lost or damaged, there is a serious danger that customers won't deal with the organization at all. Obviously, the more valuable the information being sent by the organization over the internet, the more serious the potential for a breach. In particular, banks and other financial institutions will suffer very seriously if they lose trust from their customers and counterparties.

Internet security systems today are powerful. Commercially available security is better today than even military security was only a few years ago. This is mainly because computers have become so fast that they can generate and handle levels of sophistication in encryption which were barely imaginable even five years ago.

But internet security is unlikely to be of much avail if the policies and procedures used by the organization do not work, or are not put properly in place. The nature of these policies and procedures demands considerable investigation and analysis. They should cover every aspect of the 'trust and security hygiene' of the organization. For example, a policy should indicate that users regularly need to choose a new password. Attacks by hackers using dictionaries work very well, unfortunately. This is why some systems force you to use a nonsense password such as a random selection of letters and numbers. Sometimes directives, such as frequent changes to your password can be enforced by the technology, but more often policies and procedures need human management. It is also possible to make the efforts of the hackers so inefficient that they give up. For example, in the case of dictionary attacks on a password you might employ a system that locks the user out after three failed password tries, or else features a timelock whereby after the first failure the user is locked out for ten seconds, after the second for five minutes, and after the third, for one hour, and so on. This does tend to act as a disincentive to hackers and other intruders.

Basically, the problem of security across the internet is a question of scale: what makes a threat so potent is that so many hundreds of millions of terminals are connected to the internet and any one of these terminals might be the origins of a security breach.

But it's important not to get demoralized and to feel that the internet security problem is insuperable. It isn't. For one thing, it is not usually necessary to make a system secure for ever, but rather for just long enough to cover the crucial period. Overall, the objective of the security policy and any security measures taken should be to ensure that the level of security featured in the system is appropriate to the level of sensitivity ascribed to the data held on the system. It is all basically a matter of risk analysis.

Risk analysis means that you look at the system in question and decide where the points of weakness are and how these can be rectified. You also need to decide how exactly information held on the internet may be used for illicit purposes.

Generally, I think it's indisputable that organizations in most countries, including organizations in the developed world, simply aren't doing enough to maximize the security of their installations. There have been many surveys to this effect recently.

It's not difficult to see why internet security is often given a much lower priority than it deserves. You might even argue that the very fact that organizations shy away from publicity of incidents where their e-business resources have been attacked has led to a situation where users find it dangerously difficult to believe that they themselves will become a victim of internet crime. In fact, the research we have undertaken at Charteris, as well as our personal experience of how our own internet resources at home and at work are treated, suggests that many internet systems *are more or less constantly probed by hackers* and also that *internet criminals are continually seeking to explore the margins of whatever illicit gains they can make from the internet.*

There are also some fundamental issues here which need to be considered. The following points are particularly important:

- The operating systems in PCs were originally designed to deal with the security considerations of internal networks or even stand-alone machines. The very fact of connecting a PC to the internet is itself potentially dangerous from a security point of view because these machines are designed to broadcast the fact that they are on whatever network they are connected to.
- Network systems software is often inherently insecure because it leaves 'doors' or ports open which hackers instantly recognize and are likely to target. For example, in the NetBios facility to share printers and files across a network, if you don't disable the file sharing facility someone can access the system via well-known access points, such as the infamous Port 139. File sharing is clearly very useful in a closed network, but when you connect to the internet someone can exploit the network to look at your files. It's again the same story: the very facilities which facilitate networking make true security across the internet difficult. Obviously, in a shared network there must be open ports so that computers can talk to each other. It requires considerable technical sophistication and implementation of the right defensive software to allow networking and safe internet access while protecting the organization against internet hackers and other criminals.
- At a completely numerical level, there are far more PCs now, especially in homes, that are permanently connected to the internet. This is already increasing with the introduction of Cable Modems and ADSL (Asynchronous Digital Subscriber Line). Obviously, the larger the number of PCs permanently connected to the internet, the larger the number of potential targets there are for internet criminals. These criminals often rely on a numbers game. If they hit enough terminals, sooner or later they'll find one that isn't secure. Indeed, there is freely available software that enables a hacker to scan across thousands of machines until an open door is found.

■ No matter what trust and security provisions are put in place, there are still some kinds of attacks that are still very difficult to guard against. Denial of service attacks are an example. These flood a system with requests for information such as bogus orders. The problem stems from the fact that the message is not illegitimate in itself. Its potential destructiveness is due to the sheer volume of the messages.

Ultimately, the only realistic defence against trust and security threats is eternal vigilance, which needs to follow a vigorous campaign to implement a focused and comprehensive security policy, the implementation of technical safeguards and the implementation of procedures and practices which do their utmost to protect the organization.

PriceWaterhouseCoopers – Chris Potter

Chris Potter is a partner in the Global Risk Management Solutions practice of PriceWaterhouseCoopers, the world's largest professional services practice.

The problem

We share the perception of the need to polarize the definitions of e-commerce and e-business. For us, e-commerce means buying and selling over the internet on the part of customers or businesses. E-business, on the other hand, is a much broader term covering the use of the internet, the extranet and the intranet. It's a means of improving connectivity and deals with such matters as supply-chain management, business processes, links to customers, and so on. So e-commerce can indeed be seen as a subset of e- business rather than vice versa.

PwC [PriceWaterhouseCoopers] identifies four key areas of e-business activity:

■ getting closer to the customer
■ getting closer to suppliers and managing the supply chain
■ forging new marketplaces via e-marketplaces – a particularly important aspect of this is for buyers and sellers to find each other via the internet
■ streamlining one's own company's processes through the use of technology. In practice a company can manage many aspects of its business via the internet. Human resource management, for example, can often be facilitated through use of an intranet.

But none of these hugely important benefits of e-business can achieve their potential if security is not in place. Security is a combination of integrity and availability. There can only be trust and security in place if the following questions can all be answered in the affirmative:

■ Is the person or organization with whom we are interfacing across the internet who they claim to be?

- Are we sure the message has not been tampered with?
- Can we be certain no one has eavesdropped on the message?
- Can we prove that the other person sent the message? This is the problem of non-repudiation and is a matter of great importance from a legal standpoint for buying and selling over the internet.

A recent survey we undertook and published under the title *Trust in the E-procurement Environment* suggested that only about 20 per cent of organizations feel comfortable with the trust and security of their e-procurement arrangements. And what is true of e-procurement is, in fact, true of all areas of e-business. There is no way that e-business can deliver what it might be able to deliver if individuals and organizations don't feel comfortable with the trust and security aspects of it. These issues are, beyond question, the major inhibitors in the development both of business-to-business (B2B) and business-to-consumer (B2C) activity over the internet.

A particular problem we are seeing on the B2C front is that consumers often 'chicken out' of buying online. They enter the transaction cycle and get 90 per cent there, but when it comes to giving their credit card details, or other personal details which they feel may not be secure, they back out and don't continue the transaction.

Under the circumstances, customers can hardly be blamed for this lack of confidence. The fact is that not enough organizations that wish to engage in B2C e-commerce have done enough to give customers the confidence to which they are entitled that these kind of valuable personal details will remain secure and confidential. There are plenty of scams going on across the internet, many of which receive a fair amount of publicity. Customers know about these and are understandably reluctant to engage in the danger of being the victim of one.

It's true that some credit card companies offer a full refund for goods bought over the internet if the goods aren't delivered or if some other kind of fraud has been involved. But in practice making claims is more difficult than might be imagined, partly because of the difficulty of proving loss and also because, in cases where details of a card have been stolen, it is not easy for the individual to prove that he or she was not the person who used the card. In cases where individuals have suspected that details of their cards have been compromised, they have resorted to cutting the card up and posting it to the credit card company.

Among the most serious scams on the internet at present are:

- Selling books with titles such as *How to be a Millionaire on the Internet*. These books are invariably full of advice that will *not* lead you to being a millionaire on the internet. They exploit people's beliefs that when a new technology comes along there must be some way to make easy money from it.
- Offering 'free' holidays if you visit a particular website or buy something via the internet. In practice there are almost always so many catches and conditions that you don't get your free holiday.

- Failing to deliver promised goods. It's true that delivery failure may sometimes be due to inefficiency or incompetence rather than deliberate fraud, but the effect on the consumer is much the same.
- Stealing credit card details by hacking into websites and buying goods for oneself using those stolen details.
- Hyping shares on shareprice chat groups or newgroups so that shares one has bought or obtained rights to suddenly shoot up in value.

So what is to be done about these problems?

The cure

Are organizations doing everything they can to maximize the trust and security of their internet resources? The fact that general confidence in these resources is comparatively so low would suggest that much too little is being done, and while this is the case I think it important to understand *why* too little is being done. I don't think many organizations which want to do business over the internet are completely ignorant of the need to maximize trust and security, but too often they don't know enough about how to achieve these aims, either at a technical or at a procedural level. For example, in the UK recently a survey of online banking services found that many of these had inadequate security. The story is often even worse in the retail industry. Most websites implement Secure Sockets Layer (SSL) which can constitute a good compromise between the need to control costs and the need to maximize security. SSL provides an encrypted pathway from a browser to a website that is reasonably secure for low-value transactions. Unfortunately, though, many organizations lack access to the level of expertise they need to make their systems secure. The people who are adept at designing websites and getting those websites set up are rarely also adept at maximizing the security of those websites. Inevitably this causes serious potential problems.

Generally, the weakest links in an organization's internet security tend to lie in the following areas:

- *The perimeter defence.* Firewalls are special software designed to prevent illicit incoming internet or other external traffic from entering the organization's internal IT network. They have moved on dramatically compared with even five years ago. In those days you had to custom-build a firewall. Nowadays they are commercially available.

  However, each commercial offering must be assessed on its own merits. It's dangerous to imagine that just because you buy something described by its vendors as a firewall that this will automatically do everything you want it to do. You can't assume this. Instead, you need to check the functionality to make sure you have exactly the right kind of firewall for your requirements. The firewall must also be set up correctly, otherwise there is a danger that more than the one 'official' and accepted route will be open and the firewall will fail.

Furthermore, security threats are changing *all the time*. New loopholes and weaknesses are always coming along. So a firewall configuration that is safe today may be out of date tomorrow.

■ *Denial of service attacks*. The sophistication of tools available (and freely downloadable) for these kind of attacks is increasing, just as people's skill at using these tools is also increasing. Early in 2000, for example, e-bay.com, amazon.com and other popular sites on the internet – were targeted in a major denial of service attack and inundated with hits until they crashed.

What typically happens is that seasoned hackers create ways of bringing down websites. They don't then proceed to do the dirty deed themselves but instead they post details of the techniques on the internet. Young, foolish and not terribly skilled people can now download this powerful, easy to use software and create havoc.

There is a fairly resilient type of system available to defend against denial of service attacks. It is known as an Intrusion Detection system. It usually operates by analysing attack patterns and filtering out legitimate traffic from the barrage of information used in the attack.

■ *People*. People are always a serious point of vulnerability from the security perspective, for the very obvious reason that it is people who cause security breaches! 'Insiders' – people who, due to being current or previous employees at an organization, have access privileges or know certain confidential things – are always going to be security hazards if they become disenchanted or are under personal pressure for some reason. People who work at an organization and are totally on the organization's side may also become security hazards if they become lax at implementing security procedures: something that can easily happen. An organization's IT and e-business security policy has to guard against both these eventualities.

Finally, another issue which needs addressing is that in e-business there is immense pressure to be first on the market with an idea, for the very good reason that it is often only possible to reap the rewards of an internet initiative if one is not only one of the first to bring the initiative to market but actually *the* first. In internet business there are no prizes for coming second.

But even coming second is a great deal better than launching a website which gets off the ground with enormous fanfare and PR activity and then crashes because it can't deal with the huge number of hits generated by the very launch advertising that was supposed to ensure the success of the launch. In a sense, this kind of failure is itself a kind of betrayal of trust by the organization towards customers. The customers assumed they were dealing with an organization that was competent to do business; it turned out that they weren't. Furthermore, once this kind of disaster has happened it's very difficult indeed to restore a reputation that has crashed along with the website. Resilient end-to-end processes are needed to address this.

Deloitte & Touche – Yag Kanani

Yag Kanani is a partner at the London office of Deloitte & Touche. He specializes in secure e-business.

We see e-business as fundamentally a business-to-business phenomenon. As far as terminology is concerned, we believe that e-commerce is being absorbed as a term into e-business and in due course may even cease to have an independent existence.

Yes, of course, security and trust are important facilitators of e-business. Fortunately, more and more businesses are starting to take it seriously, especially within the financial sector. Businesses recognize that if they are going to extract maximum benefits from the internet, they need to move to a twenty-four hour, seven-day service around the year and by definition, such a service cannot be rendered properly secure unless automated security solutions are in place.

On the business-to-consumer front, trust is indeed a major problem, with consumers being threatened by the difficulty that commercial sites can relatively easily be made to masquerade into being something they are not. Likewise, customers themselves may pretend to be someone who they are not. I have no doubt that in the business-to-consumer industry, the potential of e-business is being inhibited by trust and security problems. I also agree that these concepts should be kept separate in order to address them properly.

What we say at Deloitte & Touche is that security is a business issue rather than a technical issue. It is a business issue because it affects business and is likely to determine whether or not the e-initiative will succeed. Security may have technical solutions, but this does not necessarily mean that it is a technical problem first and foremost. It is an *enabler* of successful e-business. Customers are so concerned about it that if you have got your security in order you can actually advertise this fact and promote the effectiveness of your safeguards.

Nor is security in any way a theoretical or nebulous issue. Breaches of security happen all the time in IT systems generally, and e-business systems in particular. The unavoidable fact is that hackers and others bent on interfering with the integrity of a computer system are continually at work and probing for weaknesses. Why do they do this? Ask them – I suppose they have basically got nothing better to do with themselves and want to show off how clever they are.

The sad fact is that hackers have a lot going for them. Perhaps the biggest thing they have going for them is the unfortunate point that when commercial organizations set up a website, they are often in such a rush to get to market that they don't get the security right at the very beginning. From a commercial perspective I can understand this problem, although I can't condone it. If you are going to make the most of what e-business can offer your organization, you need to move quickly and ideally be the first on the block with the new idea. Also, setting up a new website and e-business initiative is exciting, and when people are in a state of excitement they overlook precautionary measures.

Unfortunately, this kind of attitude all too often leads to tears later because hackers are indifferent to the thrill and excitement of setting up a new website: all they care about is the rather pitiful pleasure they derive from interfering with initiatives that more creative and able people have set up. I don't think we must underestimate the sheer malice of some of these attacks. Take, for example, an attack launched on the website for the Norwegian newspaper *Aftenposten*. Figure 3.1 shows the *Aftenposten* website before the attack, while Figure 3.2 shows it after the attack. As you see, the website was embroidered with obscenities and cartoons. The business damage caused by this kind of attack derives not only from the offence that it can cause, but also from the loss of reputation and status stemming from the fact that the website is plainly shown to be insecure.

The simple fact is that anybody who is so excited in the rush to set up a website that they forget about the need to make their website and internet installation secure only has themselves to blame if hackers and other internet criminals take advantage of this. In the same way that it is not good enough merely to have an efficient front-end site but you must also implement robust systems for order fulfilment, you need to make security an essential part of that robustness. Because the internet is a term on everyone's lips, word of mouth is extremely important for the success or failure of a website. Good word of mouth will frequently happen if a website is known to be providing excellent products and services at a reasonable price. Unfortunately, bad word of mouth also spreads very quickly and can be a disaster. You need to get everything right from the very start and to guard against security and trust problems and to make sure that customers are properly looked

Figure 3.1 *Aftenposten* **– before the attack**

Source: Deloitte & Touche

Figure 3.2 *Aftenposten* – after the attack

Source: Deloitte & Touche

after. You can't avoid this need and there are no shortcuts to it, in a scenario where, according to the research organization Forrester, $6.8 trillion of commercial transactions will be conducted via e-business, worldwide, by 2003 out of a total of $73 trillion of total commercial activity. Represented as a proportion of a twenty-four-hour trading day, e-business will constitute 2.5 hours at that point, whereas currently it is only twenty minutes.

Is the threat to security principally an internal threat from insiders or an external threat from hackers? In 1995, about 5 per cent of the threat was from the outside, while around 95 per cent came from the inside. Today, the proportion has changed: we estimate that in the year 2000, about 25 per cent of the threat is external and the remainder comes from inside. Do note, however, that this doesn't mean that the inside threat has reduced, but rather that the external threat has got much more serious. The threat from hackers is not helped by the fact that countries have strict legislation about spying on their own citizens. I understand why this legislation needs to be in place, but it does tend to make the hackers' jobs easier.

Remember also that time factors are of the essence in maximizing security of e-business installations. To take an obvious example, if a certain type of data is of critical importance for twenty minutes, you will be safe if it is protected for, say, forty minutes – you don't need to protect it for hours on end.

Our own remedy at Deloitte & Touche is to go through a systematic and concerted process for maximizing security. Box 3.1 outlines our secure e-business process, Figure 3.3 shows the security architecture we typically would implement for a user and Figure 3.4

Box 3.1 Secure e-business process

- Perform a risk assessment
- Define secure e-business strategy and objectives
- Develop security architecture
- Define and implement scaleable solutions
  - *Security architecture*
  - *Firewalls, secure servers, intrusion detection*
  - *Public key infrastructures (PKIs), digital certificates*
  - *Incident response and escalation*
- Solution verification
  - *Pilot implementations, acceptance testing, independent penetration testing*
- Maintain the solution

Source: Deloitte & Touche

Box 3.2 The way forward

- Holistic risk-based approach to security
- Appropriate risk management strategy
- Appropriate security countermeasures
- Audit and control
- Proactive monitoring of the impact of new technologies, tools and methods
- Incident response and escalation plans

Source: Deloitte & Touche

illustrates at a diagrammatic level how our web server would actually work with the client's internet installation.

Overall, as Box 3.2 shows, we favour a holistic risk-based approach to security with specific measures that are detailed in the box.

But no amount of holistic maximization of security is going to work if management procedures are not in place which ensure that all employees of the organization are co-operating and *collaborating* to maximize security. In particular, the following are extremely important:

- *Accountability* – people must be held personally accountable for security breaches and for maximizing security in areas where they are responsible.

Figure 3.3 Defining a security architecture

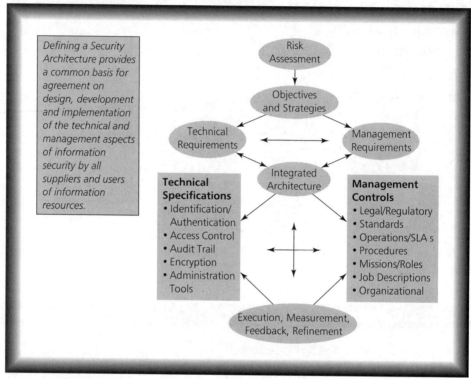

Source: Deloitte & Touche

Figure 3.4 Example secure web server (simple)

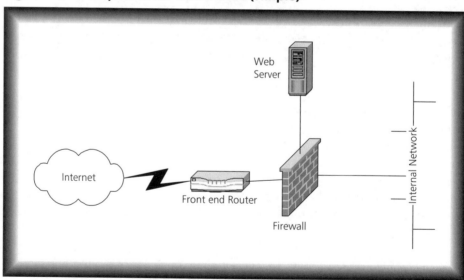

Source: Deloitte & Touche

- *Security awareness* – this needs to be maximized throughout the organization. To take a simple example, people need to be taught to be aware of opening stupid e-mails which say provocative things such as 'I love you'.
- *Knowledge* – of who is responsible for what.
- *Appropriate levels of security* must be deployed to meet the security needs in question.
- *Different hierarchies of security* must be used to add additional authentication where appropriate to the user name and password. The precise allocation of this hierarchy will depend on the overall risk assessment.

4 Secure electronic commerce in the retail financial sector?

Robert Coles

Introduction

What do you use the internet for? Many will use it for accessing the vast sources of information available or shopping, others for accessing their bank accounts and making payments. A tiny number will unfortunately abuse it for the 'fun' of causing mischief and damage or for stealing money, goods or services. You might have spotted a cause and effect here! The tiny number who use it for creating mischief and damage or stealing money, goods and services get a disproportionately large amount of publicity. This has created anxiety amongst the general public and is probably a contributing factor to the low take-up of the use of the internet for full e-commerce. Yet the facts don't seem to support some of the scare stories promulgated by the press.

KPMG recently published the results of our survey into information security. We identified that whilst retail financial institutions are consistently better at managing the risks associated with information and technology than all other organizations, including other financial institutions, the results in respect of e-commerce remained disturbing. In particular, the findings showed that full e-commerce utilization was still seriously limited, with security provisions for internet connections being inadequate.

E-commerce utilization is limited

Only 4 per cent of financial institutions responding to the survey said that they were offering fully functional corporate banking over the internet. Only a further 10 per cent said that they intended to offer this. This is in stark contrast to other KPMG feedback, where 43 per cent of the financial institutions surveyed saw e-commerce as more profitable than traditional channels of distribution, rising to 86 per cent by 2003.

So what use is being made of e-commerce at present? Most financial institutions now have a website for marketing purposes, and many use the web for browsing and e-mail. Over and above these relatively low-risk activities, a significant number now have basic internet banking. They have websites which allow simple transactions to be undertaken such as examination of balances and statements, transfers between bank accounts, payments to predefined recipients, and so on. These organizations have tried to minimize their risk by restricting the functionality available over the internet: transactions are usually limited either through a maximum value or by only allowing low-risk enquiry transactions. Traditional channels such as the high street branches or postal transactions need to take over for the higher-risk transactions. The ability to access a bank account over the web has moved from being a competitive advantage for many banks to becoming a competitive disadvantage for those who do not have it.

A few financial institutions have now set up internet-only banks. These typically offer attractive low borrowing and high investment rates to capture market share. Whilst these offerings do not yet appear to be making a profit, they have benefited from 'first mover' advantage – an important strategic factor if you believe you can cross-sell new products and services, such as the likes of Amazon.com have.

So what is holding others back from the development of these new delivery channels? High-profile press coverage of hackers and fraudsters, fuelled by lack of knowledge about the technology being used and the security measures that can be established, appears to be generating enough fear to deter many organizations from taking the plunge into full e-commerce.

> High-profile press coverage of hackers and fraudsters, appears to deter many organizations from taking the plunge into full e-commerce.

Is internet security adequate?

The fear expressed by these institutions appears to be well founded. Just over one-quarter of retail financial institutions and other financial institutions in our survey regard e-commerce as the most important issue from a security perspective. Yet little effort appears to have been made to secure current external connections. Most organizations in our survey said that they used the internet in one form or another (even if only browsing for information gathering purposes). However, coverage of security policies for external access in general is very poor, the security of internet sites is rarely tested, and provision of security violation reporting for incidents relating to external connections is weak.

Although retail financial institutions are well prepared for the more traditional security issues, such as physical and internal network security, there are serious weaknesses in the more recent areas of security introduced by the internet. Less than half had policies covering the internet/intranet, and access controls were also lacking in the majority of cases.

So what are the risks?

In addition to the basic business risks (will institutions see a return on their investment?), a number of risks have been identified by the security community as being particularly important to the internet. These are as follows:

- masquerading/spoofing (other websites pretending to be a legitimate e-commerce site; individuals pretending to be legitimate customers; 'man-in-the-middle' attack; employees pretending to be legitimate customers)
- message interception – theft of information (e.g. credit card numbers) and/or modification or duplication of messages (replay attack)
- message repudiation (legitimate customer denies a transaction/message)
- accidental disclosure of customer information leading to legal liability
- communication error leading to loss/corruption of transactions
- inability to maintain/extend the service due to technology constraints/use of non-industry standard hardware and software
  - code design error/bugs leading to software failure and loss/corruption of transactions
  - hardware failure resulting in the service not being available to customers
  - web server attack – denial of service and/or change of web server content
  - malfeasant code (e.g. viruses from e-mails; Trojan code inserted by hackers and malicious/fraudulent code inserted by internal/external programmers).

The questions that everyone seems to be asking are: are these problems all real, and if so, how often do they occur? The e-business security community will tell you that they are all theoretically possible – and if theoretically possible then someone, somewhere, will make them happen sooner or later. Whilst there may be some truth in this, there are few statistics on the actual frequency with which they occur and it is therefore very difficult to quantify this type of risk.

Does it matter? There is safety in numbers and the odds are in your favour! Many sites have virtually no security and still do

> The internet has been described as a welcome mat to any corporate network – exposing the corporate crown jewels for all to take. It is like leaving the front door to your home wide open, and the keys in the door for good measure.

not get hacked as they are not interesting or challenging enough. However, many do. The internet has been described as a welcome mat to any corporate network – exposing the corporate crown jewels for all to take. It is like leaving the front door to your home wide open, and the keys in the door for good measure.

Retail financial institutions are better at security

Not surprisingly, our survey identified that the financial sector has a better information security infrastructure and strategy than other organizations in general, and that within the financial sector, retail financial institutions are the best at managing information security. As an example, a greater proportion (84 per cent) of retail financial sector organizations had a formal information security policy than did other financial institutions (74 per cent) or other organizations (46 per cent). However, the financial sector cannot afford to be complacent. Security incidents can, and do, still occur in the financial sector. Information security breaches in the financial sector are always high profile and the reputational loss to an organization can be disastrous. For the retail financial sector, the danger is particularly acute. They cannot afford to have the credibility of their security measures questioned. High-profile court cases relating to fraudulent payment systems transfers, theft of credit card numbers over the internet and ATM withdrawals have been sensationalized in the press and caused considerable concern among the general public. The perception of the security of a financial institution is perhaps more important for the general public than for corporate investors or borrowers. Bad press could easily lead to a run on a retail high street bank, but is less likely to influence the corporate customer unless it also affects the credit rating of the financial institution. In the words of an operations director who responded to the survey, 'We have spent decades building a name that signifies trust, reliability and security – it could all be destroyed in an instant'. — *TRUST can be broken in an instant by a hacker*

Is secure electronic commerce achievable?

Until recently, use of the internet was largely limited to information browsing, e-mail and advertising. The most frequently cited reason for this was, first and foremost, the perception that e-commerce is insecure. However, it appears that among financial institutions this perception is rapidly changing. Most bank customers, however, are extremely conservative. Initially, at least, internet banking is appealing to the technologically and financially sophisticated, but banks will face a new challenge once the internet gains wider acceptance, when customers will be able to change their internet bank with a key stroke.

Banks and other types of financial institutions which underestimate the fundamental changes taking place in consumer behaviour will leave themselves seriously exposed to competition from new market entrants. The internet allows consumers to look beyond their national borders for financial services. This will require banks to be continually creative, implementing new products with a focus on customer retention and ease of use. Customers will not want to battle through a difficult website, or one that is slowed down by unnecessary graphics. They will prefer, for example, a thirty-second telephone call to check a balance rather than the four or five minutes it takes to start the PC, access the internet and log on and be authenticated to the banking site.

Banking of the future will become a commodity offered by many different types of organizations wanting to take the high ground in customer relationship management – supermarkets and insurance companies are already making inroads into the traditional banking markets. Competitive advantage will be achieved by offering safety and security – customers will only stick with the traditional banking names if they can trust them. What is the most important message for the financial sector? The risks are real, but the likelihood appears to be small. However, the consequences of a security breach are not just limited to direct monetary losses from fraud or costs of recovery. The impact from bad publicity and the consequential reaction from the general public are likely to be much more significant. So when taking the plunge into e-commerce, financial institutions need to do so with a full knowledge of the risks they are taking and how they can best be minimized through a risk management strategy and supporting security programme. They need to recognize that security may become their competitive advantage of the future. A risk management strategy should include consideration of *market*, *design*, *operation* and *security* factors. Salient issues relating to these factors are listed below:

Market

- *Achieving competitive advantage (or avoiding competitive disadvantage)* – Do you know why you are going into e-commerce, and how you are going to make a return on your investment? Is this by capturing market share, reducing costs, extending market reach, improving customer service, and so on?

- *Marketing* – How will you let customers know that you have an e-commerce offering (e.g. links from other sites, use of radio, TV, billboards, search engines)?

- *Product offering* – What will make customers come to your site? Are you offering something unique to attract new customers and keep existing customers (better rates, faster, new facilities, etc.)?

- *Profitability* – Can you tell how profitable individual customers and products are? Do you know if you are making any money out of the service as a whole?

Design

- *Web design* – Have you checked that the web pages are easy to use, attractive and fast (on all the different types of machine and browser that a customer may use)?

- *Structured development and quality control process* – Have you checked that code is of the highest quality, meets design objectives and will provide a robust and consistent service?

- *Change control* – Do you know what is on display on your web pages, and that the information is complete, accurate, timely and has been authorized?

Operations

- *Systems and business process integration* – Have the traditional 'back end' processes and systems been modified and integrated with new internet based front end?

- *Service-provider standards* – Will your ISP meet the quality, reliability and security standards that you set for yourself? (Don't let your ISP be the weak link in the chain.)

- *Compliance monitoring and audit* – Has there been an independent examination of the service? (The risks are too great for one to fall through the net.)

- *Regulatory standards* – Do you comply with all of the regulations governing electronic commerce (e.g. consumer protection, data protection, cross-border encryption regulations)?

- *Tax* – Do you know where your tax liabilities arise? (In which country will you be liable for tax? Could you be liable for tax in more than one country?)

Security

- *Internet security policies and supporting procedures, guidelines and practice statements* – Do you have a framework for security and have you checked that everyone is aware of their responsibilities?

- *Registration and authentication processes* – Do you know your customer and can you prove who generates the transactions?

- *Firewall and cryptographic solutions* – Do you have a hardware and software infrastructure including firewalls – to provide a first line of defence – and strong cryptography to ensure security can be maintained over a public network?

- *Independent penetration testing* – Have you made sure that the common routes of attack are closed by trying them? Does your security actually work in practice?

■ *Incident response and escalation process* – When the inevitable happens and an attack starts, do you know about it quickly and do you know what action to take?

An initial investment in establishing the framework for risk management and ensuring that these are embedded in all elements of the organization will reap significant benefits by providing the basis for evaluating and managing existing and new risks in a cost-effective manner. More importantly, it will provide the ability to increase the functions and facilities available to trusted users over the internet. Those who succeed in providing such services will gain the business, and it won't necessarily be those already in the market. The world needs banking; it doesn't necessarily need banks!

> The world needs banking; it doesn't necessarily need banks!

Note

Robert Coles is a partner of leading professional services consultancy KPMG.

Behavioural factors in internet crime

Introduction

We have seen that there are two principal types of threats facing organizations from the standpoint of internet crime: the *internal* threat from people – typically current or former employees – who may have, or can easily acquire, information about confidential codes or other types of security-sensitive information; and the *external* threat from hackers and other types of internet criminals. We have also seen that there is a trend for the external threat to become more serious than it has in the past, while the internal threat can in no way be said to diminish.

What is true of internet crime generally is also true of all types of IT crime: the threat comes both from outside and from within. Naturally, the more that organizations know about the motivations and attitudes of people who commit these crimes, the better. This is precisely the information that this chapter seeks to provide.

The material presented so far in this book might be said to support the argument that internet security is essentially a *management* issue rather than a technical matter, and that it is people, not computers, who constitute the real threat. It follows from this observation that guarding against the hazard of wilful interference with any kind of computer system is as much about understanding the motivation of internet criminals *and nipping their misdeeds in the bud* as it is about deploying procedural and technical precautionary measures. An understanding of the behavioural factors affecting people who misuse computers should lie at the heart of any internet security policy or strategy rather than be relegated (as is too often the case) to the status of an afterthought or an appendix.

> An understanding of the behavioural factors affecting people who misuse computers should lie at the heart of any internet security policy or strategy.

Internet technology provides many systems which are able to deal with human error and compensate for it – given that the likely types of human error which may arise can be predicted – but it is far more difficult to design a internet system which

> In internet security, prevention is infinitely better than cure.

is able to combat deliberate and wilful misuse or sabotage. Many efficient methods do exist – and have already been explored in this book – but there is no doubt that, in internet security, prevention is infinitely better than cure. Therefore, it seems to us essential for anyone involved in internet security to be aware of the factors which tend to lead people wilfully to misuse the internet and other IT resources.

Initial observations on behavioural factors

Few existing books about high-tech security look in much detail at behavioural factors influencing people to commit internet crime. Instead, the emphasis is usually placed on the power of modern software and the enormous facility which such software gives to any would-be fraudster or other internet criminal.

> The profile of the internet criminal who is prepared deliberately to initiate an internet security breach is likely to resemble that of the perfectly honest and hard-working person.

Unfortunately, behavioural science is not usually a specialization of internet security experts, except for those who have been trained within an investigative agency such as a police force or, in the US, the FBI or Secret Service. *Even those who have received investigative agency training in behavioural science find that in the real world of internet security the usefulness of their training is limited. The reason is that in practical terms the profile of the internet criminal who is prepared, for whatever reason, deliberately to initiate an internet security breach is likely in many respects to resemble that of the perfectly honest and hard-working person.*

This is precisely the point. Even though many malevolent brains behind an internet crime initiative are those of professional criminals who see crime as a way of life, most insiders – the most likely people to facilitate the fraud – are not professional criminals at all, but generally honest people who for some personal reason find themselves tempted into dishonesty.

Most standard investigative agencies, which are primarily involved in tracking down and apprehending habitual or recidivist criminals, are not really geared up to understand the thinking of such otherwise honest people who have a momentary, if devastating, lapse. (Fortunately there are investigative agencies which *are* adept at understanding how internet criminals operate; some of them are profiled in the next chapter.) Indeed, it is rare for habitual and recidivist criminals to become involved in the illicit use of the internet, simply because they are unlikely to have won the requisite level of trust which allows them to get near a sensitive and confidential internet installation in the first place. This is not to say that professional criminals have no involvement in internet security breaches; they have, but almost invariably only once the breach has been initiated by a corrupt insider (who has frequently been adversely influenced by a more experienced criminal).

As the consultants interviewed in Chapter 3 of this book implied, it is the task of anyone involved in internet security to take whatever reasonable measures can be taken in order to locate that potentially corrupt insider before he can do any damage. Ultimately the only way of doing this is to have a sufficient understanding of the relevant behavioural factors (i.e. the combination of external pressures and internal motivations) which are likely to lead an individual to become involved in internet misuse. With the sole exception of people who are seriously mentally unstable and whom the standard internal vetting processes of a financial organization would be likely to identify before they could do any damage, people who misuse internet systems do so for reasons that are perfectly rational to them and would be perfectly rational to any investigator if the investigator was able to imagine himself in their shoes. Indeed, such a process of empathy with the internet criminal's motives is essential if an understanding is to be reached of the factors which motivate such people.

In the US, where internet misuse was first recognized as a serious problem, there have been numerous studies relating to the demographics, economic and marital status and other measurable characteristics and background of people who have been caught and prosecuted for internet-related crime. These studies have not yielded much in the way of guidelines for readily predicting what kind of person is a potential misuser of high-tech resources This confirms the principle that where internet misuse is concerned, an individual's inner thinking is what matters, rather than his background and origins. Some behavioural scientists believe that, given the right combination of pressures and vulnerabilities, almost anyone is a potential misuser of the internet, and they could be right.

Wilful internet misuse falls into two fundamentally distinct categories:

■ internet misuse which is undertaken primarily for disruptive purposes
■ internet misuse which is undertaken primarily for illicit financial gain.

Recognizing the existence of these two types of internet misuse is important for an understanding of the motivation of the internet criminal. Clearly, the boundary between misuse undertaken for disruptive purposes and that undertaken primarily for illicit financial gain is a narrow one, and one type could easily become the other. However, what matters here is the prime motivation of the perpetrator: however complex the misuse becomes, a perpetrator will tend to set out aiming to initiate one type of misuse or the other.

The question of why some people cross the line between honest and dishonest behaviour in their use of the internet is similar to any question which seeks to identify why some hitherto honest and respectable people cross the threshold into dishonesty and crime. The difference is that internet security breaches can usually be initiated with little physical effort and often with so little immediate chance of detection that it is particularly easy for someone to persuade himself that the deed carried out hardly even happened; that he is 'not really' a criminal at all.

In this manner the ease with which the internet can be misused helps the illicit user to rationalize his act. The apparent subtlety and sophistication of misusing the internet appeals to many people who would not dream of committing a violent crime like taking a shotgun into a financial organization's branch and demanding money. Furthermore, the subtlety and sophistication of the internet misuse is one important reason why many countries have been so slow about passing laws against the internet crime. Yet it is usually as easy – or difficult, if the financial organization in question has taken the right precautionary measures – to steal a large sum of money via the internet misuse as it is to steal a small sum. Furthermore, the risks of apprehension or physical danger associated with the internet misuse are much less than those associated with armed robbery. This is undoubtedly why there is an alarming trend for organized criminals to become involved with the internet fraud, usually once they have found a corrupt insider to participate in a scheme.

It is useful to categorize the behavioural factors that can lead to the internet misuse into *general* and *specific* factors. The former consist of general observations which experience has shown to be helpful in considering why people misuse the internet and, in particular, commit the internet fraud, while specific factors consist of a more detailed analysis of the type of behaviour that leads to such misuse or fraud.

General behavioural factors

Research suggests that, broadly speaking, there are four principal reasons why people misuse the internet:

- desire for competitive and economic survival
- desire for social and political survival
- aggrandisement of egos
- psychotic behaviour.

The first two reasons tend to lead the person involved to commit the internet misuse for financial gain, while the third reason might also lead to this type of misuse but could equally lead to the disruptive type of misuse. The fourth reason, being irrational, is not really susceptible to analysis. It is fairly unlikely to be a serious problem within the financial sector due to the probability that a psychotic person would be identified by the organization and relieved of duties before much damage could be done. In any event, if a financial organization does not have procedures in place which would spot people who become severely disturbed, then it would only have itself to blame for any trouble they caused.

The three rational reasons listed are of help in understanding the primary motivations of people who misuse the internet. All the same, what matters here is investigating individual psychology, so these three reasons are best regarded in the light of the following comments:

■ Most people are honest most of the time.

■ Some people are dishonest all of the time.

■ Some people are dishonest most of the time.

These considerations are, in effect, corroboration of the point that what should interest anyone involved in the internet security is not so much the motivation of the habitual criminal but rather the factors which cause a person to cease to be honest.

No one can predict exactly who will make illicit use of a the internet system, and when. However, behavioural science has formulated certain axioms which are reasonably reliable in defining whether a person is likely to cross that all-important gap between honesty and dishonesty, between legitimate use of the internet system and illegitimate interference, or remain an honest person. Ten of the most useful of these rules, for anyone involved in the internet security of financial organizations, are shown in Box 5.1.

Box 5.1 Axioms indicative of dishonest, or continuing honest, use of the internet

■ People who have experienced failure are more likely to cheat.

■ People who are disliked and who dislike themselves are more likely to be deceitful.

■ People who are impulsive, destructive and unable to postpone gratification are more likely to indulge in deceitful crimes.

■ People who have a conscience (fear, apprehension and punishment) are more resistant to the temptation to deceive.

■ The easier it is to cheat and steal, the more likely it is that people will do so.

■ Individuals have different needs and therefore different levels at which they will be moved to lie, cheat and steal.

■ Lying, cheating and stealing increase when people have great pressure to achieve important goals.

■ The struggle to survive generates deceit.

Source: The author

The principles behind these axioms can be summarized in terms of three primary factors upon which often depends the likelihood that the illicit behaviour will take place:

■ *Pressure from a situation*. These pressures may be an economic need, psychosomatic incidents or conditions, or attitudinal aberrations.

■ *The opportunity to commit fraud*. This is an environmental situation resulting from a range of factors, particularly including:
  - poor internal controls
  - management apathy
  - previous unpunished incidents
  - the susceptible individual occupying a position of trust.

■ *Personal integrity*. This factor relates to the individual's personal code of conduct, that is, ethics, honesty, morality and other such generators of integrity. It also considers conscience, which is a mixture of basic moral attitudes plus a sense of apprehension relative to being caught due to a fear of sanctions and punishment. This factor also includes the act of rationalization of the misdemeanour, that is, the individual's capacity to avoid blaming himself for committing the deed. The opportunity to rationalize the act of internet misuse is extremely important for many potential misusers, who, as predominantly middle-class, white-collar workers would probably be horrified at the notion that they might be classed as common criminals. Indeed, a desire to atone for their crimes often leads such people to confess to the crime even though there would otherwise be no immediate likelihood of their apprehension. As might be expected, experience shows that an individual with low integrity easily rationalizes an actual or imaginary misdeed, while a person of high integrity finds it more difficult to rationalize an actual or imaginary misdeed, and is more likely to be affected by conscience.

Table 5.1 Example of how the 'tendency to dishonesty' factors interact

Pressure	Opportunity	Integrity	Likely result
High	High	Low	Misuse takes place
High	High	High	Temptation
Low	High	High	No misuse
Low	Low	High	No misuse
High	Low	High	Temptation

Source: The author

These three factors, while existing independently, usually interact on the individual so as to define the likelihood that the the internet misuse will or will not be committed. Table 5.1 shows some examples of how these factors interact and the results of their interaction. There are, of course, many other variations here. This table has great utility as part of a behavioural approach to preventing internet security breaches. Suggestions for practical measures which should be taken in the light of this table and the other general behavioural factors will be found in the conclusions of this chapter.

Specific behavioural factors

A study of the general behavioural factors above suggests that almost anyone in contact with an internet system has the potential to misuse it, with the likelihood that the misuse will take place depending on how the general factors of pressure, opportunity and personal integrity impinge on the individual in question. We now look more closely at the specific motivating factors, usually arising out of some social or personal pressure, which lead individuals to cross the gap between honesty and misuse.

> Almost anyone in contact with an internet system has the potential to misuse it.

The nature of motivation

In conceptual terms, motivation can be regarded as an underlying basic desire to perform. It is not the same as pressure – which is an essentially neutral reason why a particular individual feels psychologically or physically uncomfortable – although pressure may well be an important factor in someone's motivation. A man whose wife is expecting a baby may find that the prospect of the new baby gives him the motivation to look for a better-paid job. Here, the prospect of the new baby constitutes the pressure but it is unlikely to be the sole factor in the motivation. For example, a man who is not particularly ambitious or who feels that his current job is already sufficiently demanding may decide not to look for a better-paid job, even if he has good reason to suspect that when the baby comes his family may find it difficult to make ends meet.

It is difficult to prove that the impact of pressure on motivation is directly proportional to the strength of the pressure, but practical observation would suggest that this is the case, just as Table 5.1 above implies. A direct link between great pressure and the motivation to commit internet misuse is of considerable importance to anyone involved in internet security, since generally people who misuse the internet are frequently (but not always) under great pressure, and people who misuse the internet for financial gain are frequently under great financial pressure.

Anybody who is under great pressure may already have the motivation to commit internet misuse, even where the opportunity factor is low and his or her own personal integrity is otherwise high. Indeed, people with high personal integrity can represent the gravest threat to internet security, since not only are they far more likely to be employed in a position of trust, but they are also least likely to come under suspicion, at least initially.

Research carried out in the US by the Institute of Internal Auditors involved a selected group of internal auditors and other professionals being consulted with regard to various factors which they believed motivated employees to commit wilful internet security breaches. Nine factors scored particularly highly. These, listed in descending order according to the number of votes received, were:

- living beyond their means
- an overwhelming desire for personal gain
- high personal debts
- a close association with customers
- the feeling on the part of an individual that his or her pay was not commensurate with responsibility
- a wheeler-dealer attitude
- a strong challenge to beat the system
- excessive gambling habits
- undue family or peer pressure.

These items, apart from the fifth, sixth and seventh above, are not motivating factors as such, but potential causes of pressure. The pressure on the individual might or might not lead to an overwhelming motivational drive which results in the misdeed being committed. As we have seen, for practical purposes it is true that the greater the pressure, the more likely that the motivation will lead to the misdeed, but, even so, pressure is not the same as motivation. Rather, pressure is a kind of indicator which may serve as the impetus for the individual to perform in a certain way.

Behavioural scientists term pressure factors like those listed above 'red flags' and consider them very helpful in calling attention to behaviour patterns which are typically associated with illicit behaviour.

Psychological factors in motivation

Although it is important to draw a distinction between pressure and motivation, it is impossible to predict whether a particular individual will respond to a single pressure or combination of pressures by developing the motivation to commit the misdeed in question. For this reason, behavioural science has tried to look more closely at psychological factors which, if they accurately reflect a particular individual's state of mind, may render him or her more likely to commit the misdeed. It appears that where one or more of these psychological factors are strongly in evidence, the individual concerned will be under great temptation to commit the misdeed, although even here it is impossible to say with certainty that the misdeed will be committed.

Because wilful internet misuse is a relatively recent phenomenon there is little reliable empirical evidence regarding the psychological factors in the motivation of malefactors. However, the US behavioural scientist Donald R. Cressey has conducted a study of embezzlers in prisons in California and Indiana, and since the crime of embezzlement closely resembles illicit internet use in that its perpetrators tend to be trusted, predominantly middle-class, white-collar individuals, it is reasonable to suppose that Cressey's conclusions regarding embezzlement also hold good for illicit internet use.

Cressey attempted to develop a generalization as to the psychological process that underlies the embezzlement. The three steps or phases that he postulated were:

- the feeling that a personal financial problem is unsolvable by honest means
- the realization that the problem can be solved secretly by violating a position of financial trust
- the individual's ability to rationalize the act of embezzlement to him- or herself in words which do not conflict with the individual's self-image as a trusted person.

Again basing his findings on empirical evidence, Cressey went on to identify certain frequently observed causes which he believed led directly to the kind of problems which resulted in the psychological factors listed above. Examples of these causes were:

- financial speculation by the individual
- gambling and extravagant living
- the advancement of political ambitions.

However, Cressey readily acknowledges that, in the final analysis, embezzlement is not the result of the interplay of these and other causes resulting in a psychological 'blueprint' which leads to the crime, but rather the result of the moral weakness of the offender. A person of strong character would not commit the crime, whatever pressure he or she was under.

Since, ultimately, there appears no way in which a person can be identified as an actual (rather than potential) internet misuser – even if we knew the precise nature of the pressures that he or she was under – the question is whether behavioural science has anything to offer this study of the prevention of internet security breaches in financial organizations other than a few woolly generalizations. However, it does appear that behavioural science has been successful in identifying specific syndromes which are likely to lead to illicit internet use, given that the specific behavioural factor is only likely to lead to the misuse if the following three governing factors – which summarize much of the above discussion – also apply:

- A motivating force is in place which identifies the misuse as a means of responding to a psychological, social or economic need of the individual.
- An environment is available which appears to facilitate (or does facilitate) the wilful misuse.
- The would-be illicit user is able successfully to conduct a process of rationalization which attempts to identify the act of misuse as reasonable behaviour.

The different types of syndromes

The various types of specific behavioural factors are, in essence, motivating forces that constitute what might be termed syndromes: that is, complex mixtures of undesirable causes, personal reactions, environmental conditions and basic psychosocial foundations. Different names can be attached to these syndromes.

The need/temptation syndrome

This syndrome is probably the most frequent cause of fraud and embezzlement, whether or not the illicit activity is carried out by means of internet misuse. The need is most typically a personal or family economic need resulting from a variety of causes, examples of which are:

- the illness of the individual or a family member
- gambling (particularly where this has led to debt)
- the taking of illegal drugs (particularly where the individual's income is insufficient to fund the drug habit)
- extra-marital affairs (which frequently put a severe strain on the individual's finances)
- poor personal budgeting
- extravagance of the individual or his or her family
- family problems.

The common result of all these difficulties is that the individual is likely to be faced with financial needs that cannot be easily coped with except by resorting to illegal activity. The need is there, as is the temptation caused by accessibility of funds via internet misuse, and the individual, faced with extreme problems, weakens and takes the needed money, hoping that in time it can be repaid.

The 'injustice' syndrome

Here the employee is consumed by the belief that his remuneration is insufficient for the level of skill and responsibility that he brings to the job. This belief may partly be the result of comparison with the income of peers. The indignation which the employee feels dulls his sense of reason and his ability to determine what is right and wrong. Ultimately, he comes to believe that the injustice of the underpayment is greater than the act of misuse and consequent illicit financial gain. Typically, an individual who is motivated by the injustice syndrome will develop a plan to augment his remuneration. Where illicit gain is the result of this plan, the amounts concerned may not be very excessive. People involved in this syndrome often only attempt to make up the difference between the actual and the desired rate of remuneration. Over a period of time, if salary or wage increases are not forthcoming, monies stolen through internet misuse may increase so as to keep pace with the rate of pay to which the perpetrator believes he is entitled.

Because the amounts of money involved are usually small and since the theft is often a regular recurring transaction and usually fits into the normal pattern of events, the embezzlement will often be difficult to detect.

The rejection of control syndrome

It has been generally said, and the discussion earlier in this chapter would appear to confirm, that 'there is a potential criminal in many of us'. Although this statement may not necessarily be literally true, none the less most people feel some resentment against what they perceive as unnecessarily strict levels of control. There is, indeed, a normal desire to reject control and be independent. For some people, who continually experience this feeling over a period of time, this can lead them to reject the boundaries of ethics and even those of honesty. Resentment results in rationalization and the dulling of judgement between right and wrong, thus the syndrome can result in the first temptation to perform minor irregularities. These small items of dishonesty can often encourage larger acts of illicit use.

The problem here is that once the individual has embarked on illicit action spurred on by this syndrome, it is difficult to stop, since past thefts must be repaid and recovered. Frequently, this attempt at recovery requires more illicit action and so the cycle continues until some external interference stops the action. The perpetrator will be caught, will confess or will depart from the organization.

The challenge syndrome

There are unquestionably some individuals to whom any internet system is a challenge: the more complex the the internet system and the more subtle the precautionary measures embodied in it, the greater the challenge. Quite often, for such a person, the concept of the distinction between right and wrong does not enter the decision process at all. And when the 'victim' is an inanimate internet system rather than a person, there is a tendency for the internet criminal to rationalize his behaviour by regarding the whole challenge process as a game with seemingly little risk. The game offers the individuals who play it the prospects of ego gratification ('I outwitted the internet') coupled with the prospect – though probably this is less important – of financial enrichment. The perpetrator likes to think of himself as a crusading force against the big, impersonal entity, the 'management' of the financial organization which employs him. Essentially the person motivated by the challenge syndrome thinks, 'Management might be clever; but I am cleverer. There isn't an internet system in existence that I can't beat'.

Although many instances of illicit internet use that were motivated by the challenge syndrome probably started out with the perpetrator not necessarily intending to gain financially, the gap between an individual wanting to show himself to be cleverer than the management, and wanting to 'teach them a lesson' by stealing money, is a narrow one.

The 'due me' syndrome

This syndrome involves an employee who considers himself a particularly important part of the establishment for which he works. Typically, this person will have been with the organization for an extended period of time and may indeed have played a significant or major part in the organization's success. However, he does not consider that his hard work has been properly rewarded. Consequently, he may well try to make the adjustment and take what he considers to be his due, if a means for doing this is available. This has much in common with the injustice syndrome, except that here the employee has convinced himself that the current prosperity of the organization owes much to him and that therefore – if theft is involved – he is only taking what he believes to be due. The employee will frequently feel little or no guilt about what he is doing and would rationalize and defend his actions as the righting of a wrong.

The 'Robin Hood' syndrome

This syndrome, based on the concept of 'robbing the rich to help the poor', is hardly a new one. It is often the result of a related need on the individual's behalf to be loved and to rectify what he considers to be injustice. Such an individual will often go to great lengths to accomplish the illicit internet use and therefore to remedy what is seen as a social injustice. Where funds are obtained fraudulently, the individual may not use any or all of the illicitly gained funds for himself but may give the proceeds to a worthy cause.

Surprisingly, perhaps, experience has shown that individuals motivated by this syndrome are able to convince themselves that they can do good even though they can recognize that they obtained funds illegally. The rationalized approach is that the benefits from the gifts or contributions exceed the evil of the theft. Besides, since the individual may not wind up with any financial benefit himself, he is often able to convince himself that he has committed a heroic act rather than a crime.

An individual motivated by this syndrome usually has little idea of the concepts of ownership and accountability. He will typically see society as an amorphous mass whose assets ought to be distributed to areas where they will do the most good. In many instances the excitement of obtaining the illicit funds may eventually come to outweigh the desire to give these funds to worthy causes, giving rise to what might facetiously be called the 'semi-Robin Hood syndrome', where the malefactor robs from the rich but never quite manages to get round to giving to the poor.

The borrowing syndrome

A person motivated by this syndrome recognizes that it is wrong to steal but sees nothing, wrong, when faced by a short-term need (typically over a weekend), in using illicit internet access to acquire funds which he intends to pay back in the near future. Such a person may even put in a paper or the internet-based IOU slip so that the fund will stay in balance. Experience has shown that often the amounts taken will initially be repaid but that as time goes by the amounts involved become larger, while the repayments may shrink, or cease altogether.

It is difficult to halt the person motivated by the borrowing syndrome, who may continue to get into deeper and deeper water until he is finally stopped by outside interference. He may suffer pangs of conscience and may actually yearn to be caught in order to be released from the intense mental pressure to which this syndrome almost invariably leads. This subconscious desire to be caught is often seen with people who misuse internet systems for financial gain, but it appears to be particularly important within the borrowing syndrome.

The 'it will never be missed' syndrome

The person who takes this attitude does not usually have any moral compunctions about stealing. His former associations and learning, experiences have not branded theft as wrong, and he will probably be essentially amoral in this regard. His only concern is to avoid being caught. Alternatively, such a person may be naturally inclined to favour 'gentle' crimes involving the internet rather than more violent (and dangerous) crimes such as armed robbery.

To someone motivated by this syndrome, theft, fraud and embezzlement are likely to be seen as being normal. He may try to live within the law, but stepping over the line is acceptable. This attitude is a result of the individual not seeing the limits of action established by rational society as being to his advantage. If caught, the individual wants society to recognize his rights; conversely, he sees no obligation to recognize the laws and mores of society which serve to protect him and his property and rights.

Conclusions

- Since behavioural science suggests that almost anybody can be a potential internet criminal, the level of vigilance within a financial organization over people who come into intimate contact with the internet system must at all times be high.

- Prevention is infinitely better than cure. The organization must have procedures in place which serve to:
  - identify vulnerable individuals before they can do any damage
  - implement checks and safeguards which greatly limit the extent to which a lone individual can gain unauthorized access to the system and misuse it thereafter.

- Organizations can aim to identify vulnerable individuals by two principal methods:
  - by paying strict attention to recruits' credentials and financial position (as far as possible) at the recruitment stage and by taking up references before the new recruit starts work, not afterwards
  - by having in place a reliable scheme under which all employees can gain confidential access to internal or external counselling services in time of need. Some organizations might retort that they are running a highly competitive business, not a welfare service, but this is a short-sighted attitude which should be avoided. No matter how quickly the internet malefactor is apprehended, the damage which he does can be devastating; where such damage or fraud has occurred, it is of little satisfaction to know that he has received a prison sentence. Empirical evidence suggests that an effective counselling and emergency aid or loan provision system is worth a great deal to a financial organization and is a much better preventative technique than hiring many expensive internet security consultants and getting them to write lengthy and complex books. Organizations which still remain unmoved by this argument should remember that spectacular internet security breaches in the financial sector are horribly common.

- The organization should maintain a consistently strict internal policy of internet security, primarily by encouraging employees to book confidentially on colleagues whom they feel are exhibiting signs of stress, and by ensuring that employees do not become lazy regarding such essential security procedures as the use of passwords and magnetic entry cards. There is nothing iniquitous about the maintenance of strict internal internet security and nothing wrong with encouraging employees to book on each other if they believe there are valid reasons for doing so. Ultimately, it is far better for an employee who is under pressure and therefore liable to commit a dishonest act to be referred to a counselling service rather than to be allowed to commit an act of dishonesty which ruins his career and may gravely threaten his well-being and that of his family and the organization which employs him.

Computer crime investigation

Introduction

No book which focuses on e-business trust and security would be complete without providing some information about those organizations available to combat major internet fraud.

Most of these investigators, as we might expect, investigate all types of fraud and not only internet fraud. They compete vigorously on the quality of their professional expertise, sophistication of detection equipment, interviewing technique when confronting suspects, all other relevant professional skills and sheer results in terms of apprehended fraudsters and recovered funds.

We have paid particular attention to fraud investigation organizations in the UK, which is something of a pioneer in this field. We also look at one public fraud investigation agency in the United States.

There are two types of fraud investigators discussed in this chapter: public investigators and private investigators. The different organizations profiled fit into these categories as follows:

Public investigators

- The City of London Police Fraud Squad
- The Metropolitan Police Computer Crime Unit
- The Serious Fraud Office.

Private investigators

- Kroll Associates
- Network International
- KPMG's Information Security Services Department.

These organizations are now all considered in turn. Incidentally, please note that although we believe the private investigation agencies whose activities we cover in this chapter to be first-rate, their inclusion here should not be taken as a recommendation by Pearson Education or myself regarding the standard of their services.

Public investigators

The City of London Police Fraud Squad

Detective Superintendent (Det. Supt.) Ken Farrow is one of the new breed of policemen who take pride in being even brighter, more cunning and more ingenious than the criminals they hunt. He has the ebullience and groomed charm of a senior director of a public company. You feel he would be at home in any social environment, and yet there is also a vigorous determination about him which you can readily imagine coming into full force when he is tracking down or interrogating a fraud suspect.

Det. Supt. Farrow is head of the internationally renowned Fraud Squad of the City of London Police. The very nature of the activities within the City of London, where more than 500,000 people work almost entirely within the financial sector, makes it a prime site for potential fraud. The City of London is the most concentrated financial district in the world, more so even than Wall Street and Japan's financial area in terms of specialization of function, and, in the famous square mile, it occupies a much more clearly defined location compared to its US and Japanese counterparts.

The City of London Fraud Squad was formed in 1948 and initially worked jointly with the Metropolitan Police Fraud Squad. However, the pressure of work meant that diversification of function would be inevitable at some point, and in 1985 the last significant joint investigation between the two Squads took place.

Det. Supt. Farrow places immense importance on the calibre of people he recruits to the Squad, and this was the first subject we addressed in our discussion.

The City of London is an absolutely unique market. Recruiting people with the right skills is an essential part of my job and something to which the Squad devotes considerable care and effort. We look for people who are extremely well organized in a business sense; people who know where to find documents and material they need without spending time looking for them; people who are in command of their activities at every level. We also seek internet literacy, in particular an ability to use spreadsheets and to understand the importance of e-mail and international communications on the internet. We also consider an understanding of the transmission of money across international fund transfer networks of great importance. But above all, we need people who are tireless workers and good communicators. Fraud Squad work doesn't stop at 5 : 00 pm. In fact, that is often precisely when fraudsters go to work.

Det. Supt. Farrow, does not recruit his staff from the general public. They all come from within the Police Service – either the City of London Police or from outside forces on transfer. One of the basic precepts of police work is that no matter how bright and capable you may be – and many recruits are graduates nowadays, many holding doctorates – you have to start by spending two years on the beat. Det. Supt. Farrow himself began in this way, although admittedly it's quite difficult to imagine the urbane, articulate head of the Fraud Squad stomping around the City of London.

After those two years, or longer, as a Police Constable, some newcomers to the Service become interested in Criminal Investigation Department (CID) work and may also reveal an aptitude for fraud squad work. Working in the Squad is tough; there is always great pressure of work, and standards of performance are extremely high.

What makes the job difficult is the constant challenge to develop lines of inquiry even when it seems that everything has come to a dead end. It's rather like I imagine journalism to be when you are in pursuit of a good story but can't quite find a good lead; you *know* there is a story, but people will put all kinds of hurdles in your way and you mustn't be distracted from your purpose.

We went on to speak about the very nature of fraudulent activity. We agreed that many people feel that some kinds of legally definable fraud are not necessarily carried out maliciously, but because people under pressure in corporate positions might try to save their company and the jobs of their colleagues by committing an illegal act – such as artificially propping up a share price.

Det. Supt. Farrow agreed that some kinds of fraud are viewed more sympathetically by the public than others.

One of the major professional disciplines anyone in the Police Service investigating crime has to instil in themselves is an impartiality and a refusal to let their personal views on a matter get the better of them. As police officers, our job is to enforce *all* the laws: not just the ones of which we personally approve.

Det. Supt. Farrow said that, at heart, one fundamental rule can be applied to all internet fraud investigation. He emphasized that you need to search for where somebody is making a personal gain.

The whole thing is always about focusing on that matter of personal gain, because otherwise there is no point in the fraud taking place at all. Basically we want to nail the bad guy – or gal – whose motivation is normally crass in its mere simplicity. They want a big house, a fast car, a taste of the high-life, and ideally for the rest of their lives. Well, there's nothing wrong with those things, if they're honestly earned. Our job is to stop people who want to earn those things by stealing from others. We never forget that fraud is basically theft.

Det. Supt. Farrow has spent many years not only investigating fraudsters but also getting into their devious mindset. He believes that there are three major classes of fraudsters, and that all fraudsters fit into one class or another.

The first class of fraudster is the out and out con-man, or -woman. I would say, after years of observing and interviewing these people, that they suffer from a psychological illness which prevents them from ever admitting to themselves that what they are doing is fraudulent. Basically, they believe their own lies and are utterly convinced that they are right and that what they're doing is fair and reasonable. These people are unable ever to imagine that they might be wrong: I've noticed that even when they come out of prison they frequently don't believe that what they did was wrong, but rather blame their victims for the losses which the victims incurred. These con-men always have an enormous ego and are incredibly plausible. They are frequently well-spoken, often charming and fun to be with, but they tend to infect everyone with whom they have contact. They roam the world, leaving a trail of defrauded people, unpaid bills and general mayhem. Basically, as well as being appalling fraudsters, they are emotional traitors. They betray friendship, loyalty and trust. They really are extremely demoralizing people to encounter.

He continued:

The second main class of fraudster is what I would call the 'insider' fraudster. Let us never forget that about 90 per cent of all fraud is either committed by someone with an inside knowledge of an organization, or else involves somebody with that inside knowledge. Frequently, insiders are amateurs who look for the big one-off coup which will give them financial security for the rest of their lives. So often I've noticed that they are convinced they have found the opportunity to commit the perfect crime. I'm sure that they still think this even when they are walking down from the dock to start their prison sentence.

> About 90 per cent of all fraud is either committed by someone with inside knowledge or involves somebody with that inside knowledge.

I asked Det. Supt. Farrow what he thought led people to become insider fraudsters.

People can go off the rails for many reasons. All of us have some personal pressures and levels of stress: some people experience pressures and stress levels which make them behave in ways they probably would not if they were not under pressure. It's horribly easy for people to get into financial problems: credit is widely available in modern society and frequently extended to people to whom it should not really be extended. Someone who is on a fixed salary may reach a position where the cost of their living expenses and the cost of paying interest on their credit simply exceeds what they can afford. If their job is taking up many hours every day and leaving them no time to earn any other money, they are obviously going to be oppressed by financial difficulties. In such circumstances, it's quite easy to see why someone might embark on fraudulent activity: not that this makes it any more forgivable.

And he went on:

I also think that insider fraud against banks is very much a function of the changing nature of the banking business. In the old days, working for a bank was the archetypal safe and secure job. As long as you did your work well and kept your nose to the grindstone you could be confident of a secure income, regular promotion and probably receive other benefits such as cheap mortgages. But that was in the past. Today, working for a financial institution – and of course, for many other types of large organization – is no longer secure. Frequently, people are either on a specific short-term contract, or else are perfectly aware that their job is likely to be limited in duration. People frequently perceive the organizations which employ them as entirely indifferent to their own needs and not at all a source of security of any kind. On the other hand, mortgages do of course require regular payments, and generally the whole financial basis of modern life depends on people having a regular income. Staff – not unreasonably, I suppose – frequently feel little loyalty to their organization. In these circumstances you can again see why people might be prepared to commit a fraud against their organization which they would not want to commit if they saw their organization as the provider of a job for life.

Another point is that large organizations can, by their very nature, seem impersonal and indifferent. It's easier to rationalize a crime if you think of yourself as committing a fraud against an impersonal organization rather than – as would be the case if you worked for a smaller business – against a particular person. Again, I'm not suggesting that these psychological observations in any way make the fraud more forgivable; I'm just saying that they help us to understand why fraudsters do what they do. I don't think that everybody is a potential fraudster. Most people – fortunately – will remain law-abiding no matter what pressures they may be under, because they've got the sense to see that it's very likely that by breaking the law they will increase those pressures to an alarming extent rather than ease them. I do, however, think that in the modern world it's particularly easy for people to be led astray.

Talking about the third class of fraudsters, Det. Supt. Farrow says:

As well as the egocentric con-man and the insider, there is another class of fraudster who – while strictly also an insider – deserves categorization in its own class. I would describe this fraudster as the 'arrogant expert'. These people are entirely aware of what they are doing and take a positive cold-blooded pride in their ability to commit the fraud. They are usually more intelligent and perceptive than the egocentric con-man and rarely as timid as the average insider. These people are particularly dangerous, because they know that most financial institutions won't prosecute them because they fear bad publicity. These arrogant experts also know that even if they are prosecuted, as long as they can salt the money away somewhere safe and secure, they can come out of prison after – in the worst case scenario – three or four years and look forward to enjoying the proceeds of their crimes.

I know of one case where such a fraudster willingly confessed to his crime as soon as he was asked about it, and said that even if the institution prosecuted him and he went to prison, the money was safely stashed away and only he could ever enjoy it. This kind of person is particularly dangerous for institutions and organizations of all kinds, because their very technical ability and knowledge of the organization's systems – and especially internet systems – means that all too frequently they can commit their fraud and enjoy the proceeds in exactly the way that they planned.

I next asked him about the matter of opportunities for stashing money away.

Things are different now compared to how they were in the past. Countries which were once ultra-secretive banking locations are now very much amenable to being approached by law enforcement agencies. In Switzerland, for a long time renowned for the secrecy of its banking community, it is relatively easy to obtain information if one can prove criminal intent. In that case you can often get accounts frozen and gain access to details of these accounts. I should say, however, that this does not extend to queries stemming from the tax authorities. Taxation matters are still highly confidential. The Cayman Islands are also amenable to enquiries from law enforcement agencies.

Investigations in countries – such as Liechtenstein – where banking secrecy is strictly maintained can be very difficult. However, the Liechtenstein government will co-operate with the authorities over frauds and other criminal matters that are embarrassing to the government. Our strategy with Liechtenstein is to make approaches to the judicial authorities via letters of request from the Serious Fraud Office or CPS [Crown Prosecution Service]. These are passed via the Home Office and diplomatic service.

On this same subject of countries with high levels of banking confidentiality, he added that, in his experience, the three most difficult countries of access were Liechtenstein, Luxembourg and northern Cyprus (a country with which Britain does not have diplomatic relations).

I moved on to ask Det. Supt. Farrow about organizational matters, in particular, the size of the City of London Fraud Squad and its relationship with the Serious Fraud Office (SFO).

The Fraud Squad is a relatively small but nonetheless extremely dynamic and focused investigative department. As an organization, we very much see ourselves as providing a service. Much of our work is to do with fraud prevention: you really can't beat prevention as a way of dealing with fraud. It's like driving a car: the best way to avoid having an accident is to drive carefully; no matter how well you deal with the accident, it's always infinitely preferable for it not to have occurred.

Our collaborative relationship with the SFO is extremely important. Their brief is laid down very specifically and precisely: basically they have the opportunity to investigate all frauds in excess of £1 million. However, nowadays, most frauds in the City do in fact involve this amount of money or more, and the simple fact is that there are too many frauds for the SFO to investigate by itself. We therefore help with the workload and generally the SFO will nowadays only handle a fraud investigation if there is a perception that it is in the public interests for this to happen.

I moved on to ask Det. Supt. Farrow about the fundamental problem that many financial institutions – and organizations of all kinds – are reluctant to prosecute fraud suspects even where the case is very strong because they fear the bad publicity that would result from doing so. Predictably enough, he was very much against the idea of an organization avoiding prosecuting a fraudster because of the risk of receiving bad publicity. However, his reasons struck me as being extremely cogent and convincing.

I think avoiding taking prosecutions as far as you can – which in effect means avoiding calling in the police – is understandable but foolhardy. It sends out the wrong message to staff, who may feel that fraud is not really a crime and may believe that if they commit a fraud there is no danger of them being prosecuted for it. There is also the simple point that if you deal with fraud by sacking the culprit but not prosecuting, you are leaving them free to strike again, either at you or at one of your counterparties where you may well have a financial exposure anyway.

In any event, the fact of your organization having suffered a fraud will usually leak out at some point, anyway. Do you really want to have to confront angry shareholders and deny the truth of a leak regarding a fraud which did happen, or suffer shareholders' wrath when they demand why you did not book it to the police? How much better to be able to book that positive action was taken with the police to recover the funds and identify the culprit.

Finally, I discussed the issue of whether juries are always the best people to make decisions regarding culpability in fraud cases. Like most senior policemen, Det. Supt. Farrow feels strongly that they are not.

One of the big drawbacks to the jury system in Britain is that professionals and managerial people rarely have time to complete their jury service and usually ask for exemptions. The amount of expenses per day for jury service is extremely low compared with what professionals can earn from their normal activities. In addition to this, jurors, while perfectly able to understand what's gone on in a common crime case, often find fraud extremely difficult to understand. I've nothing against the jury system in general, I just don't think it works very well where serious fraud is concerned.

I tend to think that a much better system would involve a combination of judges and lay assessors, who would be people with experience of commerce. They would be well placed to provide impartial and expert advice to a judge. The Home Office recently issued a consultation document on this matter and we have responded to proposals for this type of change to the system of jury trial for serious fraud cases.

The Metropolitan Police Computer Crime Unit

Detective Inspector (DI) Phil Swinburne is head of the Metropolitan Police Computer Crime Unit. Created in 1984 as an investigative unit within the Scotland Yard Fraud Squad, the Unit books to the director of the Fraud Squad.

DI Swinburne has been in the Metropolitan Police for twenty-eight years and has been investigating for ten years, including eighteen months on secondment with the Serious Fraud Office investigating one particular crime. He has been head of the Computer Crime Unit since 1998. His main responsibility is for the day-to-day management of the Unit. He is also responsible, in conjunction with his Sergeant, for looking at the booked crimes that come in and deciding whether or not it is going to be the job of the Computer Crime Unit to investigate them. Crimes which come under the Unit's jurisdiction must have been in breach of the Computer Misuse Act 1990. The crime must also have taken place within the London Metropolitan area, although the increasingly electronic nature of these crimes means that pinning down the exact location where they have been committed is becoming correspondingly more difficult.

As well as crimes executed by internet, the Unit's jurisdiction also encompasses other high-worth internet-related crimes. 'The Unit will investigate theft of intellectual property,' explains DI Swinburne.

> This could concern, say, the theft of research and development findings by an employee who has then gone on to use this information for their own personal gain, say by setting up their own company. Another type of crime we would investigate is the large-scale distribution of counterfeit software which we know is the work of organized crime. We also investigate internet hacking cases if they have involved high value gain for the perpetrator or loss to the victim.

How is the face of computer crime changing?

> The growth in technology in all areas of industry and in all types of institution over the past ten years has been extraordinary. Within the Metropolitan Police, for example, we now have a organization-wide internet system which allows the police throughout the Metropolitan area to communicate and share information far more quickly and efficiently.
>
> Within industry, there is a huge push now for the need not only to be internetized, but to be connected on the internet. This is the same for all organizations: for businesses, for Government, and the armed forces. This increased reliance on internets is creating its own security problems.

DI Swinburne added that he was working with three other organizations to find ways to combat this escalating security risk. First, the Unit works closely with the Association of Chief Police Officers (ACPO), which has set up a Computer Crime Group. The aim of this group is to work closely with industry and to find ways for businesses in Britain to minimize their risk from computer crime. For example, this group works with telecommunications companies and internet service providers (ISPs) because these companies are often an investigator's first port of call when tracking down perpetrators of computer crime.

> The problem is that though the information these companies can provide is vital for our investigations, they often don't have the means or resources to cope with the sheer numbers of investigators who need their help. The ISP industry, for example, has exploded in the last five years. There are now over 200 internet providers in the UK alone. Investigators of crimes that have occurred via the internet need information from these companies to carry out their investigation; information, for example, like the origins of e-mails, or which internet sites a particular user has visited during a period under scrutiny. Only forty or fifty of these ISPs are big players, the rest are small firms, some with only a handful of employees. These small companies are receiving requests every day from crime investigators around the country asking for assistance to track down offenders, and that's a huge burden on their manpower.
>
> The [Computer Crime] Group is looking at ways of standardizing the amount of information that ISPs provide for investigators and the way they do it, so as to ease the burden on small companies and increase the speed and efficiency with which investigators get the information.
>
> The Group is also putting a case forward for a national Computer Crime Unit training scheme, but that is still in its early stages.

He continues:

> I am also working with a high-tech sub-group for the G8 nations, looking at ways of investigating crimes across borders. Investigators are at a disadvantage to perpetrators here because, unlike them, we are restricted by national boundaries and the legislation that governs them. This group is also encouraging dialogue with industry. We are talking with software manufacturers to influence them while new products are in their early stages to ensure that their new software is as helpful for law enforcement as possible.

He added:

> Internet software can play a vital role in tracing criminals: we can trace information logged on to a internet system and match the lines of intrusion with these logs. However, a software manufacturer may decide that this facility is not necessary, and may want to exclude this facility from a new version of his software. This would be disastrous for investigators because it would mean that there would be no logs of where the user has gone; a paedophile could view material, or swap material with his

associates, with no trace left after he had finished. By creating a dialogue with manufacturers, we can ensure that software is as helpful as possible for investigators.

The third organization that we are involved with is Interpol. Worldwide Interpol has over 150 member countries. We are involved with a European Working Group on Computer Crime. It consists of a group of experts from nine European countries in an effort to share information on how each country's law enforcement works, and find ways to create best practice to complement each other's systems. For example, an investigator may seize electronic data in one country, and find that the evidence will be inadmissible in the court of the country where the trial will be held because it was not done in a particular way. It makes sense to communicate and establish best practice procedures, for example in forensic standards, so that we can collaborate and become a force to catch internet criminals that is stronger than its parts.

The Metropolitan Police Computer Crime Unit has established a formidable track record for investigating computer crime and contributing towards the rapidly growing body of knowledge concerning how this crime should best be dealt with. In its day-to-day work, the Unit not only presents a daunting challenge to internet criminals today, but also lays the foundation of an even greater challenge in the future.

The Serious Fraud Office

Remit

As its name implies, the Serious Fraud Office (SFO) investigates 'serious' frauds which take place in the UK. The definition of what constitutes a serious fraud is based on a financial criterion. At present, as we have mentioned, it means that the SFO *may* (but will not necessarily) investigate frauds involving more than £1 million. In practice, as Det. Supt. Farrow noted above, the SFO could not possibly investigate all kinds of fraud which meet this financial criterion because, sadly, most frauds nowadays do so. Consequently, the SFO only investigates the most serious fraud frauds which exceed this amount. The criterion for what does constitute a serious fraud tends nowadays to some extent to be subjective, given that the basic financial qualifying requirement is met. Basically it usually boils down to which frauds the Office sees as being (a) especially complex in terms of the facts or the relevant law; (b) in the public interest for it to investigate.

Origins

Despite the expertise and lengthy experience of the City of London Police and other police fraud departments, the 1970s and 1980s saw a spate of huge financial frauds – typically involving investors being cheated of their savings or, as in the notorious Guinness case of the late 1980s, share prices being artificially raised by illegal purchases of shares by the company itself. Not surprisingly, considerable public dissatisfaction arose with the then existing system for the investigation and prosecution of serious and complex fraud. The public felt that too many fraudsters were 'getting away with it' merely by virtue of the extent of their ingenuity and cunning. It was also felt that the system could not cope with the prosecution of such complex cases, often because the prosecuting teams faced an insuperable difficulty in preparing all the evidence required and then presenting these in convincing fashion to a jury. The problem of the jury convicting was a serious enough one as it stood: often the length of fraud trials meant that professional people could gain exemption from jury service for such trials and consequently the jurors were often relatively poorly educated people who could readily be bamboozled by an ingenious defence counsel anxious to point out weaknesses in what might nevertheless be a strong case. If this was coupled with the problem that the police and prosecution were insufficiently expert at preparing evidence and presenting it to the jury, the chances of a successful prosecution would start to look slim indeed.

In 1986 a Government committee formed to look into this matter – known as the Fraud Trials Committee – published a book in which a major recommendation was that there existed a need for a new, unified organization responsible for all the functions of detection, investigation and prosecution of serious fraud cases. The Government accepted this book, and the need was subsequently met with the establishment of the Serious Fraud Office in April 1988. The SFO and its powers had already been created under the Criminal Justice Act of 1987.

In its early days, the SFO enjoyed considerable success. Two of the most prominent early SFO investigations and prosecutions were the Guinness trial of 1998 and the prosecution of the fraudster Peter Clowes (of Barlow Clowes) in 1992. Prosecutions were secured in these cases: Peter Clowes received ten years' imprisonment.

In the early 1990s, however, the SFO suffered several setbacks. In particular, there were various spectacular acquittals in cases that had seemed strong. Even after the careful and laborious presentation of a case, it appeared that juries could, where the trial was protracted (trials lasting many weeks or even several months were by no means rare), become weary of the whole thing and be susceptible to defence arguments that, for example, the prosecution case was so lengthy and unwieldy as to be unreliable.

There was a period in the early 1990s when the very existence of the SFO appeared threatened due to the number of major trials which collapsed after many weeks and appeared to achieve nothing apart from the spending of a considerable amount of public money. Some jurors in these trials themselves became concerned about the situation. Writing to the *Financial Times*, one juror said of one of these trials: 'Surely the legal profession will have failed society if a thief ceases to be considered a thief, or a cheat a cheat, provided that he operates with sufficient sophistication'.

This particular comment has great implications for the investigation of internet frauds, which are almost always highly complex and sometimes deliberately organized by the fraudster so as to appear even more complex than they actually are. The problem, generally, is that most countries' legal frameworks are basically designed to deal with not particularly intelligent criminals who operate in an unsubtle way: the way that most Victorian criminals tended to operate. Legal frameworks often lag well behind the reality of society, and this is especially true in the case of serious frauds.

During the early to mid-1990s the conviction record of the SFO improved slightly, but was not usually spectacular: it tended to hover around 50 per cent (e.g. in 1994–5 it was 51.6 per cent). Towards the end of the 1990s matters improved considerably due to a new focus on the part of management on getting results, widening the skill base of the SFO, and making more use of information technology as part of the investigative process. For example, the book covering the period 5 April 1997 to 4 April 1998 reported a remarkable success rate. During this year fourteen trials were conducted involving thirty-nine defendants, of whom thirty-seven were convicted and just two acquitted. Even in these two cases of acquittals, all the principal defendants were convicted. This adds up to a conviction rate of close to 95 per cent.

The SFO today

The SFO is now an integral part of the UK's criminal justice system and has been responsible for the investigation and prosecution of some of the biggest frauds in British history. The SFO is an independent Government department and the Director of the SFO exercises his or her powers under the superintendent of the Attorney General. The Director maintains contact with Government departments and with important regulatory bodies in the United Kingdom, in particular those concerned with regulating the financial industry.

The distinctive feature of the SFO approach to investigations is the use of multi-disciplinary teams. Frequently the police are one of the teams with which the SFO collaborates: the Criminal Justice Act 1987 provides for the conduct of investigations by the SFO in conjunction with the police.

When a case is accepted by the SFO, a case team of lawyers, accountants, police officers and support staff is appointed. The team is headed by a lawyer, who as case controller is responsible for ensuring a expeditious and effective investigation and for any ensuing prosecution. As the SFO told me:

Unravelling a major fraud often involves examining vast quantities of documents left in a deliberately obscure and fragmented form. A proper evaluation of such information means that the documents need to be seen by several people contributing different forms of expertise – typically including police, accountants, lawyers, bankers, stockbrokers and internet specialists – with a view to producing the information in a compact and coherent form for presentation in court.

Case conferences are held at regular intervals throughout the investigation in order to provide a forum for agreeing joint lines of action. They are attended by representatives from all the different disciplines in the case team, including prosecuting counsel, who are engaged at an early stage. At the conclusion of each case, a final conference is held to review the case and learn from the experience gained.

Note that under Section 2 of the Criminal Justice Act 1987, the SFO is empowered to order any information pertinent to its investigations to be disclosed.

In her letter to the Attorney General of June 1998, Rosalind Wright, the then-Director of the SFO, commented on the changing nature of its investigative approach and, generally, the changing nature of fraud:

We identified the use of information technology as a means of improving efficiency and effectiveness, in a changing environment, by delivering reduced overall costs per case without loss of quality. In January 1998 the Office awarded a contract to IBM to provide advanced documents and information scanning and management. This will speed up investigations and prosecutions by enabling vast quantities of material to be analyzed and cross-checked in seconds, allowing rapid identification and pursuit of the most promising lines of inquiry.

She added:

Over the last ten years we have seen types of sophisticated frauds which were once regarded as exceptional becoming increasingly common. The balance shifts according to changes in the economic climate with advance fee frauds and investment scans particularly prominent at the moment. Fraudsters seek to exploit every avenue to avoid detection and conviction. More and more are taking advantage of international jurisdictional boundaries. The unregulated internet, in which investments are being offered for sale internationally, will increasingly be used by fraudsters. Tackling such problems successfully will require even more effective international co-operation.

And she concluded:

One of my principal aims is to try and make a difference to the way complex fraud cases are investigated and trials are managed. The depressing statistic – that one per cent of cases, mostly fraud cases, use up 40 per cent of the criminal legal aid budget – is a direct result of the length of time that serious and complex fraud cases take to be tried. More tightly focused cases, resulting from well-managed investigations under the control of the lawyer responsible for the ultimate prosecution of the case, and firmly controlled trials, with strict time limits and non-contentious evidence agreed by both sides, will go a long way towards getting cases to court more quickly and disposing of them efficiently and expeditiously.

In addition to its investigative work, the SFO also supports initiatives which are directed at increasing society's awareness of the damage done by fraud and fraudsters. The SFO is particularly concerned that fraud is sometimes regarded as a 'crime without a victim' and that fraudsters are on occasion mistakenly regarded as cunning, ingenious and also almost heroic Robin Hood figures. The reality is rather different. In the words of one paraplegic fraud victim – quoted anonymously by the SFO:

> We were totally shattered. I just could not believe what had happened to us. [The broker], whom we had known for years, had come to our house and had sat on my [special paraplegic] bed and held my hand and explained to us about how this wonderful investment was as safe the as Bank of England. ... And he had told us that there was nothing to worry about and that he had put a lot of his own money into it because it was so good. He said it was particularly suitable for us because it was so safe and he knew how much we needed the money so that I could be looked after. We have always been so careful and we have never been the victims of crime or taking any risks and there we were – we had been mugged without even leaving our home.

We had been mugged without even leaving our home.

By no means all frauds are committed via the internet, but an increasing number are. Whatever the means used to carry out the fraud, the end-result is the same: misery and betrayal for the victim.

Whatever the means used to carry out fraud, the end-result is the same: misery and betrayal for the victim.

 ## Private investigators

 ### Kroll Associates

In December 1997 a hard-nosed, tremendously experienced private investigator called Jules B. Kroll combined his privately held New York-based investigation company Kroll Associates Inc. with a publicly traded armoured car maker called O'Gara Co. The deal formed a new organization called Kroll O'Gara Co, which is now one of the world's leading contract security organizations. 'It's a dangerous world out there', says Howard I. Smith, Executive Vice President of insurer American International Group Inc., Kroll's biggest clients and the holder of an 8 per cent stake in the firm. 'It's good to have Jules on your side'.

Kroll Associates is the subsidiary of the new Kroll O'Gara Co. which handles corporate investigations. Jules Kroll himself is a private eye of legendary status. Born in Brooklyn in 1941, he is believed to have tracked down Saddam Hussein's hidden assets, probed derivatives fraud at Bodywork Securities and investigated crooked schemes and frauds throughout the world. Today, he runs a major global investigation organization. There are many hundreds of professional investigator staff who provide corporate and individual clients (but only *wealthy* individuals:

Kroll Associates' fees are not trivial) with a wide range of corporate investigation services. Many of the staff are ex-police and ex-FBI; they help to create the corporate culture, which is courteous, tactful, intelligent, but deadly serious about the business of bringing investigations to a successful conclusion.

Today, the range of services offered by Kroll Associates includes:

- investigating financial fraud, intellectual property infringement and theft of trade secrets
- preparing for litigation for business dispute resolution by tracing assets in such matters as bankruptcy
- monitoring and assessing legal and ethical conduct by employees, implementing systems to assure compliance with legal and ethical standards
- performing due diligence
- conducting employment screening and insurance investigations
- reviewing environmental issues.

Internet fraud investigation is a major part of what Kroll Associates does, although distinguishing between what is an internet fraud and what isn't is by no means always easy, and in any case Kroll investigates all types of fraud. It makes extensive use of computer and information technology in its investigations whether or not the fraud was definitely carried out by internet. Where the internet *was* used in the commission of the fraud its computer fraud forensic investigation team has a brief and a budget to keep one step ahead of the fraudster at every stage.

Alan Brill, a senior managing director at Kroll Associates, commented:

> The mass media has done a definite disservice to fraud and internet misuse victims by glamorizing the work of hackers and virus merchants. Personally, I see internet criminals simply as old-fashioned criminals, however high-tech their methods might be. They disrupt business and they steal money and information that isn't theirs. They must be stopped, and we are out to stop them.

Network International

Based in Mayfair, London, and with offices in several major financial and urban centres around the world, Network International is one of the world's leading general security consultancies. It has particular expertise in internet fraud investigation and indeed in all types of fraud investigation, although at present it is focusing more on advising organizations how to develop what it terms a 'fraud risk management' strategy that is above all directed as pinpointing areas where frauds are likely to occur, and preventing them. Rather than simply reacting to a crime that has occurred this service is proactive to occur clients' needs, with the emphasis being on prevention. Network has pioneered links to convicted criminals and reformed fraudsters who will provide advice on where points of vulnerability may occur. Typically, for example, Network may say to a client, in effect: 'We know forty or fifty measures you can implement to reduce the risk of a fraud occurring', and will then work on implementing these methods within constraints of the client's budget and the overall commercial strategy which the client is pursuing.

As well as employing many highly able investigators (as with Kroll, a large percentage of these have experience in public law enforcement and investigation), Network also pioneers state-of-the-art techniques for detecting fraud. For example, it uses the very latest technology to wring the maximum amount of information out of video and surveillance cameras, no matter how poor the original quality of the image might be.

Martin Samociuk, Network's managing director, emphasizes the need for any organization in his line of work to keep one pace ahead of fraudsters all the time. He lists the following major ongoing trends in how fraudsters are becoming an ever more formidable adversary:

■ The technical ability of fraudsters is increasing all the time, and they will exploit any loophole which they can find. Samociuk instances the way in which some fraudsters are using tiny radio transmissions to pick up the keystroke which a user makes at a keyboard when he or she keys in the password. An alternative is that some fraudsters attach a small cylindrical memory unit to the keyboard which they will take away at the end of the day and which will give them details of all the keystrokes made on that keyboard during the day.

■ The internet is increasingly being used as a way of disseminating information and advice about how to commit crimes. Such crimes may be anything ranging from making a bomb to instructions on how to crack passwords.

■ Fraudsters are becoming increasingly able to defend themselves in court and will employ barristers who have many resources with which to spot holes in a prosecution case.

■ Fraudsters are continually improving their skill at laundering money.

Overall, Samociuk comments:

Fraud has become more and more like a business, and fraudsters more and more like businesspeople. Every financial district in the world abounds with criminals who sit in local pubs or bars and listen to the conversations of workers from banks and other financial institutions. These conversations often reveal important and potentially valuable information and also help criminals identify unhappy employees who might be prepared to be the insider in a fraud.

Fraud has become more and more like a business, and fraudsters more and more like businesspeople.

He adds:

> In Europe, the European Union is unfortunately making it less and less easy to obtain information. Increasingly, governments will only supply information if it is absolutely legally compulsory for them to do so. With companies being also increasingly reluctant to call in the authorities – only about 20 per cent of companies do this – because they fear negative publicity, the truth is that the debt is stacked against the good guys. Sadly, I rather think that the sophisticated international fraudsters have the advantage. Prevention is a far better tactic. It's best not to let the fraud happen in the first place.

KPMG's Information Security Services Department

KPMG is one of the world's largest accountancy firms and management consultancies. Like most such major international organizations, it has its own Information Security Services division: a discipline that rises naturally from out of the forensic accounting service.

KPMG has two IT security departments: Information Security Services, which deals with all forms of high-tech fraud, and the Forensic Accounting Department, which compiles evidence.

The Information Security Services Department offers three types of service:

- security management
- corporate continuity, including disaster recovery planning
- technical assurance, which carries out intrusive testing of networks to identify weaknesses.

Robert Coles, Director of Information Security Services at KPMG, made the following comments.

> Most security problems facing IT systems stem from the changing ways in which these systems are being used. For example, EMU, the Year 2000 problem and e-commerce mean that organizations are in a state of change and vulnerable to security problems. We can say very reasonably that there are no new threats, just new technology-related vulnerabilities.

Coles went on to add that the very fact of new technology creating new opportunities for organizations also tends to create new security hazards. He pointed out that, for example, in the financial services industry, new technology means that organizations have new channels to market, different access routes and different approaches to doing business.

He proceeded to give an example of how new technology creates new security hazards.

> When the American comedy actress Ellen revealed to the world that she was gay,

anti-gay action groups targeted the websites of all the chief executives of all the organizations which hire her for advertising promotions. One such organization was a client of KPMG. The chief executive of this organization received over 10,000 e-mails from anti-Ellen protesters. He deleted these offending e-mails, of course, but amongst these e-mails were important, even vital, business messages.

Coles argued that only a coherent and thoroughly implemented internet security strategy can deal with the new deal of technological hazard.

Most organizations don't have a unified approach to security. There are huge grey areas, leaving a situation where the 'left hand doesn't know what the right hand is doing'. Organizations need an integrated, holistic approach to dealing with all the risks.

He adds that IT security departments should communicate with their Board, and that board members frequently don't understand IT issues.

Coles places a particular emphasis on the problem that many organizations don't know how extensive are the internet networks with which they are involved.

There are applications you can use to trace the nodes on your network. KPMG tried to do this with a client and eventually gave up and turned it off after many hours because the tracing kept going and going.

He added that the organization's network had connections with other organizations with whom it had a relationship. Some of the relationships had ended, but all too often the link was not disconnected. It is essential that organizations ensure that they know exactly what networks they are involved with. He said that frequently a client organization has communications with third parties whom it does not know, and about whose security it doesn't know, organizations via which dishonest people could gain access to the client organization's network.

I think that the proliferation of e-business security consultants poses a particular problem to internet security. Most of these consultants are reputable and honest, but a few are more than happy to put logic bombs, Trojan horses and even viruses into an organization's internet system, with this rogue software frequently being used as a way of collecting money later on.

Having seen how IT fraud and security investigators operate, it is a logical step to consider the legal position relating to high-tech security. This is the subject of the next chapter.

7

High-tech security and trust – the legal position

Paul Graham

Introduction

The types of risk that are inherent in conducting electronic commerce over computer networks include the following:

- the admissibility of electronic messages
- adopting a sensible allocation of liability between the different participants in electronic commerce
- proving the party's identity
- maintaining the integrity of the parties' transactions
- preventing unauthorized transactions.

These are now discussed in turn.

The admissibility of electronic messages

The parties involved in electronic commerce need to know that, despite the fact that most of their dealings will be carried out online and that there may be an absence of paper-based records, if a dispute arises, the courts will treat the electronic evidence in a similar fashion to that adopted for paper-based transactions. The issue that arises in certain jurisdictions is that if a 'document' is to be used to establish the proof of its contents, this is 'hearsay' evidence and certain procedures may have to be followed to establish the admissibility of the evidence.

Allocation of liability

The advent of electronic commerce is predicted to give rise to new types of services such as certification services, time-stamping products and other services surrounding the authorization of electronic signatures. What obligations should be imposed on each of the participants in an electronic commerce system? Different jurisdictions have adopted entirely divergent approaches on this issue.

For example, the UK Government's Electronic Communications Act 2000 has adopted the approach that the liability of trust service providers (whether subject to the approvals regime or not) would be left to established rules on liability. However, other models impose minimum standards on both certification service providers and indeed may also impose obligations on the subscribers to these services.

Proving the party's identity

One key issue that the participants in electronic commerce must address is authenticating the parties to a particular transaction, particularly where the parties have never met. This is particularly important in the financial services industry as there is a concern that the internet could provide a perfect forum for money-laundering. The implementation of digital certificates, Public Key Infrastructure (PKI) systems and virtual private networks are designed to address the concern of authentication, although the costs of implementing these systems is not inconsiderable (*see also* Chapter 10).

In view of the areas of risk outlined in this book, the ability of organizations to rely on encryption products is crucial to processing transactions safely. The issue of security is considered to be the largest single obstacle to the adoption of electronic commerce-based services, and organizations need a regulatory framework in which security concerns are successfully addressed if they are to reassure their customer base.

> The issue of security is considered to be the largest single obstacle to the adoption of electronic commerce-based services.

There are various products available, some offering a greater level of security than others. For example, the secure electronic transactions (SET) protocol offers a form of guarantee against credit card fraud. The protocol consists of a cardholder interface resident on the customer's PC, an electronic till at the retail level, and a payment mechanism located on the bank's server which processes the encrypted transaction messages.

In contrast to SET, secure sockets layer (SSL) technology does not offer a guarantee against credit card fraud. However, the cost-benefits of this technology appear to outweigh the security risks, and many organizations are currently trailing this technology in online commerce projects.

Maintaining the integrity of the parties' transactions

It is important to be able to prove that a message has not been altered as this will prevent either party to the transaction from disputing any of the terms set out in an electronic message. There are various certification products on the market which enable parties to electronic commerce transactions to rely on the fact that their messages have remained intact during transmission.

In a financial services environment, if loss or damage is suffered by their customers and other third parties as the result of inaccurate or faulty information held on a bank's network, to which they have contractually authorized access, then the bank is likely to be liable to them. There is little or no legislation regarding liability arising from information services (electronic or conventional) providing information which is inaccurate or incomplete. Much will depend on the contractual relationship between the parties.

Preventing unauthorized transactions

The issue here is that online merchants need assurance that third parties are not capable of 'hijacking' a subscriber's private key and entering into transactions that the subscriber has not authorized. In this situation, the subscriber will almost certainly attempt to avoid the contract as they will claim that they did not enter into the contract in the first instance. Various jurisdictions have approached this issue in different ways and the legal outcome is likely to depend on factors such as the security precautions taken by the subscriber and the checks put in place by the certification authority. This problem is linked to the issue of allocation of liability as it may not be simple in any given situation to predetermine who should be liable for the loss incurred.

The legal situation in the United States

One of the first initiatives in drafting a regulatory model for digital signatures and secure electronic commerce was the Digital Signature Guidelines published by the American Bar Association's Information Security Committee (a committee of the Electronic Commerce and Information Technology Division) on 1 August 1996. The Guidelines were intended to assist in the drafting and interpretation of statutes and regulations surrounding electronic commerce. Various subsequent pieces of legislation have been drafted on similar principles to those set out in the Guidelines, and it is worth scrutinizing them in some detail.

American Bar Association Digital Signature Guidelines

The Guidelines have the following objectives:

- to minimize the incidence of electronic forgeries
- to enable and foster the reliable authentication of documents in computer form

- to facilitate commerce by means of computerized communications
- to give legal effect to the general import of the technical standards for authentication of computerized messages.

The Guidelines are based on PKI technology and largely consider the relationships and interaction between certification authorities, subscribers and relying parties. The main assumptions are that the certification authority and subscriber have a pre-existing contractual relationship whereby each party agrees to develop the subscriber's digital signature capability on a commercial basis. The relationship between certification authorities and relying parties is based upon contractual principles arising from the law of negligence, whereas the interaction between subscribers and persons relying on the subscriber's certificate, and digital signatures verified using that certificate, are founded upon both contractual and tortious principles.

Validity of certificates

If a certificate is invalid, the subscriber's digital signature is unverifiable. However, even though the certificate is not deemed valid under the Guidelines, it may still be proved to be the subscriber's signature and thus enforceable against the subscriber under traditional principles.

The requirements for a certificate are set out in the Guidelines. It is stipulated that a certificate must consist of a message which at least:

- identifies the certification authority issuing it
- names or identifies the subscriber
- contains the subscriber's public key
- identifies the certificate's operational period
- is digitally signed by the certification authority issuing it.

The operational period of a certificate begins on the date and time it is issued by a certification authority (or a later date and time if stated in the certificate), and ends on the date and time it expires or is earlier revoked and suspended. A digital signature is not verifiable unless it was created during the operational period of the certificate. A digital signature created after the revocation of a certificate is not verifiable by a public key listed in that certificate. This has the effect that reliance on such digital signatures is not deemed to be reasonable.

As noted above, the validity of a certificate is based upon issuance by the certification authority and acceptance by the subscriber and does not take account of the revocation or suspension which affect the operational period of the certificate.

Digital Signature Guidelines

The Guidelines make it clear that the persons whose duties they prescribe may more precisely define their duties amongst themselves, although this shall not affect persons with whom they have no contractual relationship. This latter category includes persons potentially relying on a certificate or on a digital signature verifiable by a public key listed in that certificate. The comments to the Guidelines note that notice of a policy or practice employed by the certification authority and subscriber may affect the reasonableness of a third party's reliance on their actions.

The Guidelines also state clearly that it is foreseeable that persons relying on a digital signature will also rely on a valid certificate containing the public key by which the digital signature can be verified (Guideline 2.3).

The Guidelines outline the two-stage process upon which reliance on a digital signature is based:

- assurance that the private key corresponding to the public key listed in the certificate was used by the signer (the verification process)
- reliance upon the accuracy of the certification authority's representations under Guideline 3.7 (in particular, to provide assurance that the signer who holds the private key corresponding to the public key listed in the certificate is in fact the subscriber identified in the certificate, and not an impostor).

The Guidelines also take account of the fact that certification services will take several myriad forms, and that it is commercially infeasible to impose a fiduciary relationship on the certification authorities in all cases. Guideline 2.4 states that a certification authority is a fiduciary to a subscriber where a certification authority holds that subscriber's private key or where provided by contract, and that a certification authority will not otherwise be in a fiduciary relationship except where provided by contract or law. The Guidelines note that the commercial marketplace will eventually determine the extent of demand for fiduciary-like certification services.

Certification Authority Guidelines

The Guidelines set out certain obligations on a certification authority:

- to use trustworthy systems in performing its services
- to use reasonable efforts to notify any persons who are known to be, or foreseeably will be, affected by the revocation or suspension of its certification authority certificate
- to use reasonable efforts to notify any persons who are known to be, or foreseeably will be, adversely affected in the event of the above, or act in accordance with procedures set out in its certification practice statement.

In relation to financial resources, the Guidelines set out that certification authorities need to maintain sufficient financial standing to maintain their operations and to be reasonably able to bear their risk of liability to subscribers and third parties relying on certificates and digital signatures. The overall risk of liability can be managed by stating that issued certificates are not suitable for transactions in excess of a certain monetary amount.

Certification authorities, by issuing a certificate, are deemed to make certain representations:

■ They have complied with all applicable requirements of the Guidelines, and if the certification authority has published the certificate or otherwise made it available to a party relying on its validity, the subscriber listed in the certificate has accepted it.

■ The subscriber identified in the certificate holds the private key corresponding to the public key listed in the certificate.

■ If the subscriber is acting through agents, the agents have authority to accept the certificate for the subscriber.

■ The subscriber's public key and private key constitute a functioning key pair.

■ All information in the certificate is accurate, unless the certification authority has stated in the certificate that the accuracy of specified information is not confirmed.

In addition, a certification authority may not publish a certificate if it knows that any of the conditions of validity of the certificate have not been met.

In relation to liability, a certification authority complying with the Guidelines will not be liable for any loss which:

■ is incurred by the subscriber of a certificate issued by that certification authority, or any other person, or

■ is caused by reliance upon a certificate issued by the certification authority, upon a digital signature verifiable with reference to a public key listed in the certificate, or upon information represented in such a certificate or repository.

Subscribers' duties

All material representations made by the subscriber to a certification authority must be accurate to the best of the subscriber's belief and irrespective of whether the information has been confirmed by the certification authority. In addition, a subscriber who provides an otherwise unpublished certificate to a relying party must disclose that fact to the certification authority.

In relation to certificates which the subscriber has not accepted, the subscriber must not create digital signatures using a private key corresponding to any public key listed in such a certificate.

The subscriber's duties mentioned above, in conjunction with the representations made by the certification authority, should ensure that all information in the certificate has either been confirmed by the certification authority or is accurate according to the subscriber's duties under the Guidelines.

In relation to safeguarding the private key, the subscriber is charged with the duty of ensuring that he/she does not compromise the private key corresponding to a public key listed in a certificate during the operational period of a valid certificate. The intent of imposing this duty was to ensure that subscribers were fixed with a stronger duty of care than that currently imposed on holders of ATM cards and credit cards but, by the same token, not to prescribe a precise standard of care applicable to a subscriber's duty not to divulge the private key. In addition to this duty, a subscriber who has accepted a certificate must request the issuing certification authority to suspend or revoke the certificate if the private key corresponding to the public key listed in the certificate has been compromised.

▪ *Relying on certificates and digital signatures*

There has been much controversy surrounding the admissibility of electronic messages. The Guidelines attempt to circumvent this by stating that a message bearing a digital signature verified by the public key listed in a valid certificate is as valid, effective and enforceable as if the message had been written on paper. In addition, the Guidelines also state that a copy of a digitally signed message is as effective, valid and enforceable as the original of the message.

In addition to the uncertainty surrounding admissibility of electronic messages, the validity of computerized signatures has been questioned. Guideline 5.2 attempts to satisfy the legal requirements for signatures by stating that where any rule of law requires a signature, or provides for certain consequences in the absence of a signature, that rule is satisfied by a digital signature which is:

- affixed by the signer with the intention of signing the message
- verified by reference to the public key listed in a valid certificate.

The Guidelines set out factors to consider when assessing the reasonableness of reliance upon certificates and digital signatures:

- facts which the relying party knows or of which the relying party has notice, including all facts listed in the certificate or incorporated in the certificate by reference
- the value or importance of the digitally signed message
- the course of dealing between the relying person and the subscriber and the available indicia of reliability or unreliability apart from the digital signature
- usage of trade, particularly trade conducted by trustworthy systems or other computer-based means.

The Guidelines also attempt to allocate the burden of proving certain matters on the party challenging a digital signature, certificate or time-stamp created by a trustworthy system. This is achieved by the presumptions that will apply under a dispute resolution scenario and which are set out in Guideline 5.6:

- The information listed in a valid certificate is correct, except for non-verified subscriber information.

- A digital signature verified by reference to the public key listed in a valid certificate is the digital signature of the subscriber listed in that certificate.

- The message associated with a verified digital signature has not been altered from its original form.

- A certificate of a certification authority, which is either published or made available to the subscriber listed in it, is issued by that certification authority.

- A digital signature was created before it was time-stamped by a trustworthy system.

These presumptions, which, in most senses, are a translation into the digital domain of those that already apply in a paper-based environment, should assist in avoiding time-consuming investigations into whether digital signatures and certificates are valid.

The ILLINOIS Electronic Commerce Security Act

This legislation was introduced to the Illinois General Assembly on 11 February 1998, was signed by the Governor of Illinois on 14 August 1998, and has been effective since 1 July 1999. The aim of this Act was to remove actual and perceived barriers to electronic commerce by:

- eliminating concerns over whether an electronic record meets the requirements of writing and signature requirements established by law or regulation

- eliminating barriers to the admissibility of records based on the medium on which they exist

- eliminating concerns whether record-keeping requirements can be met by saving records in electronic form.

Legal status and admissibility of electronic signatures

The Electronic Commerce Security Act contains the following presumptions in resolving civil disputes in relation to secure electronic records and secure electronic signatures:

- The electronic record has not been altered since the specific point in time to which the secure status relates.

- The secure electronic signature is the signature of the person to whom it correlates.

The effect of the above presumptions is to place the burden of proof in relation to the secure electronic record or signature on the person seeking to challenge their integrity or genuineness. It should be noted that, in relation to electronic records and electronic signatures that are not secure electronic records or secure electronic signatures, the normal legal and evidentiary rules regarding the burden of proving authenticity and integrity will apply and the above presumptions are not relevant.

Requirement for authorization

Section 15–220 of the Electronic Commerce Security Act states that no one may access, alter, disclose or use the signature device of a certification authority without authorization, or create an unauthorized signature using such a signature device.

Liability issues for certification authorities

Certification authorities are deemed to make the following representations when issuing a certificate with the intention that third parties will rely on them:

- The certification authority has processed, approved and issued, and will manage and revoke, if necessary, the certificate in accordance with its certification practice statement.

- The certification authority has verified the identity of the subscriber to the extent stated in the certificate or, in lieu thereof, has verified the identity of the subscriber in a trustworthy manner (see below).

- It has verified that the person requesting the certificate holds the private key corresponding to the public key listed in the certificate.

- All other information in the certificate is accurate and not materially misleading (except to the extent set out in the certificate or relevant certification practice statement).

The term 'trustworthy manner' means through the use of computer hardware, software and procedures that, in the context in which they are used:

- can be shown to be reasonably resistant to penetration, compromise and misuse

- provide a reasonable level of reliability and correct operation

- are reasonably suited to performing their intended functions or serving their intended purposes

- comply with applicable agreements between the parties, if any

- adhere to generally accepted security procedures.

This definition recognizes that the issue of security in relation to computers is one of degree and that the resources employed in relation to security need to be commensurate with the risk involved. The Electronic Commerce Security Act imposes a duty on certification authorities to perform their services in accordance with the definition of a trustworthy manner unless they clearly state otherwise in their certification practice statement.

Duties/liability imposed on subscribers

In contrast to other systems of law, the US model clearly specifies duties imposed on subscribers. In obtaining a certificate, all material representations made by the subscriber must be accurate and complete to the best of their belief. By accepting a certificate, the subscriber represents to relying parties, that:

- the subscriber rightfully holds the private key corresponding to the public key listed in the certificate

- all representations made by the subscriber to the certification authority and material to the information listed in the certificate are true

- all information in the certificate that is within the knowledge of the subscriber is true.

UNCITRAL draft uniform rules on electronic signatures

These rules take a media-neutral approach to the question of authentication, although they acknowledge that PKI has, at present, a predominant role. It was perceived that there was a need to accommodate various levels of security and to recognize the various legal effects and liability corresponding to the various types of services being provided in the context of digital signatures. It was also widely felt that, in relation to certification authorities, there was a need for a minimum set of standards particularly where cross-border certification was sought.

In relation to PKI, the Uniform Rules identify three parties (key-holders, certification authorities and relying parties) and three distinct functions (the key-issuer function, the certification function and the relying function), although it was recognized that in some PKI models the certification function and the relying function were served by the same party.

The key feature of the Uniform Rules is that they adopt a hierarchical structure with different standards for 'enhanced electronic signature' and mere 'electronic signatures'. This is similar to the approach taken by the European Commission in the Directive on a Community Framework for Electronic Signatures (see below) and in other legislation, for example the Illinois Electronic Commerce Security Act. The definition of an enhanced electronic signature is that the signature:

- is unique to the signature holder [for the purpose for] [within the context in] which it is used

- was created and affixed to the data message by the signature holder or using
- a means under the sole control of the signature holder [and not by any other person]
- [was created and is linked to the data message to which it relates in a manner which provides reliable assurance as to the integrity of the message].

The technology neutrality of the Uniform Rules is established by Article 3, which states that none of the provisions of the rules shall be applied so as to exclude, restrict or deprive of legal effect any method of signature that satisfies the requirements of the UNCITRAL Model Law on Electronic Commerce (which states that where the law requires a signature of a person, that requirement is met if a method is used to identify that person and to indicate that person's approval of the information contained in the data message, and that the relevant method is as reliable as was appropriate for the purpose for which the data message was generated).

In common with the American Bar Association Guidelines, the Uniform Rules recognize that parties are free to derogate from any aspect of the Rules except to the extent that the relevant derogation would adversely affect the rights of third parties.

In relation to the legal requirements for signature, the Working Group is still undecided as to the approach to be taken. One approach being considered is that where, in relation to a data message, an enhanced electronic signature is used, it is presumed that the data message is signed. In relation to mere 'electronic signatures', the requirement for signature will be met if an electronic signature is used which is as reliable as was appropriate for the purpose for which the data message was generated.

The requirement for originals is met by Article 7(1) of the Uniform Rules, which states that where, in relation to a data message, an enhanced electronic signature is used, it is presumed that the data message is an original.

Responsibilities of signature holders

The Uniform Rules set out the duties and responsibilities of a signature holder:

- to exercise due diligence to ensure the accuracy and completeness of all material representations made by the signature holder which are relevant to issuing, suspending or revoking a certificate, or which are included in the certificate
- to notify appropriate persons without delay in the event that [it knew its signature had been compromised] [its signature had or might have been compromised]
- to exercise due care to retain control and avoid unauthorized use of its signature, as of the time when the signature holder has sole control of the signature device.

Reliance on an enhanced electronic signature

Article 10 of the Uniform Rules sets out various factors to consider in assessing the reasonableness of relying on an enhanced electronic signature:

- the nature of the underlying transaction that the signature was intended to support
- whether the relying party has taken appropriate steps to determine the reliability of the signature
- whether the relying party knew or ought to have known that the signature had been compromised or revoked
- any agreement or course of dealing which the relying party has with the subscriber, or any trade usage which may be applicable.

Reliance on certificates

The Working Group decided to distinguish between certificates and enhanced electronic signatures when considering the reasonableness factors which applied to each. In addition, the Working Group has not decided (in relation to enhanced electronic signatures or certificates) whether compliance with the reasonableness factors conveys a right of reliance on a relying party. This should be considered alongside the American Bar Association's approach, which is that the relying party assumes the risk that a digital signature is invalid as a signature or authentication of the signed message, if reliance is not reasonable under the factors listed in Guideline 5.4 of the ABA Guidelines.

The (non-exhaustive) factors to consider when assessing reasonableness of reliance in relation to certificates are set out in Article 10:

- any restrictions placed upon the certificate
- whether the relying party has taken appropriate steps to determine the reliability of the certificate, including reference to a certificate revocation list, where relevant
- any agreement or course of dealing which the relying party has with the information certifier or subscriber or any trade usage which may be applicable.

Responsibilities of information certifiers

Article 12 sets out the duties of an information certifier:

- to act in accordance with the representations it makes with respect to its practices
- to take reasonable steps to ascertain the accuracy of any facts or information that the information certifier certifies in the certificate, [including the identity of the signature holder]
- to provide reasonably accessible means which enable a relying party to ascertain:

– the identity of the information certifier
– that the person who is named in the certificate holds [at the relevant time] the [private key corresponding to the public key] [signature device] referred to in the certificate
– [that the keys are a functioning pair]
– the method used to identify the signature holder
– any limitations on the purposes or value for which the signature may be used, and
– whether the signature device is valid and has not been compromised

■ to provide a means for signature holders to give notice that an enhanced electronic signature has been compromised and ensure the operation of a timely revocation service

■ to exercise due diligence to ensure the accuracy and completeness of all material representations made by the information certifier that are relevant to issuing, suspending or revoking a certificate or which are included in the certificate

■ to utilize trustworthy systems, procedures and human resources in performing its services.

Cross-border certification

The Uniform Rules state that in determining the legal effect of certificates [or signatures], no regard is to be placed on the location where the certificate was issued or where the issuer had its place of business. The Working Group is still considering whether the approach taken will be to establish factors to be taken into account when assessing the equivalence of two different certification practices. The factors currently being put forward include financial and human resources (including existence of assets within the jurisdiction), trustworthiness of hardware and software systems, procedures for processing of certificates and applications for certificates, retention of records, and the degree of discrepancy between the law applicable to the certification authority and the law of the enacting state.

EC Directive on Electronic Signatures

The European Parliament adopted this Directive on 13 December 1999. The aim of the Directive is to harmonize the rules in relation to electronic signatures across Member States of the European Union and to promote the inter-operability of electronic signature products. In common with the UNCITRAL Uniform Rules on Electronic Signatures, the Directive adopts a hierarchical approach, distinguishing between advanced electronic signatures and electronic signatures. In addition to these issues, the additions to the Directive indicate that, in order to increase user confidence in electronic commerce, certification-service-providers must observe data protection legislation and privacy. The Directive does not seek to govern issues surrounding the conclusion and validity of contracts which are dealt with elsewhere (e.g. in the Directive on Electronic Commerce adopted by the European Parliament on 8 June 2000).

General comments on the Directive

One of the first things to note is that the Directive states that Member States may not make the provision of certification services subject to prior authorization. This is in contrast to the position under Singaporean law and the model adopted under certain United States legislation. Article 3(2) sets out a permissive regime whereby Member States may introduce voluntary accreditation schemes aimed at enhancing the levels of certification services. It is interesting to note that the adoption of voluntary accreditation schemes has been adopted by the United Kingdom in the Electronic Communications Bill. The conditions related to such voluntary accreditation schemes must be objective, transparent, proportionate and non-discriminatory.

There are three key concepts contained in the Directive: advanced electronic signatures, qualified certificates and secure signature-creation devices.

An *advanced electronic signature* is an electronic signature which is uniquely linked to the signatory, is capable of identifying the signatory, is created using means that the signatory can maintain under his or her sole control, and is linked to the data to which it relates in such a manner that any subsequent change of the data is detectable. These criteria essentially correlate to the requirements for authenticity, integrity identifying functions that are critical for the development of secure electronic commerce.

Qualified certificates are certificates which meet the requirements set out in Annex I to the Directive and are provided by certification service providers who fulfil the requirements set out in Annex II to the Directive. Qualified certificates must contain:

- an indication that the certificate is issued as a qualified certificate
- the identification of the certification service provider and the state in which it is established
- the name of the signatory or a pseudonym, which shall be identified as such
- provision for a specific attribute of the signatory to be included if relevant, depending on the purpose for which the certificate is intended
- signature-verification data which correspond to signature-creation data under the control of the signatory

- an indication of the beginning and end of the period of validity of the certificate
- the identity code of the certificate
- the advanced electronic signature of the certification service provider issuing it
- limitations on the scope of use of the certificate, if applicable
- limits on the value of transactions for which the certificate can be used, if applicable.

The requirements for certification service providers issuing qualified certificates are set out in Annex II to the Directive and are similar to those laid down in the UNCITRAL Uniform Rules on electronic signatures and the ABA Digital Signature Guidelines. There is a slightly enhanced view taken of the confidentiality of signature-creation data; this is evidenced in criteria G of Annex II, which states that certification service providers must take measures against forgery of certificates, and, in cases where the certification service provider generates signature-creation data, must guarantee confidentiality during the process of generating such data. As noted earlier, the additions to the Directive also indicate that the provisions of data protection legislation and privacy concerns are to be upheld.

In addition, the criteria laid down in Annex II also prescribe that the precise terms and conditions governing a contractual relationship with a person seeking a certificate to support his or her electronic signature are to be set out in writing (although this may be transmitted electronically) prior to the establishment of the contract. This information should include any limitations on the use of the certificate, the existence of a voluntary accreditation scheme, and the procedure to follow for complaints and dispute resolution. Relevant parts of this information are also to be made available to third parties relying on the certificates.

Secure signature-creation devices

The criteria for secure signature-creation devices are set out in Annex III of the Directive. They must ensure, by appropriate technical and procedural means, that:

- the signature-creation data used for signature generation can practically occur only once, and that their secrecy is reasonably assured
- the signature-creation data used for signature generation cannot, with reasonable assurance, be derived and the signature is protected against forgery using currently available technology
- the signature-creation data used for signature generation can be reliably protected by the legitimate signatory against the use of others.

Secure signature-creation devices must not alter the data to be signed or prevent such data from being presented to the signatory prior to the signature process.

Legal effects of electronic signatures

In this respect, the Directive treats advanced electronic signatures and electronic signatures differently. Member States are to ensure that advanced electronic signatures based on a qualified certificate and created by a secure signature-creation device satisfy the legal requirements for signatures in the same manner as a handwritten signature, and these are to be admissible as evidence in legal proceedings. There is a slightly different emphasis to be placed on electronic signatures, which are not to be denied legal effect or admissibility as evidence in legal proceedings solely on the grounds that they are in electronic form, not based on a qualified certificate (or one issued by an accredited certification service provider) or not created by a secure signature-creation device.

Liability

The stance taken on the liability of certification service providers has a slightly different emphasis from that established in other jurisdictions, although there are certain similarities. In relation to issuing or guaranteeing a qualified certificate to the public, and as a minimum, a certification service provider will be liable for damage caused to any entity or natural person who reasonably relies on it:

■ in relation to the accuracy at the time of issue of all information contained in the qualified certificate

■ for assurance at the time of the issue of the certificate that the signatory identified in the qualified certificate held the signature-creation data corresponding to the signature-verification data given or identified in the certificate

■ for assurance that the signature-creation data can be used in a complementary manner in cases where the certification service provider generates them both.

It should be noted that the above will not apply if the certification service provider can prove that he or she has not acted negligently.

In relation to revocation of a certificate, a certification service provider will also be liable for any legal or natural person who reasonably relies on the certificate unless the certification service provider can prove that he or she has not acted negligently.

An overall derogation from the above two principles is that the certification service provider shall not be liable for damage arising from the use of a qualified certificate in excess of any limitations placed on the use of the certificate, although it should be noted that this does not alter the provisions of the Directive on Unfair Terms in Consumer Contracts.

The United Kingdom

Electronic Communications Act 2000

The UK Government's White Paper 'Building the Knowledge-Driven Economy' set the ambitious target of establishing the UK as the best environment worldwide in which to trade electronically by 2002. One of the key factors in achieving this goal was to introduce legislative measures which would create a favourable climate for electronic commerce. After much industry debate, the draft Electronic Communications Bill was published on 23 July 1999. This became an Act in 2000.

Regulation of Investigating Powers Act 2000

This Act, which came into force in October 2000, now enables law enforcement authorities to require disclosure of encryption keys if they have reasonable grounds for believing that disclosure is required

- in the interests of national security
- for the purpose of preventing or detecting crime, or
- in the interests of the 'economic well-being of the United Kingdom'.

Failure to comply with a request to disclose an encryption key is a criminal offence which may lead to two years imprisonment and/or a fine. However, a person may, in response to a request to disclose the relevant key, provide a decrypted version of the protected data rather than the actual key itself. In addition to these provisions, there is a new obligation on the providers of public postal services or public telecommunications services to maintain a reasonable intercept capability, although the full extent of this obligation is yet to be decided. This obviously has an economic impact on internet service providers and it is not yet clear what, if any, financial contribution an ISP can expect to receive from the Secretary of State for complying with an intercept notice.

Data Protection Act 1998

This Act was introduced to ensure that UK data protection legislation complied with the EC Directive on Data Protection. It should be noted that parts of the Act are not yet in force at the time of writing, such as certain provisions in relation to manual records.

The seventh data protection principle, as set out in Schedule 1, Part 1, paragraph 7 of the Data Protection Act 1998 states that 'appropriate technical and organizational measures shall be taken against unauthorized or unlawful processing of personal data and against accidental loss or destruction of, or damage to, personal data'. Data controllers must comply with the seventh data protection principle when considering the level of security offered by their banking products.

It is important to note that data controllers must take into account both the harm that might result from unauthorized processing and the nature of the data to be protected.

 ## Note

Paul Graham is an information technology solicitor at the London-based law firm Baker McKenzie.

8

Internet security – the remedy

Introduction

Internet security is, or should be, a solvable problem. As it is essentially a subset of IT security generally, we need to start by considering the challenge of IT security as a whole, and then move on to considering the special challenges of internet security. Security provisions to deal with both IT security threats as a whole and internet security threats specifically need to be in place if internet security is to be maximized throughout the organization.

So far we have looked generally at key issues relating to internet trust and security. We have seen that these two types of safety are, strictly speaking, separate. In practice, as the challenge of internet trust presents a more complex difficulty than that of internet security, it makes sense to consider the means of solving the problem of internet security first of all.

Maximizing IT security generally

The concept of the 'onion skin'

The notion of an 'onion skin' is often used by IT security practitioners to indicate the idea that protection needs to be in place at several layers, with each of the various layers acting as a kind of enclosure for the next layer. This 'onion skin' approach to IT security is depicted in Figure 8.1. The different layers of the onion skin can be described as follows:

- *Physical security*. This means the general physical security of the organization's premises and IT installations. It is reasonable to regard physical security as the first level of defence – and one that encloses all the other levels – as if the IT criminal can be prevented from physically entering the organization's premises, the likelihood is that he or she can also be prevented from committing a breach.

Figure 8.1 The 'onion skin' approach to IT security

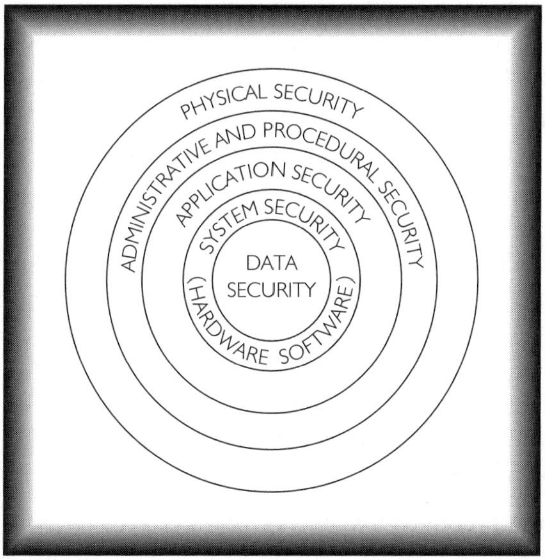

PHYSICAL SECURITY
ADMINISTRATIVE AND PROCEDURAL SECURITY
APPLICATION SECURITY
SYSTEM SECURITY
DATA SECURITY
(HARDWARE SOFTWARE)

Source: Deloitte & Touche

Physical security can also guard against IT criminals who are already working for the organization as they can be prevented from entering parts of the organization's premises to which they have no legitimate access.

Physical security is not foolproof; it can often be breached by a resourceful external IT criminal, and if the IT criminal is an insider who does have authorization to enter a particular room and/or installation, and commits the breach there, physical security is really irrelevant for this particular person. However, it is an essential initial form of protection.

■ *Administrative and procedural security*. These are those protective measures which relate to the organization's internal operating policies and methodologies. They cover any kind of protection against IT security breaches which relies on some such internal policy and methodology in order to be effective.

For example, undertaking detailed vetting of applicants before they are recruited into the organization is an important element of administrative and procedural security. Separation of function is another essential procedural control. Other specific procedural controls which have not yet been examined in detail are given later in this chapter.

■ *Application security*. This means the security of any application of the technology used by a financial organization. It would include applications used in-house by staff members as much as applications (e.g. ATMs, Electronic

Funds Transfer at Point of Sale (EFTPoS) systems) used by customers in the organization's branches or located remotely.

Clearly, the IT security of such applications will be a major factor in the overall strength of the organization's IT security.

■ *System security (hardware/software)*. This means the IT security of all IT hardware and software used by the financial organization.

■ *Data security*. This means the IT security of all data used by the organization. Note that this means all of the following types of data:
- data which are being stored in the memory of the organization's computers
- data which are being 'worked on' by a member of the organization's staff
- data which relate to transactions that the organization is currently processing.

The security of data lies at the heart of the 'onion' because ultimately IT security is all about data security. However, the other layers of the onion skin are essential in order to afford data security the level of protection it requires.

The notion of the onion skin is important for conveying how the maintenance of IT security is essentially a matter of imposing levels of protection in different layers. This is not the same, however, as the notion – often seen in texts on IT security – that there is some kind of hierarchy of IT security risk, and that guarding against some risks is more important than guarding against others.

In our view this is not a helpful approach, as it ignores or obscures one principle which is crucial to the success of any IT security strategy: understanding that *an IT security hazard can strike an organization at any part of its operation, and that consequently all points of the organization's operation must be equally well protected against hazards, that is, protected to the maximum extent possible.*

The IT security budget

How does an organization know how much money to devote to maximizing the extent and effectiveness of its IT security and what the money should be spent on? By this point in the book, the reader should be aware that this is not really the correct question to ask. A better question would be: *given that the availability, confidentiality and integrity of our IT systems are essential for our smooth, reputable and profitable operation and for the establishment and maintenance of the goodwill that is central to our relationships with our customers, can we really afford to set an unrealistically low limit to the expenditure that we allocate for IT security?*

The implications of this question are that IT security is too important an issue to be permitted to be constrained by budgetary restrictions. Quite apart from the need to protect information and customer goodwill, there is also the crucial point that the financial loss an organization suffers from even a relatively minor IT security breach can immediately wipe out, several times over, any cost savings made on skimping on the job of undertaking IT security properly, and a major breach could make those cost savings into the very worst type of false economy.

However, accepting that an organization should not skimp on expenditure for IT security is not the same thing as accepting that the organization's expenditure on IT security should be unlimited. In fact, there are several important reasons why an organization's expenditure on IT security can be fairly moderate:

- An organization can enjoy economies of scale in the implementation of IT security software, because the cost of such software will not rise significantly in proportion to the volume of data (whether stored, being worked on, or in a transaction processing system) that the software is protecting.

- Many IT security measures cost little or nothing, but are simply a matter of organizing procedures in the right way.

- The establishment and maintenance of many IT security measures will have the valuable spin-off effect that they tend to increase the organization's general efficiency anyway, thereby making it a more effective – and probably also more profitable – business entity.

  There are many instances where this would be the case. For example, storing disks, tapes and other data storage media in a locked cupboard overnight will make it much easier to find them the following morning than if they were left scattered on some desktop surface or in a drawer.

  Another example would be where an applicant's curriculum vitae was vetted and the applicant was found to have lied over where he or she had worked in the past. The vetting process would therefore very likely reveal that – apart from the applicant's honesty and therefore integrity and trustworthiness being called into question from a security viewpoint – the applicant's skills for the job were not what they were purported to be. Such an applicant would probably be less efficient in the post than expected, and his or her ability to contribute to the organization's overall efficiency and profitability would be correspondingly questionable.

Typical expenditure by organizations on IT security

There is no easy way of researching the typical expenditure which industrial and commercial organizations spend annually on IT security. The amount varies considerably between sectors, depending on the extent to which the organization regards itself as vulnerable to IT security hazards. For example, a large manufacturing plant may spend relatively little on IT security because its points of vulnerability are relatively narrow and ultimately it is not necessarily easy for an IT criminal to obtain illicit gain by penetrating into the system. We do not mean that an IT criminal can hope to gain *nothing* from such an organization, but the pickings are likely to be less rich than those of, say, an oil company or an insurance company. And since any attempt to disrupt or interfere with an IT system involves risk to the IT criminal, it is hardly surprising that he or she is more likely to seek to penetrate the systems of organizations offering more prospects for successful gain.

The only sector where, for the purposes of this book, we have been moderately successful at ascertaining levels of expenditure on IT security is the financial sector. Nevertheless, we have not been able to obtain definite information on this, because this is not a figure which organizations – least of all highly competitive financial organizations – tend to publicize, and in any case precise levels of expenditure will vary from one organization to the next. To give some idea of expenditure in this respect, however, reliable estimates from sources in the financial industry who were prepared to speak off the record suggest that a large financial organization such as one of the 'Big Four' UK clearing banks or the largest building societies would spend in the region of £25 million a year on IT security. This sounds like a large sum, but it is actually small compared to the turnover of these organizations, and compared to the kind of profit they might expect to make – up to around £1 billion in a good year. Smaller organizations would spend correspondingly lower amounts on IT security, with a medium-sized financial spending between about £5 million and £10 million annually.

Major areas of expenditure on IT security

The major areas of expenditure on IT security, in approximately descending proportion of expenditure, would typically be:

■ Measures directed against protecting the organization's IT systems against rogue software such as viruses and logic bombs. Expenditure here is always high, although this is arguably more in response to the level of media hype about these threats. Rogue software is a significant hazard and must be properly protected against, but some organizations insist on getting into something of a panic about it and devote considerably more expenditure (and anxiety) than it really warrants.

■ Consultancy advice. Many organizations feel – often with good reason – that their knowledge of IT security is woefully inadequate. They often spend considerable sums on consultancy advice which could often be obtained less expensively from a publication such as this, or from attending a well-targeted conference. However, there is no doubt that some expenditure on the advice and/or services of a good consultancy makes sense.

■ Physical security provisions.

■ Implementing stringent measures governing recruitment, training and other personnel-related matters.

■ Disaster recovery (contingency planning) facilities.

- Data communications security systems.
- Terminal access control systems.

These last three are discussed in particular detail below.

Note that this expenditure hierarchy is only a general guide to the main areas on which organizations spend their IT security budget, and is *not* supposed to constitute a recommendation regarding what they *should* be spending.

An analysis of principal methods to promote IT security

Much of the material in this book so far has provided an overview of IT security hazards and the measures which should be used to guard against them. Winning the IT security battle, however, is clearly far more than merely a matter of adopting a general perspective on IT security, and also requires detailed implementation of a methodology.

The 'onion skin' approach to IT security correctly indicates the notion of IT security depending on a number of concentric functions which, working together, maximize IT security provisions. However, the major areas of IT security measures are slightly different from the functions described in the 'onion skin'. This is a question not only of understanding IT security requirements in overview, but also of understanding them in detail.

The 'onion skin' is a schematic representation of how IT security tends to work in practice. For the following analysis of IT security measures, we need to look at things in a somewhat different light. We start by considering what – for obvious reasons – is after all a primary consideration, namely the extent to which IT security hazards can be insured against. We then move on to look at what – from a practical perspective – is the first real measure directed against the IT criminal: personnel management measures. We move on to look at procedural measures and then focus the analysis on specific technical steps which can – and should – be taken to deal with IT security hazards.

A detailed analysis follows of the following areas:

- insurance
- personnel management measures
- procedural measures
- technical measures.

Insurance

Relevant types of insurance

Insurance has an important role to play in minimizing the impact of losses arising from damage to any part of an IT installation and losses due to any of the following hazards:

- theft of any removable part of an IT installation
- wilful or accidental physical damage to any part of an IT installation
- loss or corruption of data
- interruption to the operation of an IT or IT centre
- protection against the wayward behaviour of an employee, such as an insider who commits a fraud against the organization.

Appendix I is an example of a IT crime policy, provided by Lloyd's, the leading international insurance underwriting consortium.

Drawbacks to insuring against IT security hazards

Obviously, the prospect of being able to recoup losses due to a IT security breach by the use of insurance will be attractive to any organization. We might add that this is especially so given that recent years have seen a dramatic increase in the number of insurers who are prepared to offer IT security policies, and that this has resulted in a reduction in the price of this cover. Not surprisingly, the increase in the number of insurers has also led to greater flexibility in the policies themselves, and it is now relatively easy for an organization to negotiate, for example, policies which include specific provisions to cover hazards that might occur to them. Furthermore, there are also opportunities for organizations to obtain lower premiums if they can prove to the insurer that they have put in place important IT security measures such as:

- encryption
- off-site back-ups
- password protection
- procedures for staff leaving the organization
- other specific measures to protect electronic data.

Unfortunately, one serious drawback with most IT security policies is that where the identity of a perpetrator is not known, either the policies will not be triggered at all, or else the organization faces the tough job of proving intent to commit fraud on the part of an unknown person. As one might expect, this is far from easy.

Another drawback to IT security insurance is that no matter how comprehensive the policy is, it is highly unlikely fully to compensate the organization for the entire sum of funds lost or stolen, let alone for other indirect financial loss relating to loss of goodwill among customers and public credibility if details of the fraud or breach leak out. There is no doubt whatsoever that IT security insurance is merely a form of closing the stable door after the most of the horses have bolted, with the hope that a few horses may remain in the stables. No insurance policy is better than preventing the fraud or breach from occurring in the first place.

Fidelity insurance – a form of insurance which protects an employer against the infidelity of an employee – requires further comment. Note, incidentally, that this kind of insurance does not discriminate over whether the illicit act was committed using a IT or not.

Fidelity insurance comes with its own particular problems. In no way can it be seen as an answer to fraud because any pay-out which can be obtained after the event from the insurance company is highly unlikely to be equivalent to – or even to be close to – any sum lost by the fraud. Furthermore, insurance companies attach stringent conditions to fidelity insurance policies, and will deny a claim where there is even a minor defect in the application, policy or claim.

Another unpleasant consequence of fidelity insurance is that if the insurance company does make a pay-out under a policy (which, as we have seen, is something it will only do if there really is absolutely no legal alternative), it is by no means beyond the realms of possibility that it will sue the directors of the organization personally for negligence: that is, negligence in allowing the employee breach to happen in the first place.

If the directors are sued, they must face the fact that the negligence suit will probably be a personal suit and that the insurance company may try to make recovery against their personal assets. Being the defendant in a suit where the worst that can happen is that the organization will lose some of its annual profits is one thing; running the risk of having to sell the five-bedroom detached house in a smart suburb and move to an inner-city terrace is quite another.

A further problem of an organization having a fidelity policy in place is that any accountancy firm retained by the organization may itself wind up being sued for negligence by the insurance company (or its partners be sued for negligence) if a fidelity claim is successfully made. The insurance company may try to argue that if the accountancy firm had arranged matters in another way, the fraud or other illicit act would not have happened.

The problem is that many accountancy firms – including all the largest firms – have fraud investigation teams. If the organization has a fidelity policy in place, therefore, asking the accountancy firm to investigate the fraud may be like asking them to shoot themselves in the foot. They would be unlikely to want to investigate a fraud if a fidelity policy were in place. This would, obviously, deprive the organization of a powerful ally, although it would certainly have the option of seeking investigative assistance elsewhere.

Conclusions

Generally, there is a good deal to be said for an organization taking out as a matter of course a IT security policy which covers all types of hazards relating to IT security breaches except fidelity insurance. The organization should certainly give serious consideration to taking out fidelity insurance, but should only do so after detailed scrutiny of the precise terms of the policy, and after careful weighing up of the legal pros and cons of the policy.

Above all, the organization must not get into the habit of thinking that insurance is a kind of safety net which saves it from lax attention to its information security requirements. And if insurance is a safety net, then, as the similie suggests, it is full of holes. As a back-up resource it is a lamentable substitute for maximizing IT security throughout an organization's entire infrastructure.

Personnel management measures

The hazard of the 'insider'

As I have already emphasized, most serious cases of deliberate and wilful IT misuse directed at a financial organization are committed by 'insider' IT criminals. Abundant proof of this is provided by all experience of organizations which have suffered breaches or other types of fraud: their own employees are more than likely to be responsible. Often the insider IT criminal will work alone, but in a distressingly high proportion of cases, the insider is in league with some external person or organization, often with some connection to organized crime.

> Dissatisfied, troubled, financially desperate or unhappy staff are extremely vulnerable to corruption by some external person or criminal organization.

The point is that dissatisfied, troubled, financially desperate or unhappy staff are extremely vulnerable to corruption by some external person or criminal organization. The great appeal of an 'insider' – to such persons or organizations – is that the insider will almost invariably be an amateur who will in effect be taking on all the risk. The external person or organization may supply the final means of making the fraud work – such as by giving the insider access to an overseas bank account or to some network of subterfuge – but it is the insider who has to trigger the fraud and run the risk of discovery. Furthermore, if the fraud is discovered and the insider apprehended, the external person or organization will have no compunction whatsoever about fading into oblivion and leaving the insider to face the music.

It is important to note that even where the insider is not in any way disaffected he or she can still pose a security threat to the organization, as it is perfectly possible for an external gang to kidnap his or her loved ones and force the insider to provide them with the proceeds of a fraud – whether or not IT-based – which the insider is obliged to carry out. There have been several cases of this kind of fraud in recent years. Often the victim will be the manager of a local branch of an organization rather than someone at head office. Indeed, such local managers are particularly vulnerable to this kind of fraud, for the following reasons:

- The nature of their job means that they must have access to all the main security passwords of the branch, and will know about the locations of safes and different parts of the IT system.

- The nature of their job also means that it is necessary for good customer relations that their identity is known to customers. Some organizations even go so far as to arrange for captioned photographs of local branch managers to be placed in a strategic location in the branch, thereby unwittingly giving criminals every opportunity to see what their quarry looks like.

- They will usually live locally, making it relatively easy for criminals to follow them home. Most organizations will require that their local branch managers and other key local staff are ex-directory (i.e. not listed in the telephone directory): a measure which not only increases security but also prevents them from being woken up in the middle of the night by sleepless customers anxious for a decision about a loan application. However, even the most security-conscious member of a local branch has to travel between work and home, and it is precisely this which makes them vulnerable to criminals.

Whether or not the insider is a willing or unwilling participant in the illicit act, there is always a real danger that what started out as a 'mere' IT fraud could turn into something much more serious.

Ordinary, normally law-abiding, hard-working people who – in a moment of psychological disturbance, financial embarrassment or personal unhappiness – veer from the straight and narrow and enter into cahoots with some external criminal person or organization often have no conception of how ruthless such people can be, particularly if there is a risk of detection and apprehension. These people are frequently prepared to injure or even kill in order to achieve their ultimate goal: that is, to make off with most or all of the money and not to be traced. This may particularly be the case in some legal jurisdictions, where the penalty for grievous bodily harm or murder may not significantly exceed that for committing a serious fraud.

A further extension of the 'put pressure on the local branch manager' type of crime was seen in a recent widely publicized case in the UK. In this case, the lady manager of a local building society had been found dead by a roadside in the vicinity of the branch. The culprit turned out to be the manager's husband, who had murdered his wife for the life insurance, and had then spun a complicated tale in which he maintained that she had been murdered by a gang of robbers who had burst into their home, chloroformed him, and then kidnapped her with a view to forcing her to give them access to the local branch's safes, and finally had presumably dumped her body by the roadside. On being told that no such access to the building society had been made, he said he could only imagine that they had abandoned their plan once it was in motion but had decided to kill his wife anyway.

However, the forensic evidence did not appear to support this story, which itself contained certain implausibilities, not the least of which was that the chloroform had caused the husband to be unconscious for about ten hours. An expert witness attested that chloroform could not have rendered the husband unconscious for more than an hour. He was found guilty, and sentenced to life imprisonment. After his conviction, it was revealed that he had a long criminal record.

If there is a moral to the above nasty case, it is surely that *anyone involved with maximizing IT security must harbour no illusions about the limitless potential ruthlessness, deviousness and callousness of the criminal psyche.* Taking that realization on board, and assimilating it, is an important step in ridding oneself of any illusions that protecting against the ingenuity and determination of a mind bent on nefarious activity requires anything less than an equivalent level of ingenuity and resourcefulness.

> Anyone involved with maximizing IT security must harbour no illusions about the limitless potential ruthlessness, deviousness and callousness of the criminal psyche.

Insiders represent a grave enough threat, but *collusion* between insiders is an even more serious a problem. Working together, two or more insiders can gain access to areas of the organization's activity to which no insider could have access alone. The point here – and this is always the fundamental problem with IT security as with other types of security – is that any security framework must accommodate the need for bona fide persons to do their job. *Any system or process which is absolutely secure against any kind of interference whatsoever would also be secure against access by a legitimate user.* It follows that some persons must always be permitted to use or access a IT system. Such access can be controlled, and separation of function should in most cases ensure that the power each individual has over the system can also be controlled, but where two or more individuals collude together over a fraud, there is a real danger that all the organization's IT security provisions can quickly be made to look irrelevant.

> Any system or process which is absolutely secure against any kind of interference whatsoever would also be secure against access by a legitimate user.

Unfortunately, senior managers of all types of organizations often completely fail to realize the extent to which collusion between employees can threaten the security of their IT system. This is particularly the case where the very nature of the job functions of the people involved in the collusion gives them access to levels of authorization which enable them to carry out serious frauds which they could not possibly carry out if they were working alone. For example, it is obvious that somebody working in a department dealing with overseas funds transfers could represent a serious security risk if he or she was in league with a manager who could authorize such transfers. Most organizations very reasonably insist that fund transfers must be authorized by at least two people individually or even three, but none of these safeguards will be in the least effective if all the people involved in the authorization are also in collusion with each other. It is often difficult for senior managers to imagine just how attractive illicit fraud can be to people who will never have any other prospect in their lives of making a very large amount of money.

Faced with the hazard of the insider and the danger of collusion between insiders, what type of specific precautions should an organization take to maximize its protection against the hazards posed by its own personnel?

Several of these measures have already been mentioned in the first two chapters of this book. A full list of the most important measures now follows.

Specific precautions to maximize protection against insiders

Vetting of potential new recruits. The curriculum vitae of an applicant whose application to join the organization is well advanced, and who is likely to be made an offer at some point, must be vetted for accuracy and truthfulness. Even though the organization should certainly use the vetting to make an assessment of the applicant from a perspective of honesty and integrity, there is a need to give applicants the benefit of the doubt in some cases. After all, applicants who have had a lengthy career may genuinely have forgotten the precise dates when one job ended and another began.

As for applicants who prefer to conceal a short spell of unemployment – or a bad career decision such as a short period of running their own business that failed – by extending the previous or subsequent job to fill the gap, such a small act of curriculum vitae dishonesty does not necessarily need to be regarded as an obstacle to employing someone who may be perfect for the job and may turn out to be a real asset to the organization.

Let us remember, as the Pirate King in Gilbert and Sullivan's *The Pirates Of Penzance* reminds us, that few who reach the most exalted heights of their careers have got there without committing some minor breach of ethics on the way:

> But many a king on a first-class throne,
> If he wants to call his throne his own
> Must manage somehow to get through
> More dirty work than ever I do!

Which is no doubt true enough, but hardly acceptable as an excuse. For no matter what minor ethical breaches people have committed in the past, the fact remains that an organization is entitled to expect its staff at all levels to be absolutely exemplary in their commitment to integrity, good business practice and honesty.

In practice, an organization frequently faces a choice: should it reject a talented and dynamic applicant because of a major case of inaccuracy on a CV and favour a less energetic and dynamic applicant who seems more honest from the beginning? It seems to me that the organization is right to recruit the person with the energy and commitment to make a real contribution to the organization, but that the correct course of action would be to point out to the applicant that there was an inaccuracy on the CV and that while the inaccuracy might be overlooked on this occasion, the organization pursues strict policies on honesty and will not accept any further such inaccuracies. The kind of inaccuracies we are talking about are, for example, extensions of a job in the past to cover what would otherwise be a gap occasioned either by unemployment or a brief spell at a job which did not work out. Anything more serious than this would, in my view, constitute *misrepresentation* on a CV, which *is* a serious matter and should in most cases be regarded as sufficient reason for not proceeding the application any further. Examples of such misrepresentation would be:

- Fictitious claims regarding educational qualifications. This is an alarmingly common vice, particularly in relation to claiming that a degree or degree-level qualification has been obtained when in fact one has not been. It is difficult to understand why so many applicants persist in dishonesty here, as this can be verified by the extremely simple expedient of checking with the academic organization that issued the degree. Incidentally, it is also necessary to be on guard for applicants whose degrees or degree-level qualifications have indeed been awarded, but where the 'qualification' in question has been purchased for a fee.

- Professional qualifications that the applicant claims to have obtained, but in fact has not obtained.

- Bogus professional qualifications. An unfamiliar professional qualification might just be a bogus one.

- Fictitious claims to have worked in specific areas, or to have assumed specific levels of responsibility.

- Concealment of any kind of criminal records or spells in jail. An applicant who has something to conceal in this context is hardly likely to announce it on a CV. Note, however, that, as we have seen, an applicant is entitled in most countries to conceal convictions which have lapsed under statutes directed at rehabilitating offenders.

Vetting of applicants is typically carried out by private organizations which investigate fraud and other security breaches. Examples of such organizations were provided in Chapter 6.

Note that in the UK, for example, it is illegal for any organization other than the police to check for a criminal record other than within the provisions of the Data Protection Act, which allows a search to be made to see whether an individual is listed as having a criminal record. Organizations wishing to make such a search should seek specialized advice about how to do it, ideally from the police.

IT security training. It is essential that a new recruit's induction training and ongoing training includes an in-depth introduction to the need for IT security, the kind of hazards faced in this respect and the IT security measures that must be taken throughout the organization. In short, the new recruit needs a thorough grounding in the organization's IT security policy. This grounding needs to be tested and verified at regular intervals by such methods as a written test or more informal verbal examination during a meeting to focus on IT security.

Identification of key staff. Key staff – and consultants working *in situ* – in all areas of organization's use of IT resources should be identified and the organization should train other people in their skills.

The situation which the organization must avoid at all costs is one where only one person has knowledge of a particular part of the organization's computing resources. If this is the case, the organization's operation could be badly affected by the temporary or long-term absence of the key person. Furthermore, there is the obvious security hazard here in that if the key person is corrupt, he or she could install elements in the program which render it all but unusable to anyone but themselves.

A dramatic example of what can happen if there is too much dependence on the computing skills of an IT consultant working *in situ* is shown in the film *Jurassic Park*, where a disaffected IT consultant is led by financial problems to seek to smuggle dinosaur embryos out of the Park, and deliberately deactivates some of the security programs in order to do this. His subsequent failure to return to his post (with poetic justice he has been eaten by a marauding dinosaur) is one of the reasons for the subsequent problems at the Park.

A commercial organization is not Jurassic Park, and in the financial sector the penalty for hostile activities is unlikely to be so dramatic, but the principle is the same: *do not let your IT systems become too dependent on one person.*

Monitoring of salary and other forms of remuneration. The organization should ensure that these are at all times appropriate to the skills, experience and responsibilities of the person concerned.

Comprehensive, demanding and practical training programmes, combined with performance monitoring procedures which are geared towards rewarding achievement and advancing employees where it is appropriate to do so, will help to maximize the likelihood that employees will remain loyal to the organization and not become demoralized.

Counselling services. It is a wise precaution for the organization to ensure that its personnel department has access to a counselling service to which employees with personal difficulties can if necessary he referred in complete confidence.

The employee will of course have to be willing to he referred to such a service, but an employee who was clearly troubled and who nonetheless refused such a referral can be identified as an IT security threat and it would he reasonable for his or her manager to take an interest in the situation.

Ideally, the counselling service should be provided by an external person or organization, as staff members are more likely to be frank in discussing their problems when they do not perceive the counsellor as being directly involved with the organization.

Readers of this book who find it difficult to understand why a financial organization should become involved in providing counselling services ought to reflect that giving employees confidential access to such a service is, in fact, a simple and inexpensive procedure and could stop the organization being subject to frauds which could cost it millions of pounds.

> Giving employees confidential access to such a service is simple and inexpensive and could stop the organization being subject to frauds which could cost it millions of pounds.

The intense competition throughout industry and commerce – both between staff at the same organization and between different organizations – means that staff members tend to work in a 'striving for success' climate where they perceive negativity and personal difficulties as being unwelcome. For an organization to establish such a culture is all very well, but it is futile to suppose that merely establishing such a culture will prevent employees having problems and difficulties. In fact, personal problems resulting from stress and other work-related factors, and financial problems resulting from bad financial planning as well as from taking on too much debt, are surprisingly common in the financial sector. Organizations which offer staff access to a confidential counselling service are doing themselves and their staff a big favour.

Monitoring by other staff.   Staff should be encouraged to book, confidentially, to the IT security officer or another suitable manager on any colleague who seems to be displaying abnormal degrees of stress or behaving in a manner which suggests that he or she might constitute a security risk.

Putting such a policy of encouraging monitoring of staff by staff is not the same as encouraging the creation of a climate of suspicion, but is a move which is ultimately in the interests of all the staff who work for the organization.

Dismissal and resignation procedures.   These should take into account the damage which can be caused by a dishonest or disgruntled employee while he or she is serving a period of notice.

As we have seen, an employee with access to any sensitive part of the organization – in particular its IT resources – should ideally not be allowed to work out a notice period at all, but should be given payment in lieu of notice and not allowed back on the premises. If the organization is adamant that the notice period must be worked out, it is essential that the employee's access to activities that could give the employee the chance to commit a security breach is strictly limited, or curtailed completely.

The passwords and pass cards of all employees who leave the organization's employment must be cancelled immediately they leave, not the following day. If this is not done, there is always the danger that the employee will return to the organization that evening (when a different security guard to the daytime one will probably be on duty) and use his or her password and pass card to cause havoc. There have been several cases of this occurring. The organization must understand that many departing employees regard their employer as fair game, especially if the parting was acrimonious – as many partings in the financial sector actually are.

Monitoring of holiday take-up. Generally speaking, financial sector staff who insist that they 'don't need a holiday' and refuse to take one should be viewed not as wonderfully conscientious employees who ought to have a raise and be promoted, but as people who might be up to something untoward.

Employees who consistently refuse to take a holiday may want to remain by the system or process that they are operating in order to conceal some nefarious activity. It is often only when an employee is away from the office that some such activity is discovered. Staff should therefore be obliged to take holidays, and those who stubbornly refuse to do so should be treated with deep suspicion.

Monitoring of staff morale following mergers/takeovers. When this is the case, it is likely that the overall level of morale among employees will not be high. People will probably be concerned about whether or not they will keep their jobs, and that even if they do keep their jobs, that they will lose responsibilities, seniority and possibilities for increasing their level of seniority and their incomes.

Minimizing opportunities for collusion. It is unlikely that opportunities for collusion can ever be completely eradicated, but they can be minimized by the organization implementing and enforcing the following measures:

- Employees who are married to each other must not be allowed to work in areas where, if they suddenly became IT criminals, collusion could create a IT security breach. This is an important measure, because many people meet their prospective spouses at work, and the days when women tended to leave their jobs and have a family as soon as they were married are, of course, long past.

  It will usually be clear when people at the organization have got married, but this is not always the case. People who marry each other while both are working at the organization should therefore be required to notify this to the personnel department.

■ Employees who start intimate relationships with each other should also be required to notify this fact in confidence to the personnel department. This requirement is equally valid whether the relationship is a heterosexual or homosexual one. Failure to book such a relationship should be regarded as a breach of the disciplinary code.

■ People who are related can also represent a collusion threat to the organization. No related persons should be allowed to work in areas that present an opportunity for collusion.

■ Generally, the organization should avoid employing in the same department (and ideally in the same building) people who have any kind of relationship or involvement with each other that is not strictly a professional one.

Separation of duties. These requirements must be communicated clearly to employees, who will be expected to abide by them strictly. Failure to do so must be made a disciplinary matter that the organization takes very seriously.

Procedural measures

Procedural measures are those measures which minimize the risk of the organization suffering an IT security breach because of the way it organizes its operational methodologies.

Procedural measures are an absolutely essential part of establishing and maintaining maximum IT security throughout the organization. Like personnel management measures, they act to minimize the opportunity existing for an IT security breach to take place.

We can usefully divide procedural methods into two categories: those concerned with protecting against deliberate IT security breaches by a would-be IT criminal, and those designed to present accidental damage to IT-held data and electronic media.

Procedural measures to guard against deliberate IT security breaches

The three most important procedural measures are as follows:

Separation of duties. As we have seen, this is the operational policy of ensuring that no one individual staff member has access to, or is in charge of, every element in a particular process. It applies with particular force to an activity which is facilitated by means of an IT, as such activities can involve important data being manipulated extremely quickly, and the initiation and enactment of extremely valuable transactions in short time-frames.

The challenge which computers present from the point of view of separation of duties lies in the IT being, if anything, too powerful a tool. Once access to the IT has been gained, whether by an authorized user, a IT criminal or an authorized user who is set on committing a breach, it is difficult to enforce any subsequent separation of function.

It follows that it is in most cases necessary to enforce the separation of duties before the access is gained to the computer's operation. The most obvious way to do this is require that two or more passwords are used in order to access any sensitive function. Each password will need to be given to a different individual, who will be required not to disclose it in any way.

A useful additional safeguard here is for a physical constraint to be created that would prevent one individual from activating the process even if he or she knew all the passwords involved. It is not difficult to arrange such a constraint, which might, for example, involve the users having to key in their passwords simultaneously (or within a short time-frame that would prevent one user from activating two or more terminals him- or herself) at physically separate terminals.

Separation of duties is also an enormously important resource to a financial organization in other areas of its operation that are not necessarily directly related to its IT systems. Procedures for gaining approval from a hierarchy of managers (with the number of people in the hierarchy depending on the scale of the transaction) for loans, fund transfers and other transactions involving an outflow of funds are all part of the same process to ensure that no one person has too much control over sensitive transactions.

The 'four eyes' principle. This policy, which is related in many respects to separation of duties, ensures that two pairs of eyes oversee any process where controversy could occur if only one person were overseeing it.

An example of the 'four eyes' principle in action in a process related to a financial organization's IT system is where items deposited by customers in one of the organization's ATMs are recovered and checked by two members of staff rather than one. Deposited items are an obvious area where controversy could arise, especially in relation to cash deposits; the 'four eyes' principle is extremely useful here in the event of a customer claiming to have deposited more cash than the organization actually credited to the customer's account.

The separation of duties principle, and the 'four eyes' principle, should be used liberally throughout the organization, both in its general operational activity and specifically in relation to the use of its IT systems.

Maintaining audit trails. An audit trail here means IT-based records containing information relating to who used a IT system or terminal system, when they used it, how long they used it for, and related information. These are an essential part of IT security because they greatly facilitate investigations into where misplaced or suspected stolen funds have gone and who might be responsible for taking them.

The use of passwords and pass cards greatly facilitates the creation of audit trails, as the central IT which monitors these access control systems can readily produce a print-out of this information, and will store the audit information indefinitely on file for later use.

Of course, audit information is only effective if staff members are only using the passwords that have been issued to them, and are only using their own pass keys. The audit trail cannot reveal whether the person using the password or pass card was the bona fide holder of either.

Procedural measures to deal with accidental damage to data or storage media

An organization should as part of its entire IT security strategy implement various measures throughout its operations to minimize the danger of accidental damage to the IT system and electronic storage media. These measures are an important part of IT security, even if they will seem to some readers relatively trivial and almost pedantic. But the fact is that they are necessary, and any sceptic about their importance tends to cease being sceptical after he or she has experienced the embarrassment and great inconvenience of not observing them. Typical measures which need to be implemented here are as follows:

- Rigorous procedures to back up data must be imposed to ensure that all crucial data is backed up at least twice in alternative storage media which are ideally regularly removed from the locality of the desk where the information is created and stored elsewhere to prevent a physical accident destroying both the original storage media and the back-ups. Frequently, the back-up media will be of a different nature from the original media. For example, an important file held on the hard disk of a PC might be backed up by being stored on two separate floppy disks. Some organizations also like to use special high density tape which can be used to provide regular back-ups of an entire hard disk, even of capacities of up to ten or twelve gigabytes.

- There is a need to guard against accidental switching off of computers. Although most modern computers will automatically save data which they were running if they are suddenly switched off, the organization cannot rely on this happening, and in any case, even if the data are saved, they may not necessarily be saved in the required format. As for online applications, which are especially important in certain industries such as the financial sector, data which are being processed by an online system may be lost for ever if the system is switched off. The best way to deal with this problem is to use physical methods such as taping over important electronic sockets in order to keep the plug in place and also providing notices warning people not to switch off a particular socket.

■ Measures must be taken to provide power back-ups in the event of a major power cut affecting the organization's electronic systems. Those organizations running particularly critical applications will probably prefer to set up a stand-by electric generating facility in order to ensure that there is a ready source of power in the event that normal power is lost.

■ A surprising – even alarming – amount of electronic data is lost through the vulnerability of floppy disks to accidental damage and spontaneous corruption. It must be acknowledged that floppy disks, while cheap, readily available and easy to use, are extremely unsatisfactory storage media from many perspectives. Their inherent fragility means that sometimes they spontaneously corrupt or that the delicate metallic panel which protects their disk reading sight may be damaged and that it may become lost, with the result that it may become unusable. They are also vulnerable to magnetic interference, which may come from sources that are not always readily imagined. For example, many electric railways, including light railways such as underground systems, develop comparatively strong magnetic fields as a result of the high voltage of the live rail or overhead wire. This voltage creates an electromagnetic field which can frequently corrupt or even erase data from a floppy disk. For example, travellers on the London Underground who are carrying floppy disks are well advised to keep them about their person and consequently relatively far from the field generated by the live rails, rather than place them in a briefcase which they set upon the floor of the carriage. Floppy disks can also readily be damaged by such comparatively minor accidents as having coffee or tea spilt over them.

■ Finally, staff must be educated into not abusing their IT system. Computers should not be shut down at night until all data on them have been saved, and staff need to understand that some computers will lose print jobs not yet completed once the IT system shuts down. There are also instances where staff have simply been silly with their IT system. The most common example of this in my experience is where the compact disk drive has been opened and a plastic coffee cup has been rested in the conveniently shaped hole inside the tray disk where the disk would usually lie. Needless to say, such treatment can damage the drive beyond repair.

Technical measures

I use the term 'technical measures' to describe specific techniques – usually, but not always, involving some electronic component – which an organization can use to protect its IT systems against accidental or deliberate interference.

With few exceptions, technical measures depend on placing some kind of barrier between the operation of the computer and the user, with a bona fide user generally (but not always) having the means, in effect, to unlock the barrier. This barrier is usually composed of elements that are substantially or entirely electronic. This is because, as we might expect, by its very nature an electronic system can usually only be thoroughly protected against illicit interference by electronic means.

Many organizations – especially small-to-medium sized ones – spend too little money on technical measures to prevent computer security breaches. Sometimes this is simply because they are unaware that a particular measure is available; otherwise it may be because, even though they know it is available, they fail through slackness to implement the measure sufficiently widely throughout their organization.

A familiarity with the range of technical measures available is essential knowledge for any manager who needs to know about computer security. For a manager with specific responsibility for computer security, what is required is a detailed knowledge of these measures.

These technical measures are best considered as responses to the specific hazards to which they relate, namely:

- the physical access hazard

- the electronic access hazard

- the communications security hazard

- the systems shutdown hazard

- the electromagnetic induction threat.

These are now considered in turn, with the relevant technical method to prevent a breach being discussed following the discussion of each corresponding hazard.

The physical access hazard

The hazard.   This is the threat of an unauthorized person – who it is reasonable to suppose is a computer criminal – entering any premises of the organization in order to carry out some hostile act that is directed against the organization's activities in general, or its computer security in particular.

The measures to defend against the hazard.   As we saw earlier in this chapter, physical access security is the first line of defence against the computer criminal. Comprehensive measures are required in order to maximize physical security. Box 8.1 shows the principal areas where these measures are required.

Measures to control physical access are relatively straightforward. They can be summarized as follows:

- Physical security controls in the front lobby of the building: these will usually

Box 8.1 Summary of the need for physical access controls

- Control access and exit points to and from a building, paying particular attention to tradesmen's entrances 'round the back' of the building.
- Restrict access to computer rooms and other high security areas.
- Make extensive use of staff identification procedures (e.g. passes, cards, photographs and biometric identification procedures). Ensure that habitual use of these procedures does not lead to complacency and reduced attentiveness.
- Take particular care with access control procedures for visitors.
- Take particular care with procedures relating to night shifts.
- Make extensive use of security staff and surveillance equipment.
- Locate computer facility in a secure part of the building.
- Ensure that physical security procedures cover physical transport of data or software between sites.
- Arrange alternative suppliers of critical components.
- Ensure that faulty physical access control mechanisms default to 'prevent access' mode, with the exception of fire exits and other emergency exits.
- Take particular care to avoid 'tailgating', where an *unauthorized* person confidently follows an authorized person into the building or room.

consist of one or more receptionists and/or security guards who will control access, probably in conjunction with an entry pass system.

- Physical security controls at the entrance and exits of rooms and/or other contained areas: these will usually consist of some kind of pass system, with the pass using electronic means to admit the bona fide staff member or visitor. The use of the pass can prevent access to staff not authorized to enter that particular area.

Most of these type of access control systems simply require the user to 'swipe' his or her card through a card-reading device. Other systems require that a password or code number be tapped into a keyboard located somewhere near the door.

Where physical access security to a particular room or other area is of critical importance, a further level of security can be gained by the access control system making use of **biometrics**. This is a convenient point to introduce this subject.

Obviously, any security system must meet the fundamental and related needs of allowing access to bona fide persons while denying it to other persons. This naturally raises the question of how this procedure can be arranged.

The majority of security systems devised to date by human ingenuity work by the bona fide person possessing some sort of device which he or she can use to gain legitimate access to the system or other secure installation. The most obvious such device is a key. A lock cannot be opened without a key, and the assumption is that the bona fide person will be the only person who has access to the key. Many modern access control systems – whether these concern physical access to premises or access to a computer terminal – depend on the same principle. Access may be effected by a conventional mechanical key, or more usually by an electronic key which activates the electronics controlling what is usually an electromechanical locking system. Examples of the electronic key are identity cards featuring an electronic tag or a cash card used to gain access to a cash machine.

However, electronic keys, like mechanical keys, suffer from the basic problem that there is no *inherent* connection between the key itself and the bona fide person. Obviously, a key may be lost or stolen, in which case an unauthorized person could use it.

To get around this problem, most modern access control systems – again, we are talking about access to an entire premises or to a computer terminal or computer installation – consequently make use of a secondary security system, usually involving a password or code number which the user is expected to memorize. The idea, simply, is that a more definite connection is made to the authorized person because even if the key is mislaid or lost, access can only be gained by use of the key as well as the secret word or number.

By way of introducing the concept of biometrics, we might interpret the use of the secret word or number by saying that, in effect, the system is authorizing against a modification inside the brain of the bona fide person which distinguishes that person from any other person. The modification inside the brain is, simply, the memory of the secret word or number held by the person.

This is all very well, but unfortunately there is not a *biological* connection between the security system and the bona fide person. The rather cumbersome nature of the process means that *anybody* who knows what the secret word or number is can access the system as long as he or she also has the key. For example, a serious problem facing all retail financial institutions, credit card companies, and so on, is that many of their customers have difficulty remembering their four-digit secret number associated with their bank card. This is a particular problem for financially successful people who may have several such cards, although admittedly most institutions give people the opportunity to change their personal identification number (PIN) into a more readily remembered number (such as based on their birth date) that they can use for all their cards.

Even so, the problem remains. Many people write down their PIN somewhere in their wallet – there have even been cases where people write their PIN on their bank card. In either case, it is easy to see that anybody stealing the wallet would get access not only to the key but also to the secret number.

The obvious way of dealing with this problem is to introduce a technique which *does* create a biological connection between the bona fide person and the computer system. Biometrics are personal physical details which can be incorporated into a security system and ensure that no user can gain access unless his or her biometrics are included among those already programmed into the system.

The importance of biometrics is that, as long as the system using them works properly, it can prevent access being gained by persons who have borrowed a bona fide user's card and password (whether or not with the bona fide user's connivance). The use of biometrics will restrict acceptance strictly to the bona fide user.

Examples of biometrics which feature in access control systems are:

- *Prints of one or more fingers or thumbs*. These are useful because each fingerprint or thumbprint of an individual is close to being unique for that person.

- *The sound of a voice*. Technology has already advanced to the point where the sound of an individual's voice can be digitized and tested against sample digitized voices provided at the access control point.

- *Retina scanning*. The pattern of blood vessels at the back of the retina is unique to each individual. This pattern can be scanned by the use of special scanning devices which the individual looks into at the access control point.

Retina scanning devices have achieved some success in the US, but it seems difficult to imagine that devices featuring this particular biometric could have a wide appeal, bearing in mind that many people would, not unreasonably, be suspicious of what the long-term (or even short-term) effects of use of a retina scanning device would be on their eyesight.

In all these cases, the biometric would be checked by the computer against a database of such prints, with different stored biometrics corresponding to different bona fide users. If a match was made, the user would be allowed to pass, while if no match was made, the access control system would prevent access.

Biometrics are used widely in military and law enforcement applications, where rigid physical access control is essential. They have not, however, been used extensively to date in financial organizations. The reasons for this are as follows:

- Biometric scanning devices are expensive, and many organizations feel that they constitute a level of security which is one step more than necessary.

- Some organizations feel that the use of biometric scanning devices represents an unacceptable level of intrusion into a staff member's life and into the relationship between the staff member and the organization. After all, when an organization installs biometric scanning systems it is, in effect, saying to staff members 'We don't trust you not to lend your cards to other people', even though their obligation not to do this will in many cases be written into their contracts of employment.

- Where the access control is likely to involve the organization's customers, an organization is likely to find the use of biometrics particularly unacceptable, as it might imply a lack of trust in the customer, which would hardly be likely to help the organization/customer relationship.

- Biometric scanning devices are not yet particularly reliable. They frequently reject samples that they should accept (this is more often the problem than that they accept samples they should reject) due to the technical challenge of ensuring that digitizations (i.e. computer-readable versions) of the sample biometric information are always completely accurate. This problem will probably solve itself as technology develops.

Note that even biometric systems are not foolproof but are susceptible to breaches by a resourceful and determined computer criminal. A dramatic example of this was seen in the film *Demolition Man*, where the villain gets past a retina scanning device in a prison by the expedient of attacking the prison governor and taking out his eye, presenting the governor's eye to the retina scanning device on the end of a pen. An interesting point in relation to this traumatic scene is that modern biometric systems are in fact able to distinguish between a living and dead biological part. Most fingerprint scanning systems now in use will only function if the finger is live (meaning that the person with the finger is still alive and the finger is still attached) because otherwise the absence of circulation in the finger will not give a bona fide reading. We did not investigate this matter as regards detached eyes – there are limits even to our determination to find out the truth – but presumably the same principle will apply.

At present, a considerable amount of research into biometrics is being undertaken worldwide. Unquestionably, their applications in creating reliable biological connections between bona fide individuals and computer systems are extremely useful. Research is being devoted to improving the accuracy rates of biometrics and to examining new types of biometric systems.

Accuracy is obviously an enormously important issue. The problem with any biometric-based system is that the biometric itself is not normally a discrete parameter where the input data are either right or wrong for the security verification in question. Clearly, a PIN is either correct or not: there is no grey area. However, there is such a grey area when a system is activated by biometrics. The principal requirement is that there should be no false acceptance at all: meaning that no biometric will be allowed to activate the system. For bona fide users, however, the real problem is the danger of false rejection: meaning that even if someone is a bona fide person, their biometrics still do not trigger the acceptance. Most modern biometric systems can guarantee the chance of false acceptance as zero per cent, and the chance of false rejection as down to about 0.01 per cent. However, this is still an undesirable false rejection rate and work proceeds to improve it.

New biometric methods are being developed all the time. For example, the Biometric Access Corporation in the USA is developing a form of facial recognition designed for use by surgeons just before patients come into the operating theatre. This system is designed not only to check the bona fide nature of the surgeon, but also to check that the right surgeon is working on the right patient. Fingerprints are no good because the surgeon is wearing rubber gloves; furthermore, his or her mask makes it difficult for colleagues to make an easy recognition, and so the system is being designed to recognize the part of the face not covered by the mask, from forehead to nose, including eyes and cheekbones.

Other types of biometric techniques will no doubt be developed in due course as technology evolves. In Philip Kerr's futuristic novel *The Second Angel*, a popular biometric authorization system in use involves would-be users breathing on a panel which detects minute amounts of DNA in their expelled breath. I do not know whether this is at present physically feasible, but certainly DNA appears to offer an attractive prospect for irrefutable biometric access control because of its unique nature.

The question of the future of biometrics seems to depend substantially on the motivation of the individual to use the system. Note, for example, that this motivation will vary depending on the sense of obligation. A bank's customer is highly unlikely to be prepared to have his or her retina scanned to gain access on a routine basis to a cash machine. On the other hand, even the most fastidious Government employee might be prepared to submit to this procedure in order to gain access to a room at a royal palace and meet the monarch.

Returning to the basic principle of physical access control systems, note that these must be used not only at the entrance of a room or other contained area, but also at the *exit*, in order to control access (obviously an open exit amounts to an open entrance) and also to facilitate the creation of a record of who left the room or area and when.

This need to install access controls at exits should not, of course, be allowed to inhibit the smooth functioning of emergency exits that are required by law and by common sense.

Note, too, that an essential role of all electronic physical access control systems used by an organization is to facilitate the creation of an audit trail.

The electronic access hazard

The hazard. This is the threat of an unauthorized person being able to gain access to a computer terminal that is located in the organization's premises.

The measures to defend against the hazard. In effect, measures to control electronic access are a second line of security after physical security. Electronic access security is of great importance to financial organizations, which frequently need to restrict terminal access to staff, who, while having the right to be in the room or other contained area where the terminals are located, do not have the right to access every terminal in that area.

For example, not all the traders in a dealing room will need access to every terminal in that dealing room, nor, indeed, is it desirable that they should. The organization will ideally want to control electronic access to terminals on a person-by-person basis.

Note that electronic access measures can be used to control access to one or more particular *applications* at a terminal. In other words, one or more users without authorization to access one or more applications at a terminal can nonetheless be authorized to use other applications, according to the requirements of their jobs.

Generally, electronic access control can be achieved by the use of a password or code number which is exclusive to the authorized user (or to the group of authorized users of a particular terminal or application).

Where the access control requirement is particularly stringent, an electronic pass token – increasingly likely to be a smart card rather than a magnetic strip card – can be used in conjunction with the password or code number. In this case, the electronic pass token would typically require to be swiped through a card-reader located close to the terminal, and the password or code number would typically require to be typed into the keyboard by the user. As is common practice, the password or code number would typically not appear on the screen, but each letter or digit would be cued by a hyphen or one-space line appearing there.

As with physical access control measures, there is ample scope for using bio-metric-based systems to control all aspects of electronic access. Note also that, as with physical access control, it is extremely important that the security method used should facilitate the creation of an audit trail which will provide a centralized record of who used the terminal, and when, and what application they performed on it.

The communications security hazard

The hazard.　This is the hazard of an unauthorized person being able to interfere with an data communications process which an organization sends. *Clearly, this particular hazard is especially important in relation to the security of the internet, which at heart from a technical perspective is simply a global interactive communications network.*

The message may be purely internal to the particular branch, office or premises, that is, it is sent through a local area network (LAN) or it may go to one or more external counterparties, to remotely located customers, or to staff members located in other branches, offices or premises, that is, it is sent through a wide area network (WAN).

The measures to defend against the hazard.   As we have seen, communications security, which is also often known as network security, has been the focus of considerable attention by the media in recent years, especially in relation to the communications security of financial organizations.

Communications security is without doubt a crucial priority for an organization, but it is also true that too many organizations are influenced by media hype of this kind of hazard to devote an *excessive proportion* of their computer security budget to it. In fact, the technical measures needed to maximize communications security – whether this means protecting the communications system against unauthorized access in a general sense, or paying particular attention to ensuring that viruses and other rogue software items do not enter the organization's computer system by means of its communications network – are straightforward enough: so much so that they should be capable of being deployed without much fuss.

The most important measure of all is for the organization's management to recognize that they should not be swayed by media hype of the subject of communications security, but should simply pay attention to what needs to be done in this respect.

Above all, the organization should do its best to make its computer system unattractive to prospective unauthorized users. This challenge demands some hard thinking, since many organizations rely on their computer system seeming attractive to counterparties who wish to use it, and retail organizations actively compete with each other over implementing communications systems that are easy for retail customers to use and which appeal to them.

Another important factor to discuss here is the use of the 'Welcome' message at the 'user-end' of the communications system. The use of a Welcome message may seem innocent and natural, but organizations must face the fact that it is actually double-edged. The point is that a Welcome message amounts, in effect, to a welcome to all and sundry to use the organization's computer system. If the organization insists on displaying such a message, it should hardly be entirely surprised if computer criminals, as well as authorized persons, use this as their cue to enter the system. This, at least, has been the view of several courts in the US, which have dismissed some civil and illicit computer access cases where the defendant has successfully pleaded that the use by the organization in question of a Welcome message constituted an open invitation to use the system.

In general, an organization should decide that the user interface for a computer system accessed via a communications line should not have a Welcome message, unless there are extremely good commercial reasons for having one. In addition, the point of user access should not only be kept deliberately unattractive, but should even appear mundane to the user. The point is that a bona fide user will want to gain access to the system anyway, whereas a hacker who is able to view the user contact point illicitly may be put off by seeing a screen that has no appeal.

We do not recommend using deception here, and describing the system as something which it is not, but the importance of the system can be downplayed. For example, rather than describing a funds transfer as such, it could simply be given a dull name, such as 'System A' or 'Branch system' or something similar, even assuming that it has to be named at all.

For an organization which wants to attract customers to use its systems – a retail organization, for example – this kind of approach will obviously not be possible. In this case the organization will want to do everything it can to encourage users to use the system, whether the system delivers ATM services, EFTPoS, telephone banking or other retail services. It is essential in this case that there is absolutely no way for a user to access any other of the bank's systems via the retail system.

Given that the organization has taken on board the need to deter unauthorized access, the other measures to prevent breaches of communications system security are now discussed.

There are two principal techniques for maximizing the security of data communications systems. The first technique, **encryption, encodes the communicated message in order to prevent an unauthorized person from finding out what it says**. The second, **message authentication**, **prevents an unauthorized person from tampering with the communicated message**. Without message authentication, it might be possible for an unauthorized person to tamper with the message even if this were in encrypted form. For maximum security of the message, encryption and message authentication are both required.

The need for encryption and message authentication applies equally whether the data are being communicated across a LAN or a WAN. However, some organizations do not bother to encrypt LAN communications, and others, while encrypting WAN communications, do not bother to use message authentication at all.

Encryption is an encoding procedure which takes place at the point of entry of the message that is being communicated; it uses software that can be incorporated into the home network via the entry terminal. The message is sent to the destination, where it is decoded by the same encryption process.

The software governing the encryption process at the point of data entry and the delivery of data must use the same encryption key, that is, a number which is used as the basis for generating the encrypted form of the message.

Encryption relies for its effectiveness on the fact that the encrypted form of the message is generated by a highly complex algorithm which would take so long to break through random trial and error – even if a powerful computer were used to assist in the process – that the code is for all practical purposes unbreakable. Since an encryption algorithm is only used in conjunction with a specific key, it is possible for a proprietary algorithm to be supplied, with the algorithm then being 'customized' by the use of a key.

An electronic message can be encrypted using a mathematical formula which is later used to decrypt the same document. This is the principal mechanism of symmetric key encryption because the same secret key is used at both ends of the communication channel.

In an ideal world, the sender and the recipient would have established a secure communication channel by agreeing on secret keys prior to the message being sent across the network. In practice, communication is a spontaneous process which rules out the delayed encryption process. The message needs to be sent in conjunction with the key using the same network.

This presents some drawbacks. If there are n correspondents then every participant has to keep track of $n - 1$ secret keys, one for each communication channel with the other correspondents. Otherwise, if the same key is used for more than one correspondent, one person will be able to read another's mail.

Symmetric key encryption also leaves open the other requirements for secure communications. Authenticity and the potential for non-repudiation are lacking since both communication partners possess the same key – either of them could have created and encrypted a message and claim that the other person had sent it.

A major development in encryption during the late 1970s was the introduction of what is known as public key encryption (PKE) or public key infrastructure (PKI), it is increasingly known. The beauty of PKE was that it solved the problem of the need to deliver keys to recipients in a secure way.

Public key encryption also uses a pair of keys but each is different: one is kept private and other is public and known to potentially everybody who wants to communicate with a certain person. Since both keys represent a unique pair in that only them work together, what is encrypted with one key can only be decrypted with its mate, and vice versa.

This strong link between the two keys has several advantages:

- Once a message is encrypted with a particular authorized user's public key, none other than his or her private key can decrypt the data.

- Users don't have to make available the same key to all communication partners; listing the public key in an open directory maintained by their employer or certificate authorities does not compromise the security of the private key.

- It allows users to authenticate the originator of a document; once it is signed with your private key and decrypted with your public key, then the message must have come from you.

Hence, the use of a private key on an electronic document is akin to signing a paper document, which is why public key encryption plays such a big role in authentication technologies.

The drawback of public key encryption is the slow speed with which the algorithm can be completed, due to the complexity of the process. The longer the document, the more time it takes to encrypt the whole file. To save on computer resources, a favoured solution is to combine symmetric with public key encryption.

First, the message is encrypted with a symmetric key, which is a speedy process. Since both the key and document are delivered at the same time and the recipient doesn't need to know in advance which secret key is used, the symmetric key can be generated randomly. In a second step, this symmetric key is encrypted itself, using PKE. Since symmetric keys themselves are very short, this doesn't take a long time.

Only the private key of the recipient can recover the locked symmetric key, giving only the authorized user access to the content of the message. By creating a digital equivalent to an envelope, privacy between the communication partners can be assured.

Later in this book we shall see that PKE – or public key infrastructure (PKI) – has important implications for establishing and maintaining trust over the internet.

There is a wide variety of proprietary encryption software available from computer security software vendors. If the reader has insufficient contacts at such organizations, an alternative way of identifying a suitable vendor would be to obtain advice from a computer security consultant. There are many such independent consultants, and most of the large accounting firms nowadays have specialized information consultancy divisions which are also able to provide detailed information on matters of computer security.

Whatever the encryption product, it will probably use one of the most popular encryption standards. These are commonly known by their abbreviated forms: DES and RSA.

The Data Encryption Standard (DES), which is also sometimes known as the Data Encryption Algorithm (DEA), is a standard that was developed in the 1970s by the US National Bureau of Standards. It is used extensively in all branches of commerce, and particularly in the financial sector. In view of its current wide use in international bank-to-bank networks, it is likely to be employed throughout the world's financial sectors for some time to come.

The technical specification of the DES is that it is an asymmetric block cipher employing 56-bit blocks of plan text which are transformed into 56 bits of ciphertext using a 56-bit key. DES may be implemented on microchips so that the encryption and decryption processes can be performed at high speed. DES has several modes of implementation and can be used as a block, cipher block chaining or stream cipher.

The RSA encryption system is named after its three inventors (Rivest, Shamir, Adlemann). It was initially invented to simplify the problem of maintaining the secrecy of the keys while they are being distributed.

This encryption system exploits the great difficulty of factoring certain types of very large numbers. Finding factors for such numbers is an extremely time-consuming process even if the most powerful computer is used to do this.

The technical specification of the RSA system is that it is an asymmetric block cipher. The RSA keys are several hundred bits in length; the block size varies with the parameters chosen. A user will typically require specialized assistance with the mathematically demanding process of setting up the block size, encryption and decryption keys; moreover, the algorithm is computationally more demanding than the DES. However, as with the DES, microchips are now available for the RSA algorithm, and some form of key generation service will normally be provided to users.

Sometimes the encryption process will be visible to a bona fide user at either end of the message. More often – and particularly in the financial sector, where complete confidentiality of messages is of great importance, so-called 'end-to-end' encryption will be used.

End-to-end encryption is a form of encryption where the message does not appear 'in the clear' at any point in the communication process. Where end-to-end encryption is used, the encryption and decryption processes are carried out automatically within the system, and not even a specialist member of the organization's staff who has responsibility for its computer security would be able to read the message.

End-to-end encryption should be used in all financial sector applications where the data communications concern funds transfer, whether these are inter-bank transfers or straightforward retail transfers of the kind made by ATM networks.

The use of end-to-end encryption in ATM communications is especially important, for the following reasons:

- Members of the public are entitled to have the maximum protection of their funds from any computer criminal, including a computer criminal who may be working at the organization.

- It is essential that the organization takes every possible step to ensure that only a bona fide user who carries the appropriate ATM card and has a knowledge of the PIN is able to access the ATM and conduct transactions in the account in question. End-to-end encryption maximizes the security of the transaction authorization process. (As we have seen, this process could be circumvented by a customer who handed his or her ATM card to a third party and told them his or her PIN, but that is another matter.)

Today's encryption techniques are efficient and effective, and are extremely reliable. It must be noted, however, that – as mentioned briefly above – encryption only protects against data being read by an unauthorized person; it does not protect against the data being tampered with. In order to protect against this, **message authentication** must be used.

Message authentication helps to protect an organization against its data being tampered with during the communications process by enabling a bona fide user to check when such tampering has occurred.

The message authentication technique involves a special code being put into the data at the point of entry. The recipient's message authentication software only accepts the data if the code has been transmitted along with the message, and if both are unimpaired. If anyone has tried to tamper with the message, the message authentication system will alert the bona fide recipient that this has occurred.

As with encryption, there is a standard for message authentication. This is known as ANSI Standard 9.9.

Recent years have seen the development of ever more powerful encryption systems, many of which are now freely available as 'shareware' over the internet. Perhaps the best known and most powerful example of this is the software Pretty Good Privacy (PGP). This is a highly secure commercially available encryption software package which uses different types of encryption algorithms in order to maximize its security. It also uses a network of signatures to guarantee each public key, which is called a web of trust. A key might be signed by your parents, spouse, boss and a few good friends. People who will want to verify your signature might know someone from this group and have a copy of his or her public key. Although this is unlikely, eventually they will know someone who knows someone else who links the person to the certificate. The more people who sign your public key, the smaller the number of instances that link people – revoking the law of the sixth degree whereby two people can be linked via a chain of six people.

Until such webs become widespread enough to link everybody they don't offer a practical solution to internet commerce. Many credit card companies, telecommunication companies, ISPs, governmental departments and banks are going to set up their own hierarchical networks because they need specific guarantees of identity that satisfy their models of risk, and connected, respective policies. These types of organizations all have the advantage of knowing existing customers through direct links into their homes. Thus, their strict policy may determine that a certificate is to be mailed to a new customer's house on a floppy disk. In particular, banks understand the problems involved in distributing credit cards and can use their experience to ensure that certificates are safely placed in the right hands. Table 8.1 provides an overview of cryptographic techniques.

Where a computer is sending data communications to another organization in real time it will also need to make use of two other data communications techniques: **non-repudiation and sender authentication**. These are not directed at fending off illicit external interference, but are concerned with the maintenance of the data's integrity. As such, they are part of the establishment and maintenance of computer security for an organization.

Non-repudiation is required where it is in the interests of either counterparty to be able to prove that a particular electronic message was indeed sent. Non-

Table 8.1 Overview of cryptographic techniques

Encryption technique	Advantages	Disadvantages
Symmetric key	Speed	Both keys are the same
	Deployment costs: can be easily implemented in hardware	Difficult to distribute keys
		Lack of support of digital signatures
Public key	Uses two different keys	Speed: computationally intensive
	Open distribution of keys	Greater hardware costs
	Provides integrity and non-reputability through digital signatures	

Source: Datamonitor

repudiation is a communications security technique which involves making use of a 'digital signature', which is in essence a piece of code which an organization can attach to all electronic messages which it receives from counterparties or sends to them.

The sender uses his or her private key and a digital signature algorithm such as DES or RSA to process a hash (or digest) of the message to be protected. The result is attached to the message as the digital signature. The hash is simply a means of ensuring the signature process is capable of handling a message of any length. Anyone with access to the corresponding public key can use it to check that the message and the signature match. Note that, unlike a handwritten signature, a digital signature also depends on the content of each message. This prevents the signature being copied from a genuine message to a fraudulent one. The signature itself is not normally encrypted, although the entire message (including its signature) may be encrypted in those cases where confidentiality is especially important.

Authentication of the sender only works if the person checking the signature knows who owns the public key. Thus public keys are normally distributed in the form of a certificate which binds the public key to the identity of the owner. The assumption is that only the person named in the certificate has access to the private key that corresponds to the public key. Therefore, that person must have created the signature. Clearly, there is a need for the owner of a key pair to look after their private key, otherwise, he or she may be held accountable for other people's actions.

At this point, it is appropriate to consider some further anti-hacking techniques. Deterring a hacker by making a system seem unattractive, and preventing the data in a system being read or tampered with by an unauthorized person are essential techniques, but what should the organization do to defend itself against a really determined hacker?

A most useful technique is to incorporate a dial-back modem into the user interface. This requires the system to dial back anyone who attempts to use the system. Any hacker, confronted by the possibility of his telephone number being known by a system into which he is attempting to hack, is highly unlikely to want to continue the hacking process.

An even more secure version of the dial-back modem is one which is programmed by the organization only to dial certain numbers, which would be the numbers of bona fide counterparties. No other number will be dialled back. Where this type of modem is used, there should be a provision in the user interface for new bona fide counterparties to be asked to contact some person at the organization in order to arrange for their number to be included in the modem's program. Obviously, no number should be installed there unless the organization which holds the number has first been thoroughly checked out by the organization.

Incidentally, note that in some countries the telephone system nowadays permits the recipient of a call to see on a display the source telephone number of an incoming call. Needless to say, this system, where available, is a major disincentive to hackers.

It is convenient to discuss the problem of **rogue software** here, under communications security, as the computer criminal who attempts to introduce rogue software can be seen as someone who, like a hacker, is trying to compromise the organization's computer security from a distance. This does not mean that this will always be the case, for rogue software can also be accidentally or deliberately introduced via a terminal by the staff member who works on the terminal every day.

There are various types of rogue software. The best-known types of these are **viruses**, which are designed to cause damage to data held on the legitimate software (typically deleting data irretrievably), or by impairing or corrupting the system function (system software can also be affected by a virus).

The term 'virus' is somewhat misleading, as a virus is of course a natural organism, but computer viruses are all too human in their origins, being designed as a prank or as sabotage by some unscrupulous person, or by someone who wants to show off his or her computing expertize in an immature and foolish way.

What *is* truly virus-like about viruses is their ability to replicate themselves. When a virus 'infects' a disk, it typically replicates itself by attaching itself to other programs in the disk, including system software. Like a human virus, the effects of a computer virus may not be detectable for a period of days or weeks, during which time every disk inserted into the system will come away with a hidden copy of the virus.

Incidentally, just because a virus may seem relatively innocuous because it only seems to be doing something mischievous – such as delivering a prank message – does not necessarily mean that this is all the virus can do. Often it won't be.

All types of rogue software can be described as viruses. Sometimes a particular type of virus – one that comes into play when the program reaches a particular point in its function – is known as a 'logic bomb', whereas one that comes into play at a certain time in the future is known as a 'time bomb'.

Viruses can be found in all types of software. They are particularly potent threats when they come in inside mail attachments and macros: that is, software written by someone other than the package designer. Most office applications (word processor, spreadsheets, databases, presentation packages, etc.) can have their functionality extended using macros. The leading computer security company Baltimore Technologies told me that many of their customers 'report that macro viruses are a more significant problem than conventional ones'.

Measures for dealing with all types of rogue software are similar. *Absolutely every effort must be taken to avoid introducing the rogue software into any of the organization's computer systems in the first place. Avoiding introducing the virus in the first place is an infinitely more useful computer security measure than trying to detect and defuse the virus once it has been introduced.*

There are two principal ways of combating a virus.

First, the organization must ensure that it makes daily back-ups of its data. If it does this, the risk of a virus damaging an entire bank of data is minimized.

Second, every piece of software which is being introduced into the organization's computers *must* be checked in a so-called 'checksum' program which is able to detect whether the software has been altered in any way. In practice, an extremely important part of the organization's computer security policy must be the implementation of a rigid rule that all new software must be passed through the checksum device (often known as the anti-viral device) before being used.

> Avoiding introducing the virus in the first place is an infinitely more useful computer security measure than trying to detect and defuse the virus once it has been introduced.

The importance of preventing viruses from entering the organization's computer systems is so great that even the central anti-viral device used by the organization must not be entirely relied upon. *Every* terminal on the organization's premises must also have anti-viral software installed and this should be used to check all new disks before they are loaded.

Viruses originating remotely are also a serious threat. No software offered in downloaded form or disk form by a counterparty should ever be loaded without first being checked by the organization. This applies no matter how trusted the counterparty is.

Other important anti-viral measures are as follows:

- It must be strictly forbidden for any employee to introduce into the computer system any software they have written themselves or any of their own personal software, including computer games.

- Executable programs must never be downloaded from a public bulletin board until the organization is sure that they are virus-free, which in practice means that someone else (preferably at another organization) has used the program without problems. In order to maximize security here from a centralized viewpoint, only the organization's information technology team should be permitted to download publicly sourced programs in any case.

- Similarly, executable programs from mail-order vendors of public domain pro-rams, or pro-rams from another public source (including software supplied free in magazines, and in promotional packages) must not be downloaded into the organization's computer unless the organization is completely confident that the software is virus-free.

- Never copy pirated disks of commercial programs, because these disks may contain viruses.

The systems shutdown hazard

The hazard. Systems shutdown occurs when an entire computer system ceases to be operational. The causes are numerous, typically including: power failure, fire, major physical accident, or major software or hardware failure.

The measures to defend against the hazard. As the computer security policy in the previous chapter indicated, any financial organization which is making heavy use of computers should deploy the latest methods for protecting the environment where the computers are housed and have a workable contingency plan in place if a power failure occurs. The organization should deal with these difficulties by having a fire control system in place (these often incorporate halon gas, which drives combustible oxygen away from the environment), an array of batteries for short-term power replacement and an externally situated generator for longer-term power replacement.

However, this still obliges the organization to confront the problem that its computer installation might meet with a major physical accident – such as a devastating fire, an explosion, or a crash of some kind – which puts it out of action for some time. When this happens, what the organization ideally needs is an alternative computing centre, with computers and networks already in place, to which it can transfer its existing computing needs. This is where disaster recovery facilities come in. They are operational facilities which are available in an emergency to the organization which has paid for them. Disaster recovery facilities are usually, above all, computing facilities, but they may also be other kinds of operational facility.

Broadly speaking, there are two kinds of disaster recovery facility:

- the proprietary disaster recovery facility
- the shared disaster recovery facility.

Establishing and maintaining a disaster recovery facility in a state of constant readiness is, of course, expensive. The ideal solution to the systems shutdown hazard is certainly for the organization to install a proprietary facility (i.e. one it owns itself) at a convenient location remote from the main computer centre, but generally speaking only the largest organizations can afford to do this.

An alternative is to participate in a scheme whereby the organization pays to be part of a pool with other organizations (probably no more than five or six of them altogether) which share a disaster recovery facility between themselves. The rationale for the shared facility is that the likelihood of more than one organization needing to use the facility at any one time is extremely low, and that sharing the facility with other organizations greatly reduces its cost.

Access to a shared facility is an important resource for an organization, but if the facility is to be of maximum utility, it is essential that all the following points are clarified in advance:

- The organization arranging the sharing arrangement must be reliable and fully trustworthy.

- Sharing of expenses among participants must be fair and equitable.

- The computing resources used by the facility must be fully compatible with those of all member organizations' own computers, and with their networks.

- The number of members must be strictly limited, so that the likelihood of the facility being called upon by more than one member at a time remains extremely low. Once the agreed number of member organizations has been attained, membership must be closed; it should not be open-ended.

- Members' principal computer centres should never be closer than about 250 metres, to avoid the danger that a serious incident (e.g. an explosion) could damage two or more members' main computer centres simultaneously.

- The shared facility should be regularly tested to ensure that it will work properly, and first time, in the event that it is called upon (this point of course also applies to a proprietary facility).

- Some contingency plan must be in place to deal with the eventuality that the disaster recovery facility is required by more than one member organization at a time. Such a contingency plan might involve other members offering to use their own main computer centres to assist the member, or for the operations of the disaster recovery facility to be shared in some way for a time.

■ The organization must remember to make provisions in the event that certain key staff are unable to help with the move to a stand-by facility because they are on holiday, or ill. Of course, in the worst case scenario, some members of staff may have been killed or injured in the disaster.

> Organizations should not expect their customers to sympathize with them if their main computer centres go down, because they won't.

Whether the disaster recovery facility is a proprietary or shared one, *it should ideally be ready for use right* away. The longer the delay between the organization's main computer centre going down and the disaster recovery facility coming into operation, the worse the effect of the accident or other incident on the organization's reputation, credibility, customer goodwill and profitability. Organizations should not expect their customers to sympathize with them if their main computer centres go down, because they won't. All their customer's will be concerned about will be the level of service the organization is able to provide them with.

The electromagnetic induction hazard

The hazard.   The electromagnetic induction hazard occurs when an unauthorized person gains access to, or interferes with, a computer system by deploying a variety of techniques – including installing a receiver in some kind of physical proximity to the organization's computer resources – which exploit the fact that all parts of a computer system emit electromagnetic radiation which can be 'read' by an inductive process.

There have been cases of unscrupulous persons (or television journalists eager for a good story) siting a receiving device in a car or van, parking the vehicle near the walls of a financial organization and 'reading' a customer's account details on the receiver.

This is clearly a serious, if somewhat esoteric, hazard.

Measures to deal with the hazard.   These are:

■ The organization should, as far as practicable, install its terminals away from exterior walls. This tends to reduce, or even eliminate, the extent to which the electromagnetic radiation can be picked up by an external party.

■ Where the threat is grave, or for some reason the terminals do need to be situated by exterior walls, the best defensive measure is to place a special copper screen between the source of the electromagnetic radiation and the possible location of a detection device. For practical purposes, this means that the screen should be placed along the walls. The screen will cut out the radiation.

- Alternatively, the terminal can be housed in a special, copper-sheathed office cabinet which is deliberately designed to eliminate the emission of electromagnetic radiation. Note that these cabinets are manufactured to a standard, known as 'Tempest', which originated at the UK Ministry of Defence.

Maximizing internet security specifically

To recap: I have defined **internet security** earlier as **the ideal state where all information can be communicated across the internet secure from unauthorized persons being able to read and/or manipulate it**.

In general, internet security is an easier problem to solve than internet trust and the techniques for solving it are already well established. This is because the techniques for ensuring internet security are essentially identical to those already established for ensuring the security of any data communications system. These have been discussed in detail above.

Internet security, however, requires one additional safeguard beyond encryption and message authentication. This safeguard is known as the 'firewall'.

Firewalls

The term 'firewall' describes a barrier between an organization's internal IT network and the internet, with the purpose of the barrier being only to allow authorized traffic to pass. Authorization is based on a set of rules which have the total effect of confining acceptable incoming traffic to certain specified criteria. These criteria usually relate to such matters as: acceptable incoming internet services, acceptable internet website addresses and acceptable hosts. Some firewalls allow users to check and even modify the rules whenever they wish to do so.

Clearly, a firewall is only as good as the rules relating to what it can and cannot accept. Generally, firewalls are a highly effective way of protecting a network and sensitive information from malicious attack from outside services. The point is that *only access which is explicitly permitted will be allowed to come in through the firewall*. There are no ifs, no buts, no grey areas, no opportunity for smooth-talking persuasion, no tricks and no subjective interpretations. A message is either accepted by virtue of it meeting all the acceptance criteria, or it is rejected. The technical elements of firewalls are not an important subject to us, because an organization needs specialized assistance with setting up a firewall and should leave this task to knowledgeable professionals. Suffice it to say that there are many different types of firewalls, from straightforward routers which examine packet communications coming in from website providers, to software packages which operate at the application level. As one might expect, the more thorough a firewall is, the more complete the security it provides.

Firewalls are extremely important as ways of screening an organization's internal network from any kind of internet communication. The beauty of them is that it is not necessary for the user to specify every type of *unacceptable* message: all the user has to do is specify the *acceptable* messages. This is ideal for organizations which do not want their staff to use the internet for private leisure reasons during working hours just as it is ideal for organizations which want to screen out all types of other messages.

Firewalls as defences against hackers and viruses

Firewalls play an essential role in defending an organization from people trying to gain illicit access to its internal IT network (intranet) via the internet. They provide this protection in a variety of ways, but mainly by concealing the individual addresses of users of the intranet and thereby restricting the would-be hacker to seeing information released by the firewall: that is, information which is freely available and not confidential.

Firewalls also play a key role in helping to protect an organization against viruses which it might otherwise download from the internet. The point is that downloading any data from the internet is bound to be risky for an organization because there is always the danger that the information might contain a virus. Obviously, the sick and often socially maladjusted individuals who spread viruses will try to conceal the virus within some information which may be expected to be appealing to a person browsing the web. Most internet service providers have techniques for detecting suspect information and will post warnings to accompany it to persuade users from downloading it. Merely viewing the data on your screen is not a problem. The problem arises if you try to download it.

Firewalls are in this respect what might be seen as a first line of defence: they restrict what comes into the organization to data which has been previously agreed as acceptable. But the firewall alone is not a sufficient defence against viruses: it should be used in conjunction with a good anti-virus package which detects viruses and prevents them being loaded onto the hard drive or onto the hard drive of any other hardware.

Firewalls typically work like this: the communication comes in, *in encrypted form*, via the internet and is authenticated by a digital certificate. (This is special piece of software to identify the originator of a message. It is discussed in detail in Chapter 10.) At the point of entry to the firewall, which will only accept incoming communications that have been authenticated in this way, the actual authorization of the user to specific data is provided by the user's identity and password. Only if these different elements are in place will the firewall permit the communication to continue.

Once the authenticated, authorized *but still encrypted* communication passes beyond the firewall, it is decoded by the web server using the encryption key. It is then processed within the organization's intranet and the outgoing communication embarks on a journey which is the reverse of the incoming communication. That is, it leaves the intranet, is encrypted using the encryption key and then passes through to the internet and then on to the counterparty, which will typically have its own authentication and authorization requirements and may also have a firewall in place. The counterparty will also decode the message so that it can be read in the clear (i.e. in decoded form) on the counterparty's screen.

Assuming that all these provisions are in place, there is no reason why the internet should be any less secure as a communications medium than, say, a standard bank network such as an ATM network.

The final point to make here is that some organizations do not like to use encryption for interactive communications because sometimes, as can be imagined, the very process of encryption tends to make authentication, authorization and passage through the firewall more difficult than it needs to be. However, in general, all these different security elements are used.

Internet security – conclusions

This book's conclusions about internet security are very much in line with those of official bodies such as the UK Department of Trade and Industry (DTI), which has taken considerable efforts to educate organizations about the dangers of security posed by the internet. The DTI states its conclusions on this front as follows:

■ The internet is inherently insecure because it is a public network that has no central management or control.

■ A company using the internet is responsible for the security of its own network and systems.

■ There are people on the internet who are able to attack your IT systems and information and enjoy the challenge of attempting to gain unauthorized access.

■ Organizations cannot control the route which a message will take when it crosses the internet, from, say the UK to the US.

■ It is possible for messages across the internet to be read or modified by unauthorized people.

For an organization to understand to what extent its business is exposed to the risk of internet security, it needs to consider the following issues:

■ the value of the information

■ the harm to the business which could result from a security breach

- the realistic likelihood of a security breach occurring, taking into account both current threats and existing controls.

The DTI goes on to discuss certain 'dangerous' myths about internet security. It lists these as follows:

- The service provider is responsible for the security of your information and your connection – No. It is your responsibility.

- No one with an internet connection would want to access information passing over it – No. There are a number of people who are interested in this information and capable of accessing it.

- All systems connected to the internet are secure – No. Many are inherently insecure.

- No one can divert, copy or modify information as it passes across the internet – No. There are people who are capable of doing this.

- Business financial transactions are safe when transmitted across the internet – No. This is only true if you take precautions to protect your information. Internationally agreed technologies for protecting financial transactions over the internet are emerging and some are now available.

As a final point, it is necessary to emphasize that internet security is not merely a matter of putting up the electronic shields. It is also necessary to ensure that staff understand the importance of internet security and adhere to internal procedures relating to this.

Duncan Reid, of the IT security organization Entrust comments:

With internet security, as with other types of IT security, you can't just bolt on some security software to the system and expect that to be the total answer to the problem. You must also make sure that your staff are properly educated in the actual use of the software and are motivated to make proper use of it each time rather than try to bypass it in order to avoid the small amount of inconvenience that using IT security software sometimes entails.

Internet trust: the specifics

Introduction

In our preliminary discussion we saw that the challenge which internet trust seeks to address is that of ensuring that one's counterparties (whether an individual, a corporation, or any other party using the internet) are who they claim to be. In other words, internet trust deals with the problem of authentication: the establishment of the truth or genuineness of a person or organization.

Authentication cuts both ways: the organization needs to know the customer is who he says he is, and the customer needs to know that he is providing personal information to the bona fide organization.

The hazards which may arise if authentication is abused in some way are extremely serious. From the customer's point of view, if the organization is not who it claims to be, there are two grave dangers:

- Personal information may be sent to a dishonest third party who may use it for illicit gain.
- The customer may make payments to an internet criminal who has no intention of delivering the goods or services which are being paid for.

In either case, the chances are that the whole transaction will result in loss on the part of the customer.

From the organization's point of view, there are also two serious hazards if the counterparty turns out to be someone other than who it thought it was. These apply especially if the customer is an internet criminal.

- The organization may deliver goods and services to someone who does not intend to pay for them, and who, because the person is disguising their true identity, cannot be pursued by civil debt collection methods.
- The customer may deny that he made the transaction at all. This is known as **repudiation** and means **the refusal to honour a transaction which is**

claimed not to have been made by the person or organization apparently incurring the debt.

Repudiation is one of the most serious problems facing any organization which seeks to expand its e-commerce activities.

Repudiation is not necessarily always fraudulent. There are no doubt some instances when a organization makes an error. However, evidence shows that repudiation often either indicates a fraudulent intention by a bona fide customer or else indicates that the bona fide customer's authentication details were borrowed or else used by an internet criminal. In either of these two cases, the repudiation is fraudulent and can involve the organization in very considerable loss.

Repudiation and its link to 'phantom withdrawals' via ATMs

The problem of repudiation is not a new one in the world of high-tech commerce. For example, a serious problem for financial institutions since the dawn of automated teller machines (ATMs) in the 1970s has on occasion been the problem of 'phantom' withdrawals. These are withdrawals made via an ATM network which the bona fide customer denies having made.

In the 1980s, when customers were generally still on a learning curve in relation to ATM use, phantom withdrawals were a subject which was rarely out of the newspapers. It almost always made good news copy because a fear of technology is part of human culture and the 1980s was a particularly busy time as far as introducing the general public to advanced virtual technology was concerned.

Phantom withdrawals were a controversial subject from the beginning. Generally, banks and their customers were at complete loggerheads over them. Banks and other financial institutions generally denied that phantom withdrawals happened. Customers, on the other hand, were adamant that they did happen, and regarded banks' fervent denials as merely evidence of a conspiracy or cover-up of the subject on the part of banks, who were afraid of admitting the truth.

What exactly was the truth?

Those who believed that phantom withdrawals happened maintained that the ATM system was, in effect, spontaneously generating withdrawals which had not actually taken place. Certainly, it is easy to believe that an ATM system might do this. Nobody who has any familiarity with technology – and especially new, state-of-the-art technology – can seriously doubt that such a thing could happen.

Banks, on the other hand, maintained that phantom withdrawals were not possible, any more than phantom telephone calls are possible. We have all had the odd experience of our telephone ringing and then, when we answer it, of the line going dead. But is this really a phantom telephone call? No, not really. It can usually be readily explained by the fact that the caller realized between dialling and waiting for an answer that he or she had dialled the wrong number. Alternatively, perhaps our spouse is having an affair and the wrong person answered the phone!

Very well, this is a frivolous point, but if phantom telephone calls don't happen, then it is reasonable to ask why phantom withdrawals should happen. Furthermore, an extremely strong argument which the banks advance against such spontaneous 'withdrawals' being generated by an ATM is that *the vast majority of phantom withdrawals occur from ATMs situated in the customer's locality*. The banks say that if phantom withdrawals really did happen, one might expect them to be generated spontaneously in ATMs located anywhere in the region or country covered by the ATM system, not necessarily at machines located close to where the customer lived.

It is a good argument, but not necessarily watertight. After all, if customer X makes, during a given month, thirty withdrawals from an ATM located close to his home in central London, and one withdrawal from an ATM in Edinburgh, an ATM system which was not working properly might be expected to generate a phantom withdrawal (if it was generating a phantom withdrawal at all) from the ATM which the customer used most of the time. That customer's data would be traced to that ATM more than any other.

Even so, the argument is a good one and no doubt the vast majority of phantom withdrawals are probably made by the customer, who then forgets them, or else made by a third party to whom the customer has unwisely given his or her ATM card and PIN. The truth is that many people actually find ATMs useful because if they are busy, or ill, or otherwise indisposed, they can give their card or PIN to a friend who can then withdraw funds on their behalf. This is much more difficult to arrange over the counter of a bank. Of course, any customer who allows a third party to use his or her card and PIN in this way is breaking the terms of the agreement with the bank by which the card and PIN were issued, but many customers are prepared to do this.

This discussion, which might appear to be a digression, is in fact extremely important because it shows how, generally, the threat of phantom withdrawals has not thwarted banks in their efforts to set up ATM networks. On the contrary, for sound commercial reasons, they have adopted a generally belligerent and even aggressive attitude towards customers who claim to have been the victim of a phantom withdrawal. Several banks in the UK, for example, adopted a policy in the 1980s of fighting in the courts every claim that a phantom withdrawal had happened, even if the amount involved was small. Banks obviously did not wish to have their reputations sullied by even one successful claim. Not surprisingly, most customers were reluctant to pursue the matter as far as that, although there was a handful of cases where the matter did reach the court and where the judge found in the customer's favour.

Phantom withdrawals are in the news much less often nowadays. People use ATMs far more than they did in the past, and it is possible that this greatly increased use of ATMs has made customers more familiar with the security scenario surrounding ATM use and reluctant to abuse the guidelines. A more subtle reason why phantom withdrawals are not such an issue today may be that customer bent on defrauding his or her bank has realized the futility of it. Finally, it is always possible that the less technically advanced ATM systems of the 1980s *did* generate phantom withdrawals, but that the more advanced ones of today do not.

Unfortunately for banks, and other financial institutions and organizations generally, dealing with the problem of repudiation of transactions over the internet is much trickier than dealing with phantom withdrawals.

The ideal state which organizations seek is one where their internet transaction system is proof against repudiation and consequently features **non-repudiation**.

Non-repudiation and internet trust

In internet terms, non-repudiation is an attribute of an internet trust system in which the following two features consistently apply:

- The system cannot in any practical way be exploited by a customer bent on fraud successfully claiming not to have made a transaction which in fact he or she did make.

- The system provides a sufficiently high level of evidence that a customer who has honestly forgotten that he or she made a particular transaction can be confronted with factual information which proves that he or she did make the transaction but then forgot about it.

It should be obvious that non-repudiation is actually an extremely demanding spin-off of an authentication system. The point is that non-repudiation can only be assured *if there is something inherent in the authentication system which allows the organization to prove beyond doubt that the transaction **must** have been made by the customer and **could not have** been made by anybody else.*

This notion of a particularly heavy burden being placed on an authentication system introduced a crucial notion in the area of internet trust: the principle that there are different levels of authentication available over the internet. Consider a bank which is operating a retail banking system over the internet. It is obvious that there are different types of service which a bank can deliver in this way. Furthermore, it should be obvious that these services *will vary according to the importance of reliable authentication.*

This introduces the notion of the **e-commerce service hierarchy**, in which different types of e-commerce service have different levels of authentication attached to them, depending on the risk exposure which the organization must adopt at the different levels. The e-commerce service hierarchy is shown diagrammatically in Box 9.1.

Box 9.1 The e-commerce service hierarchy – illustrative example for a retail bank

This is a hierarchy of services, presented here in ascending order of potential for serious security breaches. Those services *above* the rule on page 184 are relatively impervious to severe security breaches, but those *below* the rule are extremely vulnerable to this.

Information

This is the first level of the hierarchy. It is an extremely *neutral* level. The service here consists simply of the customer being able to obtain information about what the organization has on offer. Since this illustrative example of the hierarchy concerns a retail bank, the information would relate to such matters as mortgage rates, interest rates and details of other products on offer. Obviously, information provided in this way is basically the same as advertized information. Usually no interactive element is involved, other than that customers can click on a particular type of service in order to obtain more information about it.

Consultation

This takes the hierarchy up a notch. This service allows the customer to obtain details of his or her accounts, such as the current balances of current accounts (checking accounts in the US) and deposit accounts. The equivalent to this in a non-bank retail scenario would be the customer obtaining details of the current status of his or her account, such as information about goods in the pipeline and payments being processed.

Communication between same-customer accounts

This next level of the hierarchy is again another notch up in the *personalization* of the service being provided. Here, the customer enjoys the ability to switch funds *between his or her own accounts*, whether in a bank scenario or in some other financial scenario (such as where a retail customer has two different types of accounts with the organization). This level obviously is more demanding from a security perspective, but note that what the customer (or, by implication, a successful inter-net criminal) can do is extremely limited: there isn't much fraudulent gain potential in a situation where all you can do is transfer illicitly funds from one of the customer's accounts to another!

Communication between registered accounts

This level – the first one below the broken line which here marks a significant inten-sification of the security breach potential of the service – concerns transfers of funds between a customer's account to a *registered* account. The registered account in this context means an account *whose details the customer has already pre-registered with the bank*. Typical examples would be accounts held by suppliers to whom the customer makes regular payments. In the case of a business customer, this might be any of a wide variety of commercial suppliers. In the case of the retail customer, it would probably be such suppliers as: credit card companies, major organizations with whom the customer has an account, and utility companies such as gas, elec-tricity and water suppliers.

Note that the security breach potential here is limited in the sense that even if the internet criminal is able to intervene, the worst he can do is transfer funds illicitly from the customer's account to a pre-registered account. Obviously, it is likely that these funds could be retrieved, as the registered account-holder would want to col-laborate fully with the customer to deal with the problem, and because the customer would easily be able to show that the funds should not have been transferred. Basically, internet crime at this level of the hierarchy does not make much sense, because there is no way the fraudster can readily benefit.

Communication between *non*-registered accounts

This, the final step in the hierarchy, is obviously the ultimate step and contains very serious potential for illicit security breaches. The point is that the whole principle of this level of service is that the customer can himself key in details of any account and use his authority (which will have been established by authentication) to make the transfer. Once made, the transfer would not normally capable of being cancelled or the funds retrieved.

In the worst-case scenario, an internet criminal could, at least in principle, remove every penny from the customer's account and send it to an account of his own. If his account were located in some jurisdiction where bank confidentiality was combined with comparative inaccessibility to investigations (Liechtenstein, the Cayman Islands, and some off-shore locations would be popular here), the customer would in practice have little or no chance of retrieving the funds.

If this were to happen, and the transfer had been initiated illicitly by an internet criminal due to the bank's internet system being compromised, the customer would probably have very solid grounds for winning compensation from the bank. The potential losses which banks can incur here are consequently *unlimited*.

In practice, about 95 per cent of internet banking transactions currently made over the internet *are strictly limited to the three services above the broken line* in Box 9.1. The reason for this is easy to guess: these services present little or no serious security breach potential to the bank.

In practice, at present very few banks are offering customers an internet banking service which provides communication between registered accounts, and *no banks at all* are offering services based around communication between non-registered accounts.

A comment from Frédéric Engel, marketing director of ActivCard's operations in Europe, the Middle East and Africa, is appropriate here:

As internet trust stands at present, a bank would be out of its mind to offer communications between non-registered accounts, and it is extremely doubtful that current internet security provisions really support communications between registered accounts. The truth is that until internet security and internet trust are absolutely reliable, banks need to restrict their internet initiatives to the relatively innocuous information, consultation and communications between one account to another range of services.

Engel's perspective here makes complete sense. The question is, to what extent is this whole situation a problem for other organizations?

The answer is that it depends what kind of business the organization is in. An organization which wishes to use the internet, in effect, for advertizing purposes, and also to allow customers to check details of their accounts and the status of deliveries, will be satisfied with the relatively security-impervious services above the broken line. However, organizations which want to sell over the internet are clearly exposing themselves to a security breach in that an internet criminal could divert an order to himself while arranging for the bona fide customer to pay for this. The issue of the security breach potential here clearly depends on what is being purchased. If, say, the customer is purchasing books to a maximum order value of $100, the actual potential for security breaches is minimal because it is hardly worth the fraudster's while to try to intervene with this transaction.

On the other hand, if the organization were supplying books, or any other goods that can readily be turned into cash, to the value of several thousand pounds, the potential for security breaches would be substantial. For this reason, all internet organizations have a ceiling (which they normally keep strictly confidential to avoid giving fraudsters the opportunity to commit fraud just below the level of the ceiling) to which standard authentication procedures apply. In other words, if you want to buy a single personal computer over the internet from an internet computer supplier, you will probably be able to do this simply by using a password or pass number which the organization has issued to you. On the other hand, if you want to buy 100 personal computers, the organization will require more substantial authentication and may well not be prepared to do this over the internet at all.

Retailers who are selling goods which *are* readily convertible into cash need to adopt a completely different approach to selling via the internet. With current authentication procedures, it is, in fact, unlikely that anybody selling valuable items would wish to do so over the internet. Obviously, valuable jewels, coins, stamps, bullion, and so on, offer mouth-watering opportunities for internet criminals and such organizations would be sure to be targeted by fraudsters. All the valuable items just mentioned are so readily convertible into cash that they almost represent cash themselves. Once a fraudster had struck, it is likely he would find that crime *does* pay.

Illicit repudiation and commercial reality

In practice, organizations are vulnerable not only to internet criminals but also to bona fide customers who are being dishonest. The point is that, with current authentication procedures, it is not normally possible for an organization to prove beyond doubt that a customer did initiate a particular transaction. The customer can simply deny having done so, and usually the customer's liability here is limited very strictly to about £50. In other words, customers can easily defraud internet organizations by claiming not to have made a transaction which they have in fact made.

The organization has some come-back here. For one thing, the organization should be able to prove that goods were delivered to a particular address, and if that address is known to be held by the customer then it is difficult for the customer to repudiate the transaction. But a customer bent on fraud could quite easily arrange for goods to be delivered to a different address from his usual one and could deny that he had access to that other address. Fortunately, most customers are honest (and most, too, do not understand how easy it is to defraud a organization by illicit repudiation). In practice, of course, customers cannot usually do this more than once, and it is a fact that organizations have a 'black list' of customers whom they consider to have made illicit repudiations, and will usually share this list with other organizations.

The 'commercial reality' aspect of illicit repudiation consists of two points, the first of which is unfavourable to the organization, while the second is favourable:

- Even if illicit repudiation is proven, the commercial reality of the situation may be that the organization cannot obtain payment from the customer for the goods because the customer has either fled or has no money. It is also usually impossible to retrieve the goods, unless they are such that they are not readily portable.

- In practice, organizations are prepared to face the consequences of illicit repudiation because the advantage to their business of selling via the internet is so immense that illicit repudiation is seen simply as an occupational hazard. There is an analogy here to credit card companies, which accept that a certain proportion of their transactions (typically about 8 per cent) will be fraudulent and will involve them in loss. However, credit card business is so lucrative that they can afford to incur this loss. Similarly, if a organization is able to obtain tens of thousands of new customers via the internet – and if the vast majority of these customers behave entirely honestly – the organization will certainly be prepared to accept some loss due to illicit repudiation.

But accepting a certain of 'controlled' loss due to illicit repudiation is one thing; being prepared to offer services – in the terminology here, services 'below the broken line' – which **by their very nature expose the organization to severe potential security breaches** is quite another. As we have seen, services below the broken line have completely different authentication requirements from services above it. This raises the crucially important issue of 'strong' and 'weak' authentication.

Under the terms of reference used in this book, **strong authentication** can be defined as **authentication verified by means of any technique which makes the likelihood that the counterparty are who they say they are extremely high**.

This is, unfortunately, a somewhat vague definition, but until a clear standard for what constitutes strong authentication exists within the industry, there is little alternative but to formulate the definition in this way.

Similarly, **weak authentication** can be defined as **authentication verified by means of any technique which makes it unlikely that the genuineness of the counterparty can be verified with any serious degree of certainty**.

These definitions are useful for our discussion of e-commerce trust, but admittedly their vagueness makes them useful only as guidelines. The point is that different vendors will claim that their products feature strong authentication as much for marketing reasons as because this attribute can be proven objectively.

However, this is not to say that the terms 'strong' and 'weak' authentication have no real meaning. Indeed, they are extremely important, because they provide a way of discussing levels of internet trust and making comparisons between different types of authentication techniques.

For example, in the e-commerce service hierarchy featured in Box 9.1 above, we could say that the services *above* the broken line can be managed perfectly comfortably using a 'weak' authentication method such as a simple password. On the other hand, the services *below* the broken line cannot possibly be safely delivered using such a weak method of authentication. Instead, a more robust form of authentication is necessary. What exactly that robust type of authentication should be depends to a large extent on precisely the risk to which a organization exposes itself when it delivers the type of security-critical services which feature below the broken line. Remember that the example of the bank was only chosen for illustrative purposes; by analogy the hierarchy can be extended to other types of retail services.

As one might expect, in an industry which is so rapidly evolving and creating so many extremely exciting commercial opportunities for organizations which are successful in it, vendors tend to be extremely partisan about what constitutes strong and weak authentication. ActivCard, for example, bases much of its commercial activity on spreading the word that the only type of strong authentication which can seriously be regarded as such is the use of a smart card featuring what ActivCard terms a **dynamic password**. As we explain in the section on ActivCard in Chapter 11, this is a password which continually changes and which cannot, therefore, possibly be replicated by anybody who does not have access to the smart card. There is no doubt that this type of authentication is extremely strong, but it does admittedly suffer from the drawback that anybody who has the smart card can authenticate by means of it. As we explain, this fundamental problem lies at the heart of even the strongest internet authentication systems.

The pressing need to make existing customers a favoured, privileged group

Today, the industry created by the internet is as much a thrilling, fast-moving, pioneering industry as steam power and complex mechanical processes were at the start of the nineteenth century. Inevitably, whenever an industry is growing so rapidly and pushing ahead the boundaries of what is technically possible on an almost daily basis, the vendors are very much defining not only where the technology is going, but also what the terms of reference are for the industry.

Consequently, I avoid overt dogmatism in this book and instead I aim to provide a range of perspectives which the reader can assimilate to his or her own requirements. We have already looked in detail at issues relating to the internet's origins, its technical vulnerability to security and trust breaches and to how a kind of hierarchy of authentication can be defined which helps organizations to match authentication techniques to the levels of risk to which they are exposed when delivering a particular service.

The final element in this overview of internet trust and security is to emphasize the absolutely crucial importance of the distinction between delivering a service to a customer who is known to the organization and a potential customer who is simply surfing the internet and comes across the organization's website.

It should be easy to see why this distinction is so important. By its very nature, the internet is open to anybody; indeed, this is one of its great strengths as a delivery mechanism. But one cannot do business with *anybody*; one can only do business with a known person or organization whom one has accepted as a counterparty.

This need to sift valuable counterparties/customers/clients from the general public or from the entirety of commercial organizations in the world lies, after all, at the heart of all business activity. One of the interesting points about business today is that the larger the population of potential counterparties and the larger the business opportunities which exist, the more important personalization of service becomes and the more essential it is for an organization to deliver a completely different service to known customers compared to unknown customers who are making the acquaintance of the organization for the first time.

It is true that in many retail situations, the difference between an unknown customer and a known customer may only be a matter of minutes: once the unknown customer has 'enrolled' with the organization, that customer becomes a known customer. But the time this process takes, or the procedures which need to be followed in order for it to happen, are not the point: what is the point is the *distinction* between the unknown and known customers.

One particularly helpful way of discussing the distinction between existing customers and the great mass of potential 'anybodies' who may be surfing the internet and come across the organization's website was suggested to me by Caelen King, product manager of Baltimore Technologies. During a wide-ranging discussion with King and his colleagues at Baltimore's offices in Dublin, he explained that Baltimore Technologies used the extranet/internet model to distinguish between the type of internet-based relationships a organization has with pre-existing customers or business partners, and the type of relationship it has with 'anybody' who may come across its website.

The concept of the extranet has already been mentioned. The **extranet** can be defined here as **that part of the internet which is only available to a sub-set of people/organizations**.

The extranet is basically a kind of privileged sector of the internet. It is not, as some suppose, a special type of net of its own, but rather a privileged area of the internet covered by security and trust procedures which facilitate e-commerce.

The illustration which King provided of how the extranet works in conjunction with the internet featured a motor manufacturer such as Ford. As King explains:

> Clearly, an organization like Ford wants to use the internet to promote its cars and vehicles to the general public: anybody, or any organization, which might be searching for its website or come across it. But if Ford were to restrict its use of the internet to this 'catch-all' application, it would be denying itself another extremely valuable use of this revolutionary technology. As a result, Ford also makes use of an extranet. This serves two purposes.
>
> Firstly, it allows Ford to deliver a particular level of service to existing customers who are known to it. The type of service delivered here would obviously depend on the customer's requirements but might include information about updates to the model which the customer has, and might also involve delivering information about the state of a customer's account with Ford: say, a major organization which bought many vehicles from Ford during the year. The extranet could also be used by a customer to order individual parts from Ford.
>
> Secondly – and this is a particularly mighty benefit of the extranet – an organization like Ford could use the 'privileged' sector of the internet to communicate with its *suppliers*. Where an organization only has one or two suppliers, the extranet can still be useful as a means of communicating with them. But it really comes into its own when an organization has very many suppliers, as Ford does. In this case, the extranet provides the ideal vehicle for enabling Ford to communicate interactively with its suppliers over all types of matters, from account details to component specifications. For a major manufacturer like Ford, perhaps the most important use of the extranet of all when communicating with suppliers is the facility which it offers for enabling Ford to communicate with suppliers over component delivery timings. 'Just In Time' management of component delivery is an immensely important part of motor manufacture, just as it is essential to many other types of large-scale manufacture. The extranet provides a perfect means for a large manufacturer to liaise with suppliers over delivery, enabling suppliers to receive confirmations of delivery schedules, and also details of any changes which the manufacturer may need to make to its timetable.

King goes on to explain that much of the work which Baltimore Technologies undertakes in connection with the extranet is based around helping its customers develop internet security and trust techniques which enable them to manage their supplier relationships and their supply chain with maximum efficiency across the internet.

In summary, then, King's emphasis on the importance of the extranet is another way of looking at the e-service hierarchy. One might say in a very general sense that the services above the broken line in Box 9.1 are delivered via the internet, and the services below the broken line via the extranet. Whether you, as the reader of this book, decide to define your own commercial activities via the internet in terms of this extranet/internet distinction depends very much on whether you feel making the distinction as explicit as this will help you from a commercial standpoint. At present, when the e-commerce global industry is evolving so quickly, one ought, perhaps, not to be too dogmatic about what terms should be used and how the industry should be regarded. Ultimately, what matters is whether adopting a particular perspective on e-commerce works for you in a global sense.

The only matter on which one *most* certainly *can* be dogmatic is the need for some infrastructure which makes internet trust possible. Fortunately for all concerned, there is such an infrastructure, and it becomes more important for internet trust with every passing day. It is this infrastructure which is the subject of the next chapter.

Digital signatures and public key infrastructure

Introduction

In a famous memorandum which he sent rather belatedly to his colleagues at Microsoft in the mid-1990s, Bill Gates confessed with refreshing sincerity that he had misjudged the importance of the internet, that it was unquestionably the way ahead for Microsoft, and that much of Microsoft's activities would henceforth be orientated around it.

Since then, Bill Gates has himself become one of the gurus of the internet. Microsoft has used its commercial power and innovative strength to assume a leading position in the world's internet industry. The user metaphor employed in Microsoft's Office 97 is itself internet-based, and Microsoft's internet access program, Internet Explorer, is now the world's most popular Internet access system: a position it has assumed at the expense of Netscape.

Throughout his organization's involvement with the internet – an involvement which will only be increasing and intensifying in time to come – Bill Gates has spoken about the importance of internet trust and security. He has famously said that the fulfilment of the Internet's commercial promise depends on the trust and security issues – 'knowing who is communicating with you', as he has expressed it.

This chapter is about how public key infrastructure (referred to as PKI henceforth) provides a powerful and essential infrastructure for internet trust.

It is important to remember that the internet was never intended to provide secure end-to-end communications. When the underlying protocols and architecture which now constitute the internet were established, there were no such things as personal computers, and consequently no realistic expectation that connections would be made to the internet other than between large academic computer centres and military research establishments. There was, therefore, no particular perception that security across the internet was necessary.

Needless to say, in today's internet environment, where hundreds of millions of individuals and organizations are connecting to the internet via personal computers and a range of other interface devices, the need for security is paramount.

We have already seen that organizations connected to the internet by means of permanent connections such as servers need to take great care that they are not attacked by internet criminals whose motives may be obscure but whose potential damage and threat is not. We have provided an overview of the principal means of protecting against internet criminals, in particular by means of **firewalls**, **encryption** and **message authentication**. We have also seen how interactive transactions between retailers and their customers or between manufacturers and their suppliers can only be secure if **trust** can be established between the two counterparties. We have emphasized that internet trust represents a particularly serious challenge to organizations because it may be easy for an internet criminal to pretend to have an identity which he does not in fact possess.

In practice, e-commerce is only possible if the retailer or other organization can proceed both with confidence in the security of the transaction and a trust in the genuineness of the counterparty. The PKI system has been developed in order to maximize the likelihood that such trust can be assured.

What PKI offers

The term 'public key infrastructure' sounds intimidating, but it is in fact a thoroughly logical and sensible system which sounds more complicated than it actually is.

A PKI is **a combination of hardware and software products, policies and procedures, which provides the basic security required to carry out e-commerce activity in order that users – who do not know each other, or who are widely distributed, or who are both of these – can communicate securely through a chain of trust**.

PKI is based around digital identifications known as **digital certificates** which act rather like a form of 'electronic passport' and bind the user's **digital signature** to his or her **public key**.

In order to gain the fullest understanding of these three crucially important terms, we need to step back a moment and consider some peripheral issues.

All legally binding communications or transactions, whether electronic or paper-based, must meet four fundamental requirements:

- The sender must be able to authenticate his or her identity to the recipient in order to determine who really sent the message.

- There must be some means to ascertain that the message has integrity. The recipient must be able to determine whether or not the message received has been altered *en route* or is incomplete.

- The integrity of the message must be capable of being proven in court. This is the issue which deals with the potential problem of non-repudiation.

■ Certain signature formalities must be specified. In other words, the message must be bound in some way to the specific party who sent it.

In order to ensure internet trust, the security initiative must be directed at making *the message itself secure* rather than the transport mechanism. The technique which is directed at securing the message is known as **public key cryptography**. It is **a data encryption technique which is designed to use various methods to authenticate the message and bind it to a particular party**.

Public key cryptography makes use of **digital signatures**. In defining digital signatures and explaining how they work, it is helpful to begin by saying what they are *not*. A digital signature is *not*, for example, a digitized image of a handwritten signature. We are all familiar with the electronic pad which a person signs upon receiving a package from a delivery service such as Federal Express. What happens here is that the handwritten signature is digitized and the image transferred to the electronic document. The problem with these digitized signatures is that once they have been 'captured' by the system, they can be 'cut and pasted' onto any electronic document, making forgery a simple matter. Owing to the vulnerability of digitized signatures (as opposed to digital signatures), they are not generally recognized as legally binding in a court of law. Digital signatures are not at all the same as digitized signatures. Instead, they are **an actual transformation of an electronic message using public key cryptography**.

Throughout the process where the digital signature is being used, it is bound irrevocably to the document or message that is being 'signed' *as well as to the signatory*, and therefore cannot be falsified or reproduced. In the United States, digital signatures are already legally admissible in numerous states, and it is likely that within the next few years they will be legally recognized throughout the United States and the world.

So how exactly does cryptography work in electronic communications?

There are three basic principles which underlie the use of cryptography in electronic communications:

■ The first step, as one might expect, is that a computer reads any data as a **binary number**: that is, **a number written in Base 2**. Numbers in Base 10 are simply converted by the computer into their binary form, while verbal messages are converted by the computer into binary form using a subsidiary coding system known as ASCII.

■ Because electronic messages are represented numerically in the computer, it is possible to perform mathematical functions on them.

■ Electronic messages can thus be transformed into alternate representations that are unique to the original.

The encryption system used for converting a readily readable number or verbal message (such readily readable numbers or messages are said to be **in the clear**) is as old as the hills. Encryption techniques literally go back to the dawn of written history, and usually make use of some standard procedure for transforming the number or message into another form. Obviously, such transformations only work if both the sender and recipient understand the basis of the transformation! For example, to take an ultra-simple illustration, a transformation of a verbal message which depends on every letter in the clear being represented by the letter which is two letters on in the alphabet (with Y being represented by A and Z being represented by B) will only succeed as an encryption technique if the recipient knows that this method is the key to the deciphering.

In practice, such a simple alphabetical substitution would be relatively easy for anybody to crack, and by the 1940s – significantly during World War II) techniques were developed for encoding messages via special machines which based their alphabetical transformation not upon a simple standard procedure, but upon the output of rotor wheels which, pre-set in a certain way that was known to both the sender and the recipient (both of whom had a machine), would continually generate new transformations for each letter.

The most famous machine used to encode in this way was the notorious Enigma device: a product of German ingenuity which baffled the Allies until they were fortunate enough to capture several Enigma machines and to perceive that they themselves could build a kind of 'anti-Enigma' machine which would break the Enigma code. The problem with this approach was that initially the code-breaking took too long for the breaking to be of any useful application, for the settings of the Enigma rotors were changed by the Germans every day. However, subsequent improvements in the anti-Enigma devices (which included the creation of machines which worked electronically rather than mechanically) succeeded in cracking Enigma messages within time-frames which made the breaking of the code worthwhile. Eventually, the Allies were cracking every German message sent via Enigma. Ironically, because it was essential that the Germans did not know that there messages were being deciphered, there were some cases where the Allies deliberately took no action against German attacks which they knew from the deciphering to be imminent, but that was a consequence of being at war; it did not detract from the fact that the German codes had been broken.

Modern encryption techniques are strikingly analogous to the use of the Enigma machines. The only difference is that the sophistication and speed of computers to which internet criminals today have access require that the encryption techniques used are phenomenally more difficult to crack than those employed by the Germans. For example, it is becoming routine for state-of-the-art encryption to be based around numbers which have around fifty digits: a number which is thought to approach that of the number of atoms in the observable universe.

Here, there is no need to go into such mathematical complexities. All that is necessary to point out as far as public key cryptography is concerned, is that there are two distinct encryption techniques, and that the second is the one at the heart of PKI.

The first type of encryption technique, **symmetric cryptography**, is the most familiar and straightforward. It is based around a 'shared secret', or 'key', and works well within isolated environments. The most obvious example of symmetric cryptography is the ATM network. When you use an ATM, you gain access to your account by entering a personal identification number (PIN). You are, in effect, authenticating yourself to the bank. You and the bank share a secret, in this case your PIN, and as such can communicate securely upon revealing knowledge of this secret to each other. As we have seen, banks take great care to distribute PINs amid the greatest confidentiality. Not even a computer system technician at a bank will know a particular customer's PIN. Nor, incidentally, will the bank's chairman.

The inherent problem with symmetric cryptography is one of **scaleability**. In order for the communication to be confidential, the exchange of the key – the shared secret – must be done securely. This is comparatively easy in an ATM system, but it is not easy when the number of different people with whom you want to communicate securely escalates beyond a manageable number. A 'manageable number' in this case certainly does not cover the number of people which a retailer wants to communicate with over an internet or extranet scenario.

The second type of encryption technique is **asymmetric cryptography**, which is also known as public key cryptography. Asymmetric cryptography is known as such because it involves an **asymmetric key pair.** This key pair comprises what is usually referred to as a **public key** and **private key**. The public key, as its name suggests, *may be freely disseminated*. This key does not need to be kept confidential. The private key, on the other hand, *must be kept secret*. The owner of the key pair must guard his private key closely, *because sender authenticity and non-repudiation are based on the signer having sole access to his private key*.

There are two extremely important points to make about these key pairs.

- Even though the key pairs are mathematically related to each other, it is not possible to calculate one key from the other. Consequently, the private key cannot be compromised through knowledge of the associated public key.

- Each key in the key pair performs the *inverse function* of the other. What one key does, only the other can undo.

Digital signature components

Digital signatures are based around asymmetric, or public key, cryptography. In addition to a key pair and some type of electronic communications, the digital signing and verification processes involve what are known as a **hash algorithm** and a **signature algorithm**. These two algorithms are extremely complex mathematical equations. The hash algorithm is performed on the original electronic message's binary code, resulting in what is referred to as a **message digest**, which is **an 160-bit string of digits that is unique to the original message**. The signature algorithm is then performed on this message digest. The resultant string of digits is the digital signature.

During the signing process, the signer's private key is incorporated into the signature algorithm. During the verification process, the public key is incorporated into the signature algorithm. Se-com – a leading supplier of digital signatures – kindly provided me with the following simple example of how this works.

> For the sake of simplicity, assume that the binary number 100 (which, incidentally represents the Base 10 number 4) is the original message. Again, for simplicity, assume that the hash algorithm does nothing more complex than multiply the binary by two. The result of passing the binary of the original message through the hash algorithm is the message digest, or the unique fingerprint of the message, which is 200 in this example. This message digest is then passed through the signature algorithm, of which the signer's private key is a component. In this example, the signature algorithm has been drastically simplified to multiplying by two to the power of x, where x equals the signer's private key, in this case 2. The resulting number of 800 is the digital signature.

Just to re-emphasize what is so important: a digital signature has nothing to do with the signer's name or handwritten signature. Instead, the digital signature is an actual transformation of the message itself that incorporates a 'secret' known only to the signer, and is therefore tied to both the signer and the message being signed. **A signer's digital signature will be different for each different document he or she signs**.

End-user transparency

One of the fundamental aspects of modern advanced technology is that users want to gain the benefits of the application without being troubled by how the application is being managed from a technological point of view. We should not be surprised that this is so; after all, the whole purpose of technology is to generate useful applications, not to burden our lives with technical details.

The same process applies to digital signature software. This performs the signing and verification processes with little or no user intervention. In fact, the end-user does not even need to know what is actually happening. When the user wants to sign something, she simply clicks on a button labelled 'sign' on her computer toolbar. The software automatically retrieves her private key from wherever it is stored (e.g. on the computer hard drive, on a floppy disk, or on the drive of a portable machine such as a laptop or palmtop) and the document is signed.

On the recipient end, there is a toolbar marked 'verify'. Once it is pushed, the appropriate public key is retrieved from wherever it is stored (a local storage location on the recipient's computer, or an online public key repository), and the signature is verified by the software.

The essence of a public key infrastructure

Recent technological developments have made it possible for an individual to purchase digital signature software, or download it from a browser, and install it on his computer. The user can then generate a key pair and release his public key to the online world, using any identity he chooses, *with no guarantee that the identity is authentic*.

Understandably, this scenario is extremely alarming for retailers who want to be able to do business over the internet while trusting that their counterparties are who they say they are.

Naturally enough, this scenario underscores the need for some type of entity to serve as a **trusted third party (TTP)** to vouch for individuals' identities, and their relationship to their public keys. This entity, in PKI terminology, is referred to as a **certification authority (CA)**. The CA – which is also discussed below in the section on managing the components of a PKI – is **a trusted third party which issues digital certificates to its subscribers, binding their identities to the key pairs they use to sign electronic communications digitally**.

Digital certificates

Digital certificates contain the following information:

- the subscriber's name
- the subscriber's public key
- the digital signature of the issuing CA
- the issuing CA's public key
- other pertinent information about the subscriber and his organization, such as his authority to conduct certain transactions.

These certificates have a default life cycle of one year, and can be revoked upon private key compromise, separation from an organization, and for other, similar, factors which change the status of the user.

Certificates are stored in an online, publicly accessible repository. The repository also maintains an up-to-date listing of all the unexpired certificates which have been revoked. This is referred to as a certificate revocation list (CRL). The repository also maintains an electronic copy of the certification practice statement (CPS) of each CA that publishes certificates to it. The CPS outlines the policies and procedures of each CA's operations from registration of a subscriber to the physical security surrounding their CA system.

The following is a representation of the PKI process flow:

- *Step 1* – Subscriber applies to CA for digital certificates.
- *Step 2* – CA verifies identity of subscriber and issues digital certificates.
- *Step 3* – CA publishes certificates to repository.
- *Step 4* – Subscriber digitally signs electronic message with private key to ensure sender authenticity, message integrity and non-repudiation and sends to reliant party.
- *Step 5* – Reliant party receives message, verifies digital signature with subscriber's public key, and goes to repository to check status and validity of subscriber's certificate.
- *Step 6* – Repository returns results of status check on subscriber's certificate to reliant party.

Figure 10.1 shows this process flow graphically.

The different grades of digital certificates

It should be obvious that not all digital certificates are equally trustworthy. The situation here is perfectly analogous to that of documentary identifications. There are, clearly, different grades of these. For example, it is well known that certain types of documentary ID are widely available via illicit means, such as ID

Figure 10.1 The PKI process

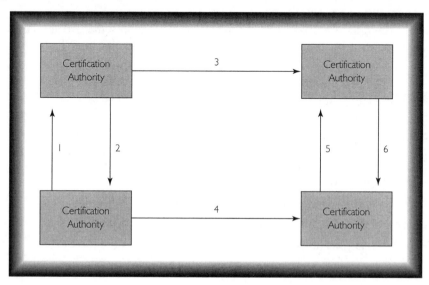

purporting to show that a young person has attained the age of 18 and can therefore visit bars and public houses. On the other hand, passports are not normally issued without checks being made of the user's identity and without a person with some official status in a community vouching for the applicant.

It would be unfair, and pointless, to mention here different types of digital certificate and the trustworthiness which they should be regarded as extending. It is, obviously, a matter of common sense that a CA which simply issues digital certificates over the internet without taking any effort to compel the applicant to prove that his or her identity is not conferring the same level of trust as a CA which requires personal visits from applicants, with the applicant being required to bring his or her passport along to prove identity. Any organization seeking to establish internet trust needs to know exactly what grade of digital certificate is being offered as part of the PKI process. Furthermore, if the type of certificate being offered does not seem particularly trustworthy, the organization should take care over what services it offers via the internet or the extranet.

Obligations and legalities

The effective use of digital signatures imposes certain heavy obligations on the parties involved.

The signers of electronic messages must protect their private key from compromise. After all, *this private key is the fundamental building block of the PKI*. If a signer's private key is compromised, he or she must book this immediately, so the CA can revoke his or her certificate and place it on a CRL.

CAs are obliged to use due diligence to verify the identity of their subscribers and their relationship to their public keys. The CA must also promptly suspend or revoke a certificate at a subscriber's request.

Finally, the reliant parties must actually verify the digital signature and check its validity against the current CRL maintained by an online repository.

Managing the public key infrastructure

Overall, a PKI should consist of:

- a security policy
- a certification authority (CA)
- a registration authority (RA)
- a certificate distribution system
- PKI-enabled applications.

These are now discussed in turn.

Security policy

A security policy sets out and defines an organization's top-level direction on information security, as well as the processes and principles for the use of cryptography. Typically, it will include statements on how the organization will handle keys and valuable information and will set the level of control required to match the levels of risk.

Some PKI systems are operated by commercial certificate authorities (CCAs) or trusted third parties, and therefore require a certificate practice statement (CPS). This is a detailed document containing the operational procedures on how the security policy will be enforced and supported in practice. It typically includes definitions on how the CAs are constructed and operated, how certificates are issued, accepted and revoked, and how keys will be generated, registered and certified, where they will be stored, and how they will be made available to users.

Certification authority (CA)

The CA system is the trust basis of a PKI as it manages public key certificates for their whole life cycle. The CA will:

- issue certificates by binding the identity of a user or system to a public key with a digital signature
- schedule expiry dates for certificates
- ensure certificates are revoked when necessary by publishing certificate revocation lists (CRLs).

When implementing a PKI, an organization can either operate its own CA system, or use the CA service of a commercial CA or trusted third party.

Registration authority (RA)

An RA provides the interface between the user and the CA. It captures and authenticates the identity of the users and submits the certificate request to the CA. The quality of this authentication process determines the level of trust that can be placed in the certificates.

Certificate distribution system

Certificates can be distributed in a number of ways depending on the structure of the PKI environment: for example, by the users themselves, or through a directory service. A directory server may already exist within an organization or one may be supplied as part of the PKI solution.

PKI-enabled applications

A PKI is a means to an end, providing the security framework by which PKI-enabled applications can be confidently deployed to achieve the end benefits. Examples of applications are:

- communications between web servers and browsers
- e-mail
- electronic date interchange (EDI)
- credit card transactions over the internet
- virtual private networks (VPNs).

Smart cards and secure storage media for digital certificates

It should be evident that the effectiveness of a PKI system is closely linked to the difficulty which any person other than the bona fide user has in using the digital certificate. One might, indeed, say that this precept is at the very heart of how a PKI operates.

It follows, therefore, that the ideal token for accessing a PKI system is one which incorporates the digital certificate within its very essence and which is thus inextricably bound up with the bona fide user.

It is true that this binding process is not of a *biological* nature: there is still nothing to stop an illicit user employing the bona fide user's token and user identity in order to initiate a transaction, even across an ultra-secure and ultra-trustworthy PKI system. However, in practice it is extremely unlikely that an illicit user would be able to get hold of a genuine user's token and also user identity, unless some foul play or collusion between a bona fide user and an illicit user were taking place. The difficulty is increased because it is likely that the genuine user will only be able to access the internet – given that the PKI system is in place – via a small number of computer terminals. In other words, an illicit user not only needs the token and the user identification, he or she also needs to know which terminal is the access point.

Smart cards – also known as **chip cards – literally incorporate a computer chip in their physical make-up**. The power of this chip varies according to the application. For example, smart cards used as stored value cards for telecommunications systems have a much less powerful chip than smart cards used in ATM banking operations. However, as might be expected in these days of ever-increasing microchip power, the general tendency is for the chips in smart cards to be increasingly powerful and for smart cards to feature increasingly high levels of functionality.

Smart cards are the *ideal token* to gain ultra-secure and ultra-trustworthy access to the PKI system. The chip of the smart card can contain the user's digital certificate and can also contain other identification data which may be used to increase the security of the authentication process. The smart card is readily portable, is easy for the user to conceal somewhere where it is unlikely that an illicit user would find it, and is generally culturally increasingly acceptable, especially as most ATM systems in developed countries are in the process of switching over to a smart card infrastructure.

Vendors of smart card solutions for PKI, such as ActivCard (whose attitude to the importance of smart cards in the PKI methodology is profiled in Chapter 6), argue that a PKI system *is simply insufficiently secure or trustworthy if smart cards are not used as the access tokens*. While it is certainly true that such vendors have a vested interest in promulgating this argument, there is little real doubt that it is a valid one.

Mobile commerce

Closely related to the ideal use of smart cards as access tokens for a PKI system is the increasing importance of mobile commerce via this system. It is important to bear in mind that mobile telephones already extensively use smart cards to ensure that only mobile telephones which are covered by an airtime agreement and other agreed provisions are able to access mobile telephone networks. In effect, a mobile telephone is a system with a smart card built in, and as such is itself ideal for accessing am electronic commerce system featuring PKI.

The only drawback to using mobile telephones for this purpose at present is that in order to access an electronic commerce system one needs an interface screen which can provide far more information than is currently available in most mobile telephones. However, this problem is already being rectified by vendors and there are already models of mobile telephone available which are ideally suited to interface with a bank's electronic commerce system. It is likely that in due course the screens of mobile telephones will become even more suitable for internet interface, although no doubt much of the interface will also be supplied by a laptop or palmtop linked directly to the mobile telephone. A mobile phone can simply be used as the smart card-integrated access vehicle to a PKI system, with the actual message-sending and interface taking place via a conventional portable computer.

Digital certificates

The point here is that any suitable token which incorporates a digital certificate can be used to access the PKI system. It seems certain that in time to come, internet users will make use of the digital certificates without even being aware of it, much as users of mobile telephones make use of the smart card every time they make a call, but are not usually aware of this fact until they replace the battery in their mobile telephone and see the smart card in the back.

Implications for internet banking systems

The implications for banks of the principle that smart cards and other secure storage media are the ideal way of accessing a PKI system are extremely exciting. Banks are already experienced in issuing bank cards; it is only a small step for them to incorporate smart cards into the same infrastructure. There is a very strong likelihood that banks can steal a march on their rivals when it comes to making the most of the potential which smart cards offer in secure electronic commerce. But unquestionably, banks need to move fast here because many of their rivals – such as supermarkets, which issue loyalty cards – also have experience in issuing cards and are often demonstrably better at branding these cards and making customers aware of them than banks are themselves.

Standards

Standards are always the focus of discussion when a new type of technology is coming into being, but tend to become increasingly less important as one standard starts to predominate, just as hardly anybody nowadays remembers that there used to be two railway gauges in Britain (and in many other countries) until the narrow gauge proved its superiority over the broad gauge.

Today, there is still considerable work necessary to ensure that different PKI systems are compatible with each other. However, there appears to be an increasing consensus that of the various standards currently available – X.509v3, SMS, WAP and VMTS – X.509v3 is starting to predominate.

Secure sockets layer (SSL)

One of the organizations that has done more than any other to popularize the world wide web and make it more accessible to the general public is Netscape (inventors of the web browser). An early innovation that it developed was a security protocol which would be able to work with any application that needs secure collections across the internet.

This protocol, **secure sockets layer (SSL)**, has been widely adopted by many other major suppliers of internet software – including Microsoft – and has thus become a security standard. **It enables two devices (such as a customer's personal computer and a retailer's server) to communicate in privacy, with optional authentication of the counterparties**. On the world wide web, it is easy for a retailer to ensure that pages with order forms and payment details can be protected using SSL. It requires no effort on the part of the consumer to use SSL to protect transactions initiated on such pages. Many suppliers offer merchant server software packages that not only make setting up and maintenance of an online shop/catalogue very easy, but also provide SSL protection as a matter of course.

It must, however, be remembered that SSL provides no protection to the transaction data beyond the communication itself. Using SSL securely to communicate with an otherwise insecure server is widespread, *and offers a false sense of security to the consumer*.

The SET protocol and strategic questions for SET implementation

As we have seen, SSL does not offer authentication but only security. The secure electronic transactions (SET) protocol, a joint initiative between Visa and Mastercard, is designed to fill this gap and provide a PKI-based authentication system for payment cards. It is the only standard of its kind in the world, and likely to become a global standard for bank payment cards..

The importance of other elements in establishing trust

It is extremely important for a bank, or any other retailer who is involved with e-commerce, to bear in mind that *PKI does not need to be the only trust-establishing element in an organization's activities via the internet*.

As Caelen King of Baltimore Technologies told me:

Ways of doing business in the real world have been developed over thousands of years and have been found to work. Obviously, establishing the authenticity of a particular counterparty is much easier in the real world than in the virtual world. In the real world there is a physical presence and people can be recognized by sight or according to some physical element of their business activity. For example, there's not much danger of delivering 500 personal computers to a fraudulent impostor if the supplier of those PCs is familiar with the geographical location of the customer and is delivering them there by lorry.

Unfortunately, where there is no physical presence, the job of establishing trust by means of verifying identity is more difficult.

Unquestionably, a public key infrastructure system is extremely helpful as a means of establishing trust over the internet. It tries hard, and uses state-of-the-art encryption techniques, to provide the same level of security in the virtual world that is already available in the real world.

But of course PKI still involves no physical verification between counterparties and its trustworthiness can consequently be compromised in extreme situations.

He added:

> The way to deal with this is to remember that *PKI only addresses a small part of the problem of internet trust*. It facilitates a system where messages can be signed digitally by a verifiable party. But it's important – indeed essential – to bear in mind that a retailer does not need to limit its trust-establishing procedure to the PKI system and the digital signature.

King went on to argue that a retailer or other organization doing business over the internet should be able to look at other indicators when making a decision about trustworthiness. He pointed out, for example, that when an organization is deciding about the trustworthiness of an e-mail it has received, it does not need to limit its trust-establishing investigation to the question of whether the e-mail has the correct digital signature on it.

> For example, when I receive an e-mail from a friend, I can easily tell whether this is a genuine e-mail from references in the message to things with which I and the sender are familiar. By extension, a retailer could quite easily deploy techniques for ascertaining the likely trustworthiness of a message even with the PKI system in place.

King accepted that the real problem of internet trust occurs when a retailer is deploying an automated system for communicating to known customers across an extranet. On the face of it, automated systems are very bad at making any kind of intelligent assessment of whether a message is trustworthy or not. However, automated systems can certainly make some authentication decisions: in the US, for example, authentication is often based around verification of postal addresses, and this is a process which can easily be automated.

During my discussion with King, I raised the question whether it might be possible to programme an automated system with certain low-grade (or even high-grade) artificial intelligence which would allow it to make its own assessment of whether a message was likely to be valid. There was agreement between us that such techniques could be highly effective for spotting unusual transactions. (Indeed these techniques are already used by telecommunications companies to permit prompt spotting of unusual usage of telephone systems.) King pointed out that banks are also good at identifying a customer's shopping profile and that such techniques could be used to identify unusual types of spending which may indicate fraudulent behaviour.

▓▓ ▓▓ Conclusion

In today's burgeoning e-commerce market, PKI systems are essential in maximizing the likelihood that counterparties are who they say they are, but only if the certificate on which the PKI authentication is based has a high grade of trustworthiness.

Organizations seeking to use PKI to ascertain trust should remember that it is only one element of the trust-ascertaining process and that other commercial pointers need to be used in conjunction with PKI to maximize the likelihood that the granting of trustworthiness is safe.

Lloyd's electronic and IT crime policy

▮▮ Schedule

ITEM 1. **Policy No.:**

_____

ITEM 2. **Name of Assured:**

_____

              Principal Address:

_____

ITEM 3. **Policy Period:**

              From: _____

              To: _____

ITEM 4. **Retroactive Date:**

_____

ITEM 5. **Premium:**

_____

ITEM 6. **Proposal Form dated:**

_____

The Proposal Form together with any correspondence relative thereto signed by or on behalf of the Assured shall be the basis of the Insurance.

ITEM 7. **Policy Limits:**

_____

Aggregate Limit of Indemnity:
The Limit of Indemnity under the Policy subject to General Condition 8, shall be _____ in the aggregate for the Policy Period.

    PROVIDED, however, that if lesser amounts are inserted against the several Insuring Clauses shown below, the Underwriters' liability in respect of Loss or Losses falling within such Insuring Clauses is limited to such lesser amounts which are also in the aggregate (herein referred to as the 'Sub-Limits') which are considered as part of and not in addition to the above-mentioned Aggregate Limit of Indemnity.

Sub-Limits Applicable to the Aggregate Limit of Indemnity stated above

Insuring Clause 1

IT Systems in the aggregate

Insuring Clause 2

Electronic IT Programs in the aggregate

Insuring Clause 3

Electronic Data and Media in the aggregate

Insuring Clause 4

IT Virus in the aggregate

Insuring Clause 5

Electronic and Telefacsimile Communications in the aggregate

Insuring Clause 6

Electronic Transmissions in the aggregate

Insuring Clause 7

Electronic Securities in the aggregate

Insuring Clause 8

Voice Initiated Instructions in the aggregate

If 'not covered' is inserted opposite any specified Insuring Clause, such Insuring Clause and any reference thereto in this Policy shall be deemed to be deleted therefrom.

ITEM 8.   **Deductible:**
The amount of the deductible under this Policy for each and every
Loss, subject to General Condition 16, is as follows:

_____

ITEM 9.   **Service of Suit:**

_____

_____

_____

ITEM 10.   **Losses to be Notified to:**

_____

_____

ITEM 11.   **Endorsements:**

_____

Dated in London

_____

▉ ▉ I Insuring clauses

▉ Insuring Clause 1
IT Systems

By reason of the Assured having transferred, paid or delivered any funds or property, established any credit, debited any account or given any value as the direct result of

(a) the fraudulent input of Electronic Data directly into:
   (i) the Assured's IT System, or
   (ii) a Service Bureau's IT System, or
   (iii) any Electronic Funds Transfer System, or
   (iv) a Customer Communication System; or
(b) the fraudulent modification or the fraudulent destruction of Electronic Data stored within or being run within any of the above systems or during Electronic Transmission to the Assured's IT System or a Service Bureau's IT System; or
(c) the fraudulent input of Electronic Data through a Telephone Banking System directly into the Assured's IT System

which fraudulent acts were instructed by or committed by a person who intended to cause the Assured to sustain a loss or to obtain financial gain for himself or any other person.

▉ Insuring Clause 2
Electronic IT Programs

By reason of the Assured having transferred, paid or delivered any funds or property, established any credit, debited any account or given any value as the direct result of the fraudulent preparation or the fraudulent modification of Electronic IT Programs which fraudulent acts were instructed by or committed by a person who intended to cause the Assured to sustain a loss or to obtain financial gain for himself or any other person.

▉ Insuring Clause 3
Electronic Data and Media

By reason of

(a) malicious alteration or destruction or attempt thereat of Electronic Data by any person while the Electronic Data are stored within the Assured's IT System or a Service Bureau's IT System or while recorded upon Electronic Data Processing Media within the offices or premises of the Assured or in the custody of a person designated by the Assured to act as its messenger (or a person acting as messenger or custodian during an emergency arising from the incapacity of such designated messenger) while the Electronic Data Processing Media upon which such Electronic Data are recorded is in transit anywhere, such transit to begin immediately upon receipt of such Electronic Data Processing Media by said messenger and to end immediately upon delivery to the designated recipient or its agent, provided that the Assured is the owner of such Electronic Data or Electronic Data Processing Media or is legally liable for such loss or damage;

(b) Electronic Data Processing Media being lost, damaged or destroyed as the direct result of robbery, burglary, larceny, theft, misplacement, mysterious unexplainable disappearance or malicious act while the Electronic Date Processing Media is lodged or deposited within offices or premises located anywhere, or in the custody of a person designated by the Assured to act as its messenger (or a person acting as a messenger or custodian during an emergency arising from the incapacity of such designated messenger) while the Electronic Data Processing Media is in transit anywhere, such transit to begin immediately upon receipt of such Electronic Data Processing Media by said messenger and to end immediately upon delivery to the designated recipient or its agent, provided that the Assured is the owner of such Electronic Data Processing Media or is legally liable for such loss or damage; and

(c) malicious alteration or destruction of Electronic IT Programs while stored within the Assured's IT System, provided that the Assured is the owner of such Electronic IT Programs or is legally liable for such loss or damage.

Insuring Clause 4
IT Virus

By reason of

(a) the Assured having transferred, paid or delivered any funds or property, established any credit, debited any account or given any value as the direct result of the destruction or attempt thereat of the Assured's Electronic Data due to a IT Virus caused by any person while such Electronic Data are stored within the Assured's IT System or a Service Bureau's IT System; and

(b) the destruction or attempt thereat of the Assured's Electronic Data as the result of a IT Virus caused by any person while such Electronic Data are stored within the Assured's IT System or a Service Bureau's IT System.

Insuring Clause 5
Electronic and Telefacsimile Communications

By reason of the Assured having transferred, paid or delivered any funds or property, established any credit, debited any account or given any value on the faith of any electronic communications directed to the Assured authorizing or acknowledging the transfer, payment, delivery or receipt of funds or property which communications were transmitted or appear to have been transmitted

(a) through an Electronic Communication System, or

(b) by Telefacsimile, telex, TWX or similar means of communication

directly into the Assured's IT System or to the Assured's Communications Terminal and fraudulently purport to have been sent by a customer, Automated Clearing House, an office of the Assured, or another financial institution but which communications were either not sent by said customer, Automated Clearing House, an office of the Assured, or another financial institution or were fraudulently modified during physical transit of Electronic Data Processing Media to the Assured or during Electronic Transmission to the Assured's IT System or to the Assured's Communications Terminal.

Special condition

All Telefacsimile, telex, TWX or similar means of communication referred to in paragraph (2) above must be Tested or subject to a call-back to an authorized person other than the individual initiating the transfer request and any such Telefacsimile must also bear a Forged Signature or Fraudulent Alteration.

Insuring Clause 6
Electronic Transmissions

By reason of a customer of the Assured, an Automated Clearing House or another financial institution having transferred, paid or delivered any funds or property, established any credit, debited any account or given any value

(a) on the faith of any electronic communications purporting to have been directed by the Assured to its customer, an Automated Clearing House or a financial institution authorizing or acknowledging the transfer, payment, delivery or receipt of funds or property which communications were transmitted or appear to have been transmitted through an Electronic Communication System, or by Tested Telefacsimile, Tested telex, Tested TWX or similar means of Tested communications directly into a IT System or a Communications Terminal of said customer, Automated Clearing House or financial institution and fraudulently purport to have been sent by the Assured or were the direct result of the fraudulent modification of Electronic Data during physical transit of Electronic Data Processing Media from the Assured or during Electronic Transmission from the Assured's IT System or the Assured's Communications Terminal; or

(b) as the direct result of the fraudulent input, the fraudulent modification or the fraudulent destruction of Electronic Data stored within or being run within the Assured's IT System or during Electronic Transmission from the Assured's IT System into the customer's IT System while the Assured is acting as a Service Bureau for the said customer; and

for which loss the Assured is legally liable to the customer, the Automated Clearing House or the financial institution.

Insuring Clause 7
Electronic Securities

By reason of a Central Depository having transferred, paid or delivered any funds or property or debited any account of the Assured on the faith of any electronic communications purporting to have been directed by the Assured to the Central Depository authorizing the transfer, payment or delivery of said funds or property or the debiting of the Assured's account in connection with the purchase, sale, transfer or pledge of an Electronic Security which communications were transmitted or appear to have been transmitted

(a)   through an Electronic Communication System, or

(b)   by Tested Telefacsimile, Tested Telex, Tested TWX or similar means of Tested communication

directly into a IT System or a Communications Terminal of said Central Depository and fraudulently purport to have been sent by the Assured to the Central Depository but which communications were either not sent by the Assured to the Central Depository or were fraudulently modified during physical transit of Electronic Data Processing Media from the Assured or during Electronic Transmission from the Assured's IT System or the Assured's Communications Terminal to the Central Depository and for which loss the Assured is legally liable to the Central Depository.

Insuring Clause 8
Voice Initiated Instructions

By reason of

(a)   the Assured having transferred any funds or delivered any property on the faith of any voice initiated instructions directed to the Assured authorizing the transfer of finds or delivery of any property in a Customer's account to other banks for the credit to persons allegedly designated by the Customer and which instructions were made over the telephone to those employees of the Assured specifically authorized to receive said instructions at the Assured's offices and fraudulently purport to have been made by a person authorized and appointed by a Customer to request by telephone the transfer of such funds or delivery of such property but which instructions were not made by said Customer or by any officer, director, partner or employee of said Customer or were fraudulently made by an officer, director, partner or employee of said Customer whose duty, responsibility or authority did not permit him to make, initiate, authorize, validate or authenticate Customer voice initiated instructions, which fraudulent acts were committed by said person who intended to cause the Assured or the Customer to sustain a loss or to obtain financial gain for himself or any other person;

(b) the Assured having transferred any funds or delivered any property on the faith of any voice initiated instructions purportedly communicated between the Assured's offices authorizing the transfer of funds or delivery of any property in a customer's account between the Assured's offices for the credit to persons allegedly designated by the Customer and which instructions were purportedly made over the telephone between the Assured's offices to those employees of the Assured specifically authorized to receive said inter-office instructions by telephone, and fraudulently purport to have been made by an employee of the Assured authorized to request by telephone such transfer of funds or delivery of property but which fraudulent acts were committed by a person, other than an employee of the Assured, who intended to cause the Assured or the Customer to sustain a loss or to obtain financial gain for himself or any other person.

■ *Special definition*

'Customer' as used in this Insuring Agreement means any corporate, partnership or trust customer or similar business entity which has a written agreement with the Assured for customer voice initiated funds transfers, which agreement shall be in the form of a corporate resolution containing a list of individuals authorized to initiate and authenticate voice initiated funds transfers, which list must specify the telephone numbers as well as monetary limits for all initiators/authenticators. Such written agreement shall also outline the terms and conditions under which the service is provided including a limitation of liability accepted by the Assured.

■ *Special condition*

All voice initiated instructions purportedly received from a customer for the transfer of funds or property must be Tested or subject to a call-back to an authorized person other than the individual initiating the transfer request.

■ II Definitions

1 'Assured' means the Assured first named in the Schedule and any wholly

owned companies engaged in banking that are named in the Proposal Form and Schedule. It does not mean or include any

(a) non-wholly owned banking subsidiary company, or

(b) non-banking subsidiary company,

unless such subsidiary company is named in the Proposal Form and Schedule with its principal business activity and the first named Assured's shareholding interest so indicated.

2 'Assured's IT System' means those IT Systems operated by the Assured and which are either owned by or leased to the Assured or are declared in the Proposal Form.

3 'Automated Clearing House' means any corporation or association which operates an electronic clearing and transfer mechanism for the transfer of preauthorized recurring debits and credits between financial institutions on behalf of the financial institutions' customers.

4 'Central Depository' means any clearing corporation, including any Federal Reserve Bank of the United States, where as the direct result of an electronic clearing and transfer mechanism entries are made on the books reducing the account of the transferor, pledgor or pledgee and increasing the account of the transferee, pledgee or pledgor by the amount of the obligation or the number of shares or rights transferred, pledged or released, which clearing corporation is declared in the Proposal Form.

5 'Communications Terminal' means any teletype, teleprinter, video display terminal, or telefacsimile machine or similar device capable of sending and/or receiving information electronically, whether or not equipped with a keyboard or mouse.

6 'IT System' means an IT suitable for multi-use applications that is capable or directing hardware, software and data resources according to Electronic IT Programs formulated and introduced to the computer's operating system by the user. All input, output, processing, storage and communication facilities including related communication or open Systems networks which are physically connected to such a device, as well as the device's off-line media libraries, are deemed to be part of said IT system. It does not include those computers suitable solely for single use applications.

7 'IT Virus' means a set of unauthorized instructions, programmatic or otherwise, that propagate themselves through the Assured's IT System and/or networks which instructions were maliciously introduced by a person other than by an identifiable employee.

8 'Customer Communication System' means those communications systems as declared in the Proposal Form which provide customers of the Assured with direct access to the Assured's IT System.

9　'Electronic Communication System' means electronic communication operations by Fedwire, Clearing House Interbank Payment System (CHIPS), Society for Worldwide Interbank Financial Telecommunication (SWIFT), Clearing House Automated Payment System (CHAPS), the funds transfer system for the transfer of preauthorized recurring debits and credits of an Automated Clearing House Association which is a member of the National Automated Clearing House Association and similar automated communication systems as declared in the Proposal Form.

10　'Electronic IT Programs' means IT programs, i.e. facts or statements converted to a form usable in an IT System to act upon Electronic Data.

11　'Electronic Data' means facts or information converted to a form usable in a IT System and which is stored on Electronic Data Processing Media for use by IT programs.

12　'Electronic Data Processing Media' means tapes or discs or other bulk media, whether magnetic or optical, on which Electronic Data are recorded.

13　'Electronic Funds Transfer Systems' means those systems which operate automated teller machines or point of sale terminals and include any shared networks or facilities for said system in which the Assured participates.

14　'Electronic Security' means a share, participation or other interest in property of or an enterprise of the issuer or an obligation of the issuer which
  (a)　is a type commonly dealt in upon securities exchanges or markets; and
  (b)　is either one of a class or series or by its terms is divisible into a class or series of shares, participations, interests or obligations; and
  (c)　(i)　is not represented by an instrument, or
  　　(ii)　is part of a master or global certificate; or
  　　(iii)　represents a paper certificate that has been surrendered by a financial institution and which paper certificate has been combined into a master depository note and the paper certificates are immobilized and such security is shown as an electronic entry on the account of the transferor, pledgor or pledgee on the hooks of a Central Depository.

15　'Electronic Transmission' means the transmission of Electronic Data through data communication lines including by satellite links, radio frequency, infrared links or similar means used for the transmission of Electronic Data.

16　'Evidences of Debt' means instruments executed by a customer of the Assured and held by the Assured which in the regular course of business are treated as evidencing the customer's debt to the Assured including records of charges and accounts receivable.

17　'Forged Signature' means the hand-written signing of the name of another genuine person or a copy of said person's signature without authority and with intent to deceive; it does not include the signing in whole or in part of one's own name, with or without authority, in any capacity, for any purpose.

18 'Fraudulent Alteration' means the material alteration to a Telefacsimile for a fraudulent purpose by a person other than the person who signed and prepared the instrument.

19 'Service Bureau' means a natural person, partnership or corporation authorized by written agreement to perform data processing services using IT Systems.

20 'Service Bureau's IT System' means those IT Systems operated by a Service Bureau and which are either owned by or leased to a Service Bureau.

21 'Telefacsimile' means a system for transmitting written documents by means of electronic signals over telephone lines to equipment maintained by the Assured within a specially secured area for the purpose of reproducing a copy of said document.

22 'Telephone Banking System' means a telephone banking communications system as declared in the proposal form which provides customers of the Assured with direct access to the Assured's IT System via an automated touch tone telephone service and which requires the use of a Tested code in order to effect any banking transactions but does not mean a private branch exchange, voice mail processor, automated call attendant or an IT system with a similar capacity used for the direction or routing of telephone calls in a voice communications network.

23 'Tested' means a method of authenticating the contents of a communication by affixing thereto a valid test key which has been exchanged between the Assured and a customer, Automated Clearing House, Central Depository, another financial institution or between the offices of the Assured for the purpose of protecting the integrity of the communication in the ordinary course of business.

WHENEVER ANY OF THE ABOVE TERMS, 1 TO 23 INCLUSIVE, APPEAR IN THIS POLICY, THE WORDS 'AS DEFINED' SHALL BE DEEMED TO BE INCORPORATED IN THE TEXT IMMEDIATELY FOLLOWING EACH OF THE SAID TERMS.

III Exclusions

This Policy does not cover:

1 Loss resulting from any of the perils covered by the Assured's Financial Institution Bond.

2 Loss caused by an identifiable director or employee of the Assured or by a person or persons in collusion with said director or employee of the Assured.

Prior knowledge by any employee that a fraudulent act by a person or persons, not in the employ of the Assured, has been or will be perpetrated, shall for the intent and purpose of this Policy be deemed to be collusion should said employee wilfully or deliberately withhold this knowledge from the Assured. The withholding of knowledge from the Assured by an employee because of a threat to do bodily harm to any person or to do damage to the premises or property of the Assured shall not be deemed to be or to constitute collusion.

3 Loss of potential income, including but not limited to interest and dividends.

4 Indirect or consequential loss of any nature.

5 Liability assumed by the Assured by agreement under any contract unless such liability would have attached to the Assured even in the absence of such agreement.

6 All fees, costs and expenses incurred by the Assured
   (a) in establishing the existence of or amount of loss covered under this Policy; or
   (b) as a party to any legal proceeding except as provided by General Condition 6.

7 Any loss or damage which arises directly or indirectly by reason of or in connection with war, invasion, act of foreign enemy, hostilities or warlike operations (whether war has been declared or not), civil war, rebellion, revolution, insurrection, civil commotion assuming the proportion of or amounting to a popular uprising, military or usurped power, martial law, riot or the act of any lawfully constituted Authority.

IN ANY CLAIM, and in any action, suit or other proceeding to enforce a claim under this Policy for loss or damage, the BURDEN OF PROVING that such loss or damage does not fall within this General Exclusion shall be upon the Assured.

8 Any loss or destruction of or damage to any property whatsoever or any loss or expense whatsoever resulting or arising therefrom or any consequential loss or legal liability of whatsoever nature directly or indirectly caused by or contributed to by or arising from:
   (a) ionizing radiation or contamination by radioactivity from any nuclear fuel or from any nuclear waste from the combustion of nuclear fuel, or
   (b) the radioactive, toxic, explosive or other hazardous properties of any explosive nuclear assembly or nuclear component thereof.

9 Loss as a result of a threat
  (a) to do bodily harm to any person, except loss of Electronic Data Processing Media or Electronic Data in transit in the custody of any person acting as messenger provided that when such transit was initiated there was no knowledge by the Assured of any such threat, or
  (b) to do damage to the premises or property of the Assured.

10 Loss of Electronic Data Processing Media or Electronic Data while in the mail or with a carrier for hire other than an armoured motor vehicle company.

11 Loss of Electronic Data, Electronic Data Processing Media or Electronic IT Programs except as valued under General Condition 11.

12 Loss resulting directly or indirectly from
  (a) written instructions or advices, or
  (b) telegraphic or cable instructions or advices, or
  (c) instructions or advices by voice over telephone, unless such instructions are covered under Insuring Clause 8, or
  (d) Telefacsimile instructions or advices unless said Telefacsimile instructions or advices are covered under Insuring Clauses 5, 6 or 7.

13 Loss resulting directly or indirectly from forged, altered or fraudulent negotiable instruments, securities, documents or written instruments used as source documentation in the preparation of Electronic Data or manually keyed in a data terminal.

14 Loss of negotiable instruments, securities, documents or written instruments except as converted to Electronic Data and then only in that converted form.

15 Loss resulting directly or indirectly from the accessing of any confidential information including but not limited to trade secret information, IT programs or customer information.

16 Loss resulting from mechanical failure, faulty construction, error in design, latent defect, wear or tear, gradual deterioration, electrical disturbance, Electronic Data Processing Media failure or breakdown or any malfunction or error in programming or errors or omissions in processing.

17 Loss resulting directly or indirectly from the fraudulent preparation, fraudulent modification, alteration or destruction of Electronic IT Programs unless covered under Insuring Clauses 2, 3 or 4.

18 Loss by reason of the input of Electronic Data at an authorized electronic terminal of an Electronic Funds Transfer System or a Customer Communication system by a customer or other person who had authorized access to the customer's authentication mechanism.

19 Loss resulting from fraudulent features contained in Electronic IT Programs developed for sale to or that are sold to multiple customers at the time of their acquisition from a vendor or consultant.

20 Loss resulting directly or indirectly from any IT Virus unless covered under Insuring Clause 4.

21 Any loss

    (a) sustained prior to the Retroactive Date or any loss involving any act, transaction, or event which occurred or commenced prior to the Retroactive Date, or

    (b) discovered prior to the inception date of the Policy Period stated in the Schedule, or

    (c) discovered subsequent to the termination of the Policy, or

    (d) notified to a prior insurer.

22 Loss resulting directly or indirectly from a Telephone Banking System or from or arising out of the authorized or unauthorized use of a private branch exchange, voice mail processor, automated call attendant or an IT system with a similar capacity used for the direction or routing of telephone calls in a voice communications network or a cellular phone system, unless covered under Insuring Clause 1(c).

IV General conditions

1 Companion Policy

The Lloyd's Electronic and IT Crime Policy is designed to be a companion policy to the Assured's Financial Institution Bond and is intended to provide coverage for IT related crime as defined in the Insuring Clauses which is not covered under the Assured's Financial Institution Bond. Since certain Underwriters who are underwriting the Lloyd's Electronic and IT Crime Policy may also be underwriting the Assured's Financial Institution Bond by either primary insurance, excess insurance or other contributing insurance or reinsurance and since it is their intention not to increase or double up their coverage to the Assured it is agreed that this Policy will not be deemed to be excess or co-insuring coverage.

2 Nominees

Loss sustained by any nominee organized by the Assured for the purpose of handling certain of its business transactions and composed exclusively of its officers, clerks or other employees shall, for all the purposes of this Policy, be deemed to be loss sustained by the Assured.

3 Additional offices, consolidation, merger or purchase by the assured of another business

If the Assured shall, during the Policy Period, establish any new branch offices, or add to the Assured's IT system, other than by merger or consolidation with, or purchase or other acquisition of the assets of another business, such branch offices or addition to the Assured's IT system shall be automatically covered hereunder from the dates of their establishment, without the requirement of notice to the Underwriters or the payment of additional premium for the remainder of the Policy Period.

In the event that the Assured shall during the Policy Period merge or consolidate with, or purchase, or otherwise acquire, the assets of another business, this Policy shall not afford any coverage of any kind for loss which either:

(a) has occurred or may subsequently occur in any offices or premises; or

(b) has arisen or may arise out of the assets or liabilities or other exposures acquired by the Assured, as the result of such merger, consolidation, purchase or acquisition unless the Assured shall:

    (i) give written notice to the Underwriters, prior to the effective date, of such merger, consolidation, purchase or acquisition, and

    (ii) promptly provide the Underwriters with all such further information as the Underwriters may require, and

    (iii) obtain the written consent of the Underwriters to extend the coverage provided by this Policy in respect of such merger, consolidation, purchase or acquisition, and

    (iv) give written notice to the Underwriters of its agreement to the terms and conditions of coverage which are required by the Underwriters consequent upon such merger, consolidation, purchase or acquisition, and

    (v) pay to the Underwriters any additional premium.

Failure to give notice to the Underwriters in accordance with paragraph (i) above or failure of the Assured to notify the Underwriters of its agreement in accordance with paragraph (iv) above shall be an election by the Assured not to continue coverage.

Notification to the Underwriters, as herein required, shall not have been accomplished unless provided by the Assured in writing and acknowledged in writing by the Underwriters.

4 Change of control of the assured

(a) Liquidation, Etc.

In the event of the liquidation of the Assured, either voluntary or compulsory, or the appointment of a Receiver or Manager, or the entering into of any Scheme of Arrangement or composition with creditors, or the control of the Assured being taken over by any Government or by officials appointed by any Government or Governmental Authority or Agency, then this Policy shall immediately cease to afford any coverage of any kind for loss subsequently discovered and notified to the Underwriters.

In the event of the liquidation, etc., as aforesaid, of any subsidiary of the Assured named in the Proposal Form and the Schedule, then this Policy shall immediately cease to afford any coverage of any kind for loss subsequently discovered and notified to the Underwriters which arose in any manner from such subsidiary.

(b) Change of Assets or Share Ownership

The Assured shall immediately advise the Underwriters of any consolidation or merger with another business entity or any purchase, assignment, transfer, pledge or sale of assets or shares occasioning any change in ownership or control. As used in this General Condition, control means the power to determine the management or policy of a controlling holding company of the Assured by virtue of voting share ownership. A change in ownership of voting shares which results in direct or indirect ownership by a shareholder or an affiliated group of shareholders of ten per cent (10%) or more of such shares shall be presumed to result in a change of control for the purposes of the required notice.

As a condition to continuation of this Policy, the Assured shall:

(i)   give written notice to the Underwriters within thirty (30) days of the event, and

(ii)   promptly provide the Underwriters with all such further information as the Underwriters may require, and

(iii) obtain the written consent of the Underwriters to continue some or all of the coverage provided by this policy, and

(iv)   give written notice within ten (10) days to the Underwriters of its agreement to the terms and conditions which are required by the Underwriters consequent upon such change, and

(v)   pay to the Underwriters any additional premium.

Failure to give notice to the Underwriters in accordance with paragraph (b)(i) above or failure of the Assured to notify the Underwriters of its agreement in accordance with paragraph (b)(iv) above shall be an election by the Assured not to continue coverage.

Notification to the Underwriters, as herein required, shall not have been accomplished unless provided by the Assured in writing and acknowledged in writing by the Underwriters.

5 Joint assured

(a) If two or more Assureds are covered under this Policy, the first named Assured shall act for all Assureds. Payment by Underwriters to the first named Assured of loss sustained by any Assured shall fully release Underwriters on account of such loss. If the first named Assured ceases to be covered under this Policy, the Assured next named shall thereafter be considered as the first named Assured.

(b) Knowledge possessed or discovery made by any Assured shall constitute knowledge or discovery by all Assureds for all purposes of this Policy.

(c) The liability of Underwriters for a loss or losses sustained by all Assureds shall not exceed the amount for which Underwriters would have been liable had all such loss or losses been sustained by one Assured.

(d) Underwriters shall not be liable for loss sustained by one Assured to the advantage of any other Assured.

(e) It is agreed that the Insurance granted herein shall be for the exclusive benefit only of the first named Assured herein, and that in no event shall anyone other than said Assured have any right of action under this Policy.

6 Legal fees and legal expenses

The Underwriters shall indemnify the Assured against reasonable legal fees and legal expenses incurred and paid by the Assured with the prior approval of the Underwriters in the defence of any suit or legal proceeding brought against the Assured, with respect to which the Assured establishes that the act or acts which have been committed, or the events which have occurred, would entitle the Assured to recover under this Policy. Legal fees and legal expenses paid by the Underwriters in defending any suit or legal processing shall be applied subject to General Condition No. 8 to the reduction of the Aggregate Limit of Indemnity and the Sub-Limit for the applicable Insuring Clause.

The Assured shall promptly give notice to the Underwriters of the institution of any suit or legal proceeding referred to above and at the request of the Underwriters shall furnish them with copies of all pleadings and other papers therein.

If multiple causes of action are alleged in any such suit or legal proceeding some of which causes of action, if established against the Assured, would not constitute a collectible loss under this Policy, including without limitation claims for punitive, consequential or other non-compensatory damages, then the Assured shall bear for its own expense the legal fees and legal expenses insured in the defence of such alleged causes of action.

If the amount of the Assured's loss is greater than the amount recoverable under this Policy, or if a Deductible is applicable, or both, the liability of the Underwriters under the first paragraph of this General Condition is limited to the proportion of the legal fees and legal expenses incurred under his Policy bears to the total of such amount plus the amount which is not so recoverable. Such pro-rated amount shall be applied in reduction of the Aggregate Limit of Indemnity and the Sub-Limit for the applicable Insuring Clause.

The Underwriters shall not be liable to indemnify the Assured for legal fees and legal expenses until after final judgement or settlement of any suit or legal proceeding.

The Underwriters are not obligated to conduct the defence of such suit or legal proceeding referred to in the first paragraph of this General Condition. At the Underwriters' election the Assured shall permit the Underwriters to conduct the defence of such suitor legal proceeding, in the Assured's name, through legal representatives of the Underwriters' selection. The Assured shall give all reasonable information and assistance that the Underwriters shall deem necessary to the defence of such suit or legal proceeding.

Legal fees and legal expenses paid by the Underwriters in defending any suit or legal proceeding shall be applied to the reduction of the Aggregate Limit of Indemnity and the Sub-Limit for the applicable Insuring Clause.

If having elected to defend, the Underwriters pay legal fees and legal expenses in excess of their proportionate share of such fees and expenses the Assured shall promptly reimburse the Underwriters for such excess.

The Assured shall not unreasonably withhold consent to a settlement by the Underwriters of any suit or legal proceeding.

7 Notification and discovery of loss

As a condition precedent to its right to be indemnified under this Policy, the Assured shall, as soon as possible and in any event within thirty (30) days after discovery by the Assured of any loss hereunder, give written notice thereof to the Underwriters.

For the purposes of this Policy, discoveries are deemed to occur at the time when the Assured first becomes aware of facts which would cause a reasonable person to believe that a loss of the kind covered by this Policy has been or will be incurred, regardless of when the acts, transactions or events causing or contributing to such loss occurred, and regardless of whether the Assured's knowledge is sufficient at such time to prove that such loss meets the terms and conditions of this Policy, and even though the amount of details of loss may not then be known.

Discovery is also deemed to occur when the Assured receives notice of an actual or potential claim in which it is alleged that the Assured is liable to a third party under circumstances which, if true, might constitute a loss of a type covered by this Policy, even though the amount of details of loss may not then be known.

All loss or losses discovered by the Assured which are attributable to the acts of omissions of one person, whether or not an Employee, or in which such person is concerned or implicated, shall be deemed to be one loss.

8 Limit of indemnity

(a) The total liability of the Underwriters for all loss or losses discovered during the Policy Period set forth in Item 3 of the Schedule of this Policy and including legal fees and legal expenses is limited to the Aggregate Limit of Indemnity stated in Item 7 of the Schedule of this Policy irrespective of the total amount of such loss or losses. The Sub-Limit of any applicable Insuring Clause is part of and not in addition to the Aggregate Limit of Indemnity and the total liability of the Underwriters for all losses, including legal fees and legal expenses, concerning any such Insuring Clause with a Sub-Limit is limited to the amount of the Sub-Limit, irrespective of the total amount of such loss or losses.

The Aggregate Limit of Indemnity shall be reduced by the amount of any payment made under this Policy. Upon exhaustion of the Aggregate Limit of Indemnity by such payments the Underwriters shall have no further liability:

   (i)   to indemnity the Assured under any Insuring Clause(s) of this Policy for any loss or losses, and

   (ii)   to indemnify the Assured for any legal fees and legal expenses, and

   (iii)   to continue the defence of the Assured in the event that the Underwriters elected to conduct the defence of any suit or legal proceedings. Upon notice by the Underwriters to the Assured that the Aggregate Limit of Indemnity has been exhausted, the Assured shall assume all responsibility for its defence at its own cost.

(b) In addition to the Aggregate Limit of Indemnity being reduced, the Sub-Limit of any applicable Insuring Clause(s) stated in Item 7 of the Schedule shall be reduced by the amount of any payment made in connection with said Insuring Clause(s). Upon exhaustion of the Sub-Limit applicable to said Insuring Clause(s) by such payments the Underwriters shall have no further liability:

   (i)   to indemnify the Assured under said Insuring Clause(s) of this Policy for any loss or losses, and

   (ii)   to indemnify the Assured for any legal fees and legal expenses incurred in connection with said loss or losses or in connection with said Insuring Clause(s),

   (iii)   to continue the defence of the Assured in the event of the Underwriters' election to conduct the defence of any suit or legal proceeding in connection with said loss or losses. Upon such notice by the Underwriters to the Assured that the Sub-Limit has been exhausted, the Assured shall assume all responsibility for its defence at its own cost.

If by reason of payments made under this Policy the Aggregate Limit of Indemnity is reduced to an amount less than the amount stated for any Sub-Limit in Item 7 of the Schedule of this Policy, then the amount of any such Sub-Limit shall be reduced accordingly so that the total amount available under any Sub-Limit for any loss or losses, including legal fees and legal expenses, does not exceed the reduced amount remaining available under the Aggregate Limit of Indemnity.

The Aggregate Limit of Indemnity and any Sub-Limit shall not be reinstated in whole or in part by any recovery effected subsequent to any payment made under this Policy, unless such recovery is actually received by Underwriters during the period stated in Item 3 of the Schedule or within twelve (12) calendar months thereafter.

If a loss is covered under more than one Insuring Clause the maximum amount payable with respect to such loss shall not exceed the largest amount remaining available under any one applicable Insuring Clause.

(c) Lost Securities: In the event that a loss of a security is settled through the use of a lost securities bond or indemnity agreement pursuant to General Condition 11(d), such loss, to the extent that during the Policy Period the Underwriters are not called upon to pay under said lost securities bond or indemnity agreement, shall not reduce the Aggregate Limit of Indemnity or any Sub-Limit remaining for the payment of any loss or losses. However, any payment by the Underwriters of such loss or under such lost securities bond or indemnity agreement shall be deemed to be a payment under this Policy.

The exhaustion or reduction of the Aggregate Limit of Indemnity or any Sub-Limit shall not affect the Underwriters' obligations in connection with any lost securities bond or indemnity agreement issued prior to the exhaustion or reduction of the Aggregate Limit of Indemnity or any applicable Sub-Limit.

9 Proof of loss

Within six months of discovery of loss, the Assured shall furnish affirmative proof of loss to the Underwriters, in writing, duly sworn to by the chief financial officer of the Assured together with full particulars. The onus of proof is upon the Assured in preparing its proof of loss with respect to a loss for which claim is made under any Insuring Clause to establish that such loss directly resulted from the insured peril and not from economic conditions or other contributing causes.

10 Legal proceedings for recovery of loss

If the Underwriters, after completing their investigation, do not pay a loss for which the Assured believes the terms, conditions and other provisions of this Policy entitle it to recover hereunder, the Underwriters at the request of the Assured, shall submit to the jurisdiction of any court of competent jurisdiction of the United Kingdom.

Service of process in any such legal proceedings shall be made upon the person(s) named in the Schedule who are duly authorized to accept Service of Process on behalf of the Underwriters. In such legal proceedings instituted against any one of the Underwriters, the other Underwriters hereon shall abide by the final judgement of such Court or of any Appellate Court in the event of appeal.

Legal proceedings for recovery of loss hereunder shall not be brought until after three months from the Assured furnishing proof of loss, as stated in General Condition No. 9, nor after the expiration of two years from the discovery of such loss.

If the said two year limitation period is prohibited by any law controlling the construction of this Policy, such limitation shall be deemed to be amended so as to equal the minimum period of limitation permitted by such law.

11 Basis of valuation

(a) Computation

In determining the amount collectible under this Policy for any loss, all money received from any source whatsoever in connection with any matter from which a claimed loss has arisen, including payments and receipts of principal, interest, dividends, commissions and the like, whenever received, shall be deducted from the amount actually paid out, advanced, taken or otherwise lost. The value of all property received from any source whatsoever in connection with any matter from which a claimed loss has arisen, whenever received, shall likewise be deducted from the Assured's claimed loss.

(b) Funds

The value of any foreign funds or currencies for the loss of which a claim shall be made, shall be determined by their closing market value on the last business day prior to the date of discovery of the loss. If there is no market price or value for the same on such day, then the value shall be as agreed between the Assured and then Underwriters or in default thereof by arbitration.

(c) Deductible

If this Policy is subject to a Deductible, or the aggregate Policy Limit in Item 7 of the Schedule remaining for the payment of any loss or losses is not sufficient in amount to indemnify the Assured in full for the loss of securities for which claim is made hereunder, the liability of the Underwriters under this Policy is limited to the payment for, or the duplication of, so much of such securities as has a value equal to the amount collectible under the applicable Insuring Clause of this Policy.

(d) Lost Securities

In the event of a claim in respect of a loss covered under this Policy of securities, the Assured shall, subject to the conditions stated below, first attempt to replace the lost securities by use of a letter of indemnity issued by it. In the event that it is unable to replace the lost securities by a letter of indemnity, the Assured shall, subject to the Underwriters' prior consent, secure a lost securities bond for the purpose of obtaining the issuance of duplicate securities.

(e) Electronic Data Processing Media

In case of loss of, or damage to, Electronic Data Processing Media used by the Assured in its business, Underwriters shall be liable under this Policy only if such items are actually reproduced by other Electronic Data Processing Media of the same kind or quality and then for not more than the cost of the blank media plus the cost of labour for the actual transcription or copying of data which shall have been furnished by the Assured in order to reproduce such Electronic Data Processing Media, subject, of course, to the applicable Limit of Indemnity.

(f) Other Property

In case of loss to, or damage to, any property other than foreign funds, securities or Electronic Data Processing Media, Underwriters shall not be liable for more than the actual cash value of such property. Underwriters may, at their election, pay the actual cash value of replace or repair such property. Disagreement between Underwriters and the Assured as to the cash value or as to the adequacy of repair or replacement shall be resolved by arbitration.

(g) Electronic Data/Electronic IT Programs

In case of loss of Electronic Data or Electronic IT Programs, Underwriters shall be liable under this Policy only if such Electronic Data or Electronic IT Programs are actually reproduced by other Electronic Data or Electronic IT Programs of the same kind or quality and then for not more than the cost of labour for the actual transcription or copying of data or programs which shall have been furnished by the Assured in order to reproduce such Electronic Data or Electronic IT Programs subject, of course, to the applicable Limit of Indemnity.

However, if such Electronic Data cannot be reproduced and said Electronic

Data represents securities, or financial instruments having a value, including Evidences of Debt, then the loss will be valued as indicated in the Securities and Other Property paragraphs of this section.

12 Co-operation

As a condition precedent to its right to be indemnified under this Policy, the Assured shall co-operate fully with the Underwriters and their appointed representatives in all matters pertaining to any loss notified hereunder. The Assured shall, upon request and at times and places designated by the Underwriters, provide for examination all pertinent records including audit records of its accounts and provide for interview any of its Employees or other persons, to the best of its ability and power. The Assured agrees to execute all papers and render all assistance to secure all rights, title, interest and causes of action as it may have against any person or entity in connection with any loss notified hereunder, and to do nothing to prejudice such rights or causes of action.

13 Subrogation, salvage and recovery

It is agreed that the Underwriters upon payment of any loss hereunder shall become subrogated to all rights, title, interest and causes of action of the Assured in respect of such loss.

In the case of recovery after payment of any loss hereunder, the amount recovered, after deducting the actual cost of obtaining or making such recovery but excluding the Assured's own labour or establishment costs, shall be applied in the following order:

(a) to reimburse the Assured in full for the part, if any, of such loss which exceeds the amount of loss paid under this Policy (disregarding the amount of any Deductible applicable).

(b) the balance, if any, or the entire net recovery if no part of such loss exceeds the amount of loss paid under this Policy, to the reimbursement of the Underwriters.

(c) finally, to that part of such loss sustained by the Assured by reason of the Deductible specified in the Schedule and/or to that part of such loss covered by any policy(ies) of Insurance of which this Policy is excess.

14 Other insurance or indemnity

It is agreed that in the event of loss, this Policy, insofar as it covers loss also covered by other insurance or indemnity, shall only pay claims (not exceeding the Aggregate Limit of Indemnity or any applicable Sub-Limit) for the excess of the amount of such other insurance or indemnity. As excess insurance this Policy shall not apply or contribute to the payment of any loss until the amount of such other insurance or indemnity shall have been exhausted.

15 Ownership

This Policy shall apply to loss of property and loss of Electronic Data Processing Media and Electronic Data owned by the Assured, held by the Assured in any capacity or for which the Assured is legally liable. This Policy shall be for the sole use and benefit of the Assured named in the Schedule.

16 Deductible amount/notice of loss within Deductible

The Underwriters shall be liable only in excess of the Deductible stated in Item 8 of the Schedule. The Deductible shall apply to each and every loss, irrespective of the number of such losses during the Policy Period.

The Assured shall, in the time and in the manner prescribed in this Policy, give Underwriters notice of any loss of the kind covered by the terms of this Policy, whether or not Underwriters are liable therefore, and upon the request of Underwriters shall file with it a brief statement giving particulars concerning such loss.

17 Termination provisions

This Policy shall terminate with or without the tender of unearned premium
(a) immediately upon
    (i) the happening of any of the events relating to a change in control of the Assured as set forth in General Condition No. 4(a),
    (ii) the failure by the Assured to notify a change of assets or share ownership or otherwise comply with the terms as set forth in General Condition No. 4(b).
    (iii) refusal by the Underwriters to continue coverage following a change in ownership or control as set forth in General Condition No. 4(b).
(b) immediately as to any subsidiary of the Assured upon the happening of any event with regard to such subsidiary relating to a change in control or ownership of such subsidiary as set forth in General Condition No. 4.
(c) thirty (30) days after receipt by the Assured of written notice from the Underwriters of their decision to terminate this Policy. If sent by prepaid registered post and addressed to the Principal Address of the Assured, as stated in the Proposal Form, such notice shall be deemed to have been received when sent.

(d) immediately upon receipt by the Underwriters of a written notice from the Assured of its decision to terminate this Policy.

(e) at noon local standard time at the Principal Address on the expiration date stated in Item 3 of the Schedule.

The Underwriters shall refund any unearned premium computed at short-rate of the Annual Premium if terminated pursuant to paragraph (a) or (d) of this General Condition but pro-rata of the Annual Premium if terminated by the Underwriters as provided in paragraph (c) of this General Condition.

This Policy shall terminate immediately upon exhaustion of the Aggregate Limit of Indemnity by one or more payments of loss hereunder, in which event the premium is fully earned.

This Policy shall be terminated as to any Service Bureau

(a) as soon as any Assured, or any director or officer not in collusion with such person, shall learn of any dishonest or fraudulent act committed by any partner, director, officer or employee of any such Service Bureau at any time against the Assured or any other person or entity, without prejudice to the loss of any property then in transit in the custody of such person, or

(b) fifteen (15) days after the receipt by the Assured of a written notice from Underwriters of their desire to terminate or cancel this Policy as to such person.

Termination of this Policy as to any Assured terminates liability for any loss sustained by such Assured which is discovered after the effective date of such termination.

18 Action against Service Bureau or Customer

This Policy does not afford coverage in favour of any Service Bureau or customer as aforesaid, and upon payment to the Assured by the Underwriters on account of any loss through fraudulent or dishonest acts committed by any of the partners, directors, officers or employees of such Service Bureau or customer whether acting alone or in collusion with others, an assignment of such of the Assured's rights and causes of action as they may have against such Service Bureau or customer by reason of such acts so committed shall, to the extent of such payment, be given by the Assured to the Underwriters, or to one of the Underwriters designated by Underwriters, and the Assured shall execute all papers necessary to secure to the Underwriters, or to one of the Underwriters designated by Underwriters, the rights herein provided for.

19 Fraud

If the Assured shall make any claim knowing the same to be false or fraudulent, as regards amount or otherwise, this Policy shall become void and all claims thereunder shall be forfeited.

20 Interpretation

The construction, interpretation and meaning of the terms, exclusions, limitations and conditions of this Policy shall be determined in accordance with the common law of England and in accordance with the English text as it appears in this Policy.

Source: Lloyd's

SafeStone Technologies: combining advanced technology with entrepreneurial vision

John Todd, chief executive and founder of SafeStone Technologies, is unequivocal about the enormous importance of security and trust in the bid by any organization for maximized revenue and profitability from e-business initiatives.

> E-business cannot grow without security, and if you can't trust who you are dealing with over the internet you are not going to make progress at all. I see security and trust for e-business as among the most fascinating areas of commercial activity right now.

As readers of this book will have already noticed, the world of security and trust for e-business is filled with personalities who are larger-than-life. To the layperson, expecting that people professionally involved with internet security and trust would be rather passive, introverted types who prefer to focus on encryption algorithms rather than the real world of business, this might be surprising. But in fact it is precisely because these issues are so fundamental to any e-business initiative that the security and trust industry attracts people with hot entrepreneurial blood in their veins.

SafeStone's John Todd is emphatically one of them. Formerly a founder of the information technology training organization CBT Systems, he ended his ten years with CBT at the age of thirty-seven with a handsome financial reward for building up that organization.

> For a year I took things easy and nurtured various minority stake investments I had initiated, but I found that being a minority investor gave me too little clout with the organizations with which I was involved. I wanted to lead from the front not from the back. Semi-retirement did not suit me at all.

Once an entrepreneur, always an entrepreneur. Todd looked around for a new opportunity which would harmonize with his fundamental career plan of building and energizing sales forces that target chief information officers (CIOs).

> I have always been involved in this particular area: developing new initiatives for CIOs

of the world's top 2,000 organizations. This is the world where I flourish. The question was, what opportunity would fascinate me and make my target market cry out for what I could offer?

He found the answer in the provision of security for the heterogeneous IBM enterprise market – not, on the face of it, an opportunity that seems immediately glamorous, but Todd emphasizes how important this particular niche really is.

The heterogeneous IBM environment, which includes operating platforms such as Windows NT, Novel, UNIX and AS/400, is at the hub of most major organizations' information technology resources. Making these resources secure is not only a major and extremely important technological challenge, it is also an enormously important commercial opportunity. I bought an organization named CCT and changed its name to SafeStone Technologies. SafeStone is basically focused on building the security management infrastructure which allows every aspect of an organization's overall operations and e-business initiatives to function properly. The security solutions we offer may be described in the industry as 'back office', but they are only back office in terms of their location in a schematic diagram of the organization's operations. When it comes to functionality, everything depends on them.

There are several types of security application where powerful security at the hub of the organization's operations is, Todd argues, of enormous importance.

Recent estimates in connection with the workplace efficiency of middle and senior executives have thrown up the alarming fact that about two and a half per cent of all office employees' productivity during the average week is likely to be devoted to inputting secure passwords to sign on to different computer systems used by his or her organization. It is perfectly possible for office staff to be obliged to know up to one hundred passwords in order to gain access to carefully controlled areas of their organization's operations. Certainly, this kind of precise and rigorous access control is an essential part of good housekeeping and good security management; one can't simply discard it or dismantle it without risking a very serious compromise to the organization's activities. On the other hand, how can an organization possibly maximize profitability if such a significant amount of time is being consumed by office staff merely in order to *get access to the opportunity to work*? Unquestionably, what is needed is a powerful back-office security resource which facilitates rigorous access control while allowing office staff to use only a small number of passwords at a time, or even only one.

Todd also points out that about fifty per cent of technical calls made to IT systems vendors are in connection with password problems – further evidence that inefficient or cumbersome access control based around an executive using dozens of different passwords is extremely costly in terms of time and energy.

Todd emphasizes that a powerful central resource is essential for any organization wishing to make the most of digital certificates and to handle internet trust with maximized flexibility.

SafeStone's view of the internet security and trust marketplace is that you cannot possibly have real security, or effective trust, unless you have a powerful infrastructure in place that is able to handle all the sophisticated security and trust resources needed today to provide organizations with the three-way protection they need: confidentiality, integrity and authenticity. Todd explains:

> At present, digital certificates, and the role they play in PKI [public key infrastructure], are correctly regarded as a major step forward for internet trust. The problem, though, is that different organizations are using different digital certificates, with little standardization between these certificates. Some certificates are deliberately designed to be effective only for a few minutes or seconds; others may have a life expectancy of months or years. Again, a powerful central computer resource is absolutely essential for managing the complex range of digital certificates used by the organization itself and by its counterparties. At SafeStone we are aiming to create a back office security resource that amounts to a Universal Registration Authority [URA] that will handle all the digital verification for the entire enterprise. The fact that these systems do not yet exist in my view explains why PKI has been so slow to take off. There is a fundamental and serious digital certificate management problem. Solving it is one of our major commercial objectives during the next few years.

SafeStone's philosophy is that what maximizes an organization's competitive edge is effective management of computing power. The company believes that a secure and reliable IT environment is the supreme goal of every IT director, and that an organization's investment in, and reliance upon, e-business systems emphasizes the need to protect the IT infrastructure from potential disaster and expensive downtime, which is not only costly to the bottom line, but which also alienates customers and counterparties, possibly forever.

Today, SafeStone's vision for the future of e-business trust and security is still being implemented as the organization moves from its primary current activities as a supplier of AS/400 security systems. Todd regards these supply activities as undergirding his vision of the security needs of all types of large organizations – and the security needs of e-businesses in particular – in the first decades of the twenty-first century. They certainly constitute a secure foundation: SafeStone's suite of AS/400 security applications has to date sold more than 20,000 licences in over forty countries. The goal of the AS/400 solutions is to provide a suite of professional systems management software which eliminates the complexity of security for AS/400, eases the pressure on resources, and brings simple manageability to the environment.

In order to achieve his vision of how powerful back-office computer strength in the IBM environment can transform an organization's security and trust capabilities, and therefore the organization's e-business resources, Todd has managed an important partnership agreement with Axent Technologies Limited, a global leader in information security which provides e-security solutions that maximize its customers' business advantage. Axent delivers integrated products and expert services to assess, protect, enable and manage business processes and information assets. The partnership agreement was signed in 1997, and in December 2000 was strengthened to facilitate the cross-selling of products for the multi-platform environment by both organizations. The idea of the multi-platform security solution was to unite two of Axent's solutions – Enterprise Security Manager (ESM) and Intruder Alert – with SafeStone's DetectIT modules to provide an enterprise wide security management system.

'The branding of the solutions is not as important as the overall objective', says Todd. 'This overall objective of producing a powerful, integrated security platform on which organizations can base flexible, security-enabled e-business activities and then go out to conquer the world is what our partnership with Axent is all about'.

How SafeStone Technologies DetectIT Provides Credit Lyonnais with central control of its AS/400 security resources.

This case study illustrates how a major bank – Credit Lyonnais – makes use of the DetectIT solution to provide itself with a comprehensive AS/400 security resource. Credit Lyonnais has been in existence since 1863 and today has a presence in more than sixty countries, employing 40,000 people. It supplies an extensive line of banking products and services to individuals, self-employed professionals, small- to mid-size businesses and major corporations around the world.

Credit Lyonnais has an information security department in New York that is responsible for the bank's IT security throughout the Americas. As well as its US responsibility, this department also has regional responsibility for Canada, South and Central America.

As one might imagine, this department is mission-critical. It is also multi-platform, with at least eight different operating systems, including three flavours of UNIX, VMS, NT4.0, Windows 2000 and AS/400. It is, in other words, a typical example of a heterogeneous IBM environment, where a number of different platforms need to be integrated from the security perspective and work together.

Sean Mahon, vice president of information security, takes up the story:

We needed the ability to monitor security on all platforms, including AS/400. We use Axent's ESM to cover UNIX, VMS, NT and Windows 2000, but we wanted to extend this coverage to the AS/400.

ESM facilitates the monitoring and measuring of security throughout the enterprise – except for the AS/400. Sean Mahon's requirement was to control AS/400 security centrally, which would lead to valuable productivity savings for his department. 'We did not have a good method for monitoring security on the AS/400 without someone actually having to log on to the machines – this was obviously using up a lot of time.'

They turned to Axent for advice. 'Axent suggested two products, one of which was DetectIT, by SafeStone Technologies', Mahon explains. 'After careful investigation, we came to the conclusion that DetectIT was the right choice. SafeStone had the better-established relationship with Axent, and was more committed to the AS/400 platform than the other company. I had a better feeling about them'.

One of the reasons Credit Lyonnais went for DetectIT is that, as Mahon emphasizes, it has a seamless interface into ESM, allowing powerful interrogation of the AS/400, managed from a single enterprise consul.

Mahon summarizes the situation:

I have been very impressed with the stability of the product, both during the pilot test and since then. It has been up and running for some time now, and is rock solid. I also like the fact that DetectIT does not interfere with any other applications on the AS/400. This is obviously extremely important for us because any compromise to our service would be bad news indeed. In all our time of using DetectIT, there has never been any conflict between it and any other of the AS/400 applications – it is a very well-behaved product. I'm also impressed by the support we have received from SafeStone.

Now that the solution has been implemented, Sean Mahon's team can monitor AS/400 security around the clock without taking the time to log on to individual machines. Importantly, security has not been compromised. Mahon reports that with DetectIT, Credit Lyonnais can monitor the AS/400 platform much more efficiently, and can also increase monitoring capability on that platform. DetectIT allows companies such as Credit Lyonnais to manage AS/400 security easily and comprehensibly.

Also making use of the DetectIT solution ist Kleinwort Benson, a private off-shore bank based in the Channel Islands, one of the world's foremost private financial centres, ultimately owned by the Dresdner Bank Group, which is among Europe's leading banking institutions, employing over 49,000 people in the major financial centres of over seventy countries. Private banking – looking after the banking needs of people with high net worth – is a key business area for Dresdner. Through Kleinwort Benson (Channel Islands) Limited, it is able to offer a wide range of off-shore products and services that provide global solutions for private wealth. The bank has been in operation since 1963, and since that time has become renowned for its track record in the private banking area.

Kleinwort Benson's head of information security is André Gorvel, who is responsible for maximizing security levels within the bank's operations in the Channel Islands. He explains that the IT systems must be protected from both inside and outside the organization.

Security and confidentiality are absolutely essential to our business. Our customers need to know that their data and assets are protected by a truly effective security solution.

Kleinwort Benson chose the DetectIT solution from Safestone because it was the only product which fulfilled all its criteria.

All of the competitive products we considered lacked key elements for our stringent security policy. However, DetectIT passed our evaluation with flying colours.

Gorvel and his team are now thoroughly confident about their AS/400 security. DetectIT allows the bank to monitor its AS/400 platforms much more efficiently than it was able to in the past.

SafeStone Technologies can be contacted at:

SafeStone Technologies Inc.
600 Alexander Park
Suite 303
Princeton
NJ 08540
USA
Tel: 001 609 750 8502
E: enquiries@safestone.com

SafeStone Technologies Plc
UK Head Office
SafeStone House
Church Street
Old Amersham
Bucks HP7 0DB
UK
Tel: +44 1494 723372
Fax: +44 1494 723377
E: enquiries@safestone.com

SSE Ltd – Promoting Secure E-business Communications

Internet security, like many concepts rising to prominence in modern, high-tech society, remains shrouded in secrecy until implemented by market leaders for market leaders. In order for such concepts to catch on in the marketplace, they must simultaneously deliver cost reductions, improve business processes and increase corporate revenues.

SSE Ltd, a subsidiary company of Infineon, is headquartered in Dublin, a city which has established itself as a leading location for high-tech organizations in general and internet security providers in particular. Today SSE is a major vendor of state-of-the-art internet security software solutions. The organization offers a powerful suite of products and services for secure online business communications and e-commerce.

What SSE sells, like many successful providers of e-business security, is confidence. SSE promotes the ability to communicate securely: the confidence that the customer – and the customers own customer – can buy and sell on the internet or simply transfer sensitive information without falling victim to the fraudulent, the unscrupulous or the plain untrustworthy.

Paul Dhesi, CEO of SSE, comments:

> SSE is acknowledged globally as a leader in secure military messaging, and as one might expect from such an organization, our expertize in developing and furnishing our customers with secure solutions is extremely extensive. SSE can provide corporations of all sizes with the infrastructure they need to achieve a trustworthy network within which to communicate. Today this is based upon PKI applications.

On the subject of e-business he says:

> The possible applications of e-business are endless. However, unless people can communicate safely and securely, these opportunities will never be leveraged. The difference between insecure and secure communications is enormous. To use an analogy: an open message on the internet is similar to a postcard, with the message easily readable by everyone en route. Secure mail can be compared to a letter in a

sealed envelope. The implications of this for trust on the internet are obvious. People who want to use electronic commerce have a perfectly justifiable need to feel not only that their transaction will take place securely but also that they can take this for granted and not even have to think about it. Fortunately, PKI provides a remarkably useful infrastructure for doing precisely this. A good way to understand PKI is to separate the 'PK' from the 'I': to separate the Public Key *technology* from the *trust* Infrastructure builds for business. Many of the important issues underlying PKI can also be resolved into technical and business aspects.

Technically, one of the most important issues is to be able to demonstrate interoperability. SSE is playing its full part in major initiatives, such as those run by the PKI Forum and the UK government's 2001 CESG interoperability trials.

Business issues span the spectrum from the need to invest and support a new infrastructure, to the cultural acceptance of PKI amongst users. For instance, only when PKI is used like credit cards will we know that it is culturally accepted.

Dhesi adds:

What organizations need from a vendor of security solutions is a new suite of products which can be integrated into a comprehensive trust infrastructure that ensures that every area of the organization is secure for e-business. The organization/customer link must also be backed by a completely reliable trust system which guarantees that each party can ensure that they are dealing with whom they think they are. Business conducted across the internet is always going to be virtual business by definition. In order for the parties involved to feel secure about what they are doing they need to enjoy the same level of security and trust that we enjoy in face-to-face encounters in comfortable surroundings. SSE provides the means to make that level of trust happen. We support our network of products with a comprehensive consultancy service that covers every aspect of making an e-business fully secured and giving it a trust capacity. For example, we can write a security policy for an organization from scratch and then provide the tools which let the organization implement that policy. And furthermore, because we are a virtual company operating globally we have a comprehensive understanding of what makes an e-business tick and how fundamental security and trust requirements are if an organization's success is to be maximized.

SSE has an extensive customer base, spanning multiple geographical and vertical markets, including some of the largest projects in the world. The Siemens TrustCentre, for example, was set up by SSE and enabled by SSE technology. In order fully to understand and appreciate the tasks and processes involved in implementing a security framework for trustworthy communications, an examination of real-life business scenarios is required. Many of these real-life scenarios are enabling new business models and enhancing business competitiveness.

Case Study 1: Telia Telecom – web security

Today's telecommunications companies face ever-increasing competition. This is due, first, to the remarkable developments in technology, which have created a dynamic and fast-moving market where technical excellence is a must, and, second, to the global deregulation of the telecommunications industry itself.

Telecom's service providers must offer leading-edge services in order to retain current customers and attract new ones. Increasingly these companies are implementing web-based services to enable rapid information dissemination, while simultaneously simplifying business processes in both B2B and B2C scenarios.

Headquartered in Stockholm, Sweden, one of the world's most innovative and progressive telecoms markets, Telia Telecom is a leader in the field. Consequently, Swedish customers expect high-quality products and services from the organization. Telia, in turn, is committed to the delivery of customer-focused network products and services to a rapidly growing domestic and international client base. The organization's executives recognize that it is its ability to remain at the forefront of innovation in secure online communications, and, particularly, secure web-based applications, which is fundamental to its continued growth and success.

In the past, Telia operated a conventional help-desk for its corporate data communications customers. With this method, the organization could book and report fault calls, check network status and order new network services. This help-service was adequate in meeting immediate requirements, but Telia recognized the value of service improvements by the implementation of innovative leading-edge technology.

Thus, Telia developed a vision of opening up its internal networks to allow its corporate data communications customers instant access to individual account information. To achieve this, it needed to ensure that exchange of information took place in a secure environment. It also needed to be certain that confidential customer information would not end up in the wrong hands. Like all major innovators utilizing new internet technologies, Telia has put security at the top of the list of its system development priorities.

Telia found the solution in TrustedWeb, SSE's intra/extranet security product. TrustedWeb has given Telia exactly the security framework it needs to create its innovative service. Working together SSE and Telia provide the customer with a first-class service which is both user-friendly and cost-efficient. With this in mind, Telia is migrating from TrustedWeb to SSE's new authorization and access control solution TrustedAuthorizer, a client-less solution based on new innovative attribute certificate standards, in order to reap the benefits of advanced networked applications.

Headquartered in Munich, Germany, Siemens has become number twenty-four in corporation size globally, employing more than 400,000 people worldwide. The company's success is attributable to its continuous innovation and wide service offering.

An integral part of Siemens' business objectives is to achieve consistent business processes by improving the workings between inter-groups and inter-regions as well as integration of its customers, suppliers and partners in business operations globally. Given the enormity of Siemens and the distribution of its offices on a global scale, it faces many challenges when it comes to secure business communications both internally and externally between employees, customers and business partners alike.

The internet is inherently an insecure network, and so this objective can be easily undermined. E-mail messages can be intercepted, viewed and even modified without the knowledge of the sender or the recipient. Therefore, what Siemens required was a product which guaranteed to protect corporate information against loss of confidentiality, while simultaneously protecting against falsification of information through authentication of the sender, especially when communicating with customers and suppliers.

SSE's TrustedMIME, an advanced, state-of-the-art product for securing e-mail, fully met Siemens' requirements by providing an extremely cost-effective means of establishing a highly secure channel for internal and external business communications. TrustedMIME is a simple-to-install plug-in, to Microsoft and Lotus e-mail products and provides strong (128-bit) encryption and strong authentication with smart card support.

This advanced technology allows Siemens to encrypt and digitally sign messages, thus ensuring the authentication of the sender whilst also protecting sensitive data and providing complete message integrity. This is achieved through a strong 128-bit encryption feature (RC2, Triple DES) which ensures the confidentiality of data sent and received from both within and outside Siemens.

TrustedMIME is compliant with S/MIME, the *de facto* industry standard for secure e-mail over the internet. It allows Siemens to exchange encrypted or signed messages with a wide range of e-mail products from other vendors.

Using a packaging tool supplied by SSE gives Siemens the option to define and enforce an enterprise-wide policy for secure e-mail. This enabled administrators to pre-configure encryption and digital signature policies from a central point. This has reduced the cost of administration and support involved in the deployment of enterprise-wide secure e-mail. Importantly, TrustedMIME can also seamlessly import public keys directly from Siemens' corporate directory, which greatly eases administration and enhances usability.

Case Study 3: Svenska Handelsbanken (SHB) – internet banking

In recent years the improvements brought about by the internet both at home and in the office never cease to amaze. One area which has benefited substantially from the rise in networked applications is banking and financial services.

Internet banking is now a must for financial institutions everywhere as standard customer expectations become more complex and demanding. In order to remain competitive, banks must provide potentially costly and time-consuming services such as 24-hour banking, international monetary transfers and 24-hour loan approval. By switching to online banking, however, financial institutions are now realizing they can meet and exceed their customers' demands at significantly reduced cost.

Nevertheless, in order for such online banking services to be both efficient and effective, customers and service providers alike must be able to rely on the systems and technologies they use. Trust is the facilitating factor in this business. Customers must be assured that they are communicating in a safe and secure manner in order for the potential benefits of online banking to be fulfilled.

SHB is one of the largest banks in the Nordic region, employing approximately 8,400 people and concentrating its business in Sweden, where there are almost 500 banking offices. It offers a complete range of financial services: traditional corporate services, investment banking and trading as well as private banking including life assurance.

Owing to the highly sensitive information that clients need to access and exchange, real-time security was a high priority for SHB. A powerful and scalable solution was required that was designed to eliminate information security risks and ensure that increasing demand for internet banking did not compromise the bank's system.

Having evaluated a range of competing products, SHB chose SSE's certification authority TrustedCA for its secure internet banking solution based on its performance guarantees, standards-based technology approach, flexibility and reliability. Moreover, SSE's adaptability in accommodating all of the bank's needs proved paramount. In addition, TrustedCA's advanced technology base and scalability features provide numerous benefits for SHB customers.

As part of the SHB total solution, the company operates as a certification authority and offers online certificate management services to issue and manage digital certificates.

SHB's internet service has continued to grow from strength to strength. Today, over 300,000 customers have digital certificates in order to conduct their banking business via the internet. TrustedCA represents the second and most exciting growth phase of this project. As new services are marketed, TrustedCA will be expected to scale up to two million digital certificates.

By partnering with SSE, SHB can now provide a safe and secure medium to its customers allowing highly sensitive financial transactions to take place in a trustworthy environment.

There are four major products in the SSE portfolio. These include:

■ *TrustedMIME*: This is a seamless, award-winning e-mail security plug-in for Microsoft Exchange, MS Outlook and Lotus Notes. It ensures the complete confidentiality of e-mail messages and file attachments using strong (128-bit) encryption and authentication, together with smart card support and an extremely cost-effective way of establishing a highly secure channel for internet and external business communications. With the TrustedMIME/Corporate SDK, an organization can easily customize TrustedMIME for its own use and automatically link into the corporate directory of e-mail users.

■ *TrustedDoc*: This product combines market-leading digital signature technologies and standards to produce digitally signed documents which can be securely transmitted via the internet. Smartcard support allows the identification of the person signing the digital communication and the authentication of the data which were signed. Furthermore, the product also features a 'trusted timestamp' and trusted archive. Together these allow validation of the document years after signing. TrustedDoc offers leading global corporations powerful, secure management of documents within a PKI.

■ *TrustedAuthorizer (Attribute Authority)*: This state-of-the-art access control and authorization solution is easily deployed in any enterprise, organization or service provider, to control access to information resources whether web-enabled or not. On request, TrustedAuthorizer will securely issue an X.509 Attribute Certificate (AC) for an authenticated user. The AC will contain a list of the user's security attributes. If the user subsequently attempts to access a protected resource, the attributes within the user's AC are used to make an access control decision, either to grant or to deny access to the resource.

■ *TrustedCA*: This provides a scalable certification authority solution for organizations of all sizes. The product's great strength is that it allows its users to create and manage the public key infrastructure needed to run network services such as secure e-mail, digital signatures and secure web access. TrustedCA supports multiple applications and multiple vendors; this is achieved through its standards-based approach and highly modular design.

In the increasingly competitive and demanding e-business arena the rewards for organizations that can offer customers what they need across the web can be prodigious. But if there has been one message of this book it is that e-business cannot exist without proper security and trust provisions, any more than conventional business can exist without a secure method for banking payments received and collecting payment due. SSE is an outstanding example of a security and trust vendor which ultimately achieves its objectives, first, by obtaining a comprehensive knowledge of the customer's agenda and, second, by using extensive resources of expertize and technical excellence to ensure not only that organizations are able to trade comfortably and securely and on a basis of trust, but also that these organizations' customers enjoy the same benefits.

For further information please contact:

SSE Ltd
Fitzwilliam Close
Leeson Court
Dublin 2,
Republic of Ireland.

Telephone: +353 1 216 2900
Telefax: +353 1 216 2082

E-mail: *info@sse.ie*
internet: *http://www.sse.ie*

Index